CHEMICAL SLAVERY
Understanding Addiction and Stopping the Drug Epidemic

Books by Robert L. DuPont, MD

Getting Tough on Gateway Drugs: A Guide for the Family

A Bridge to Recovery: An Introduction to 12-Step Programs
coauthored with John P. McGovern, MD

The Selfish Brain: Learning from Addiction

The Anxiety Cure: An Eight-Step Program for Getting Well
coauthored with Elizabeth DuPont Spencer, LCSW-C
and Caroline M. DuPont, MD

The Anxiety Cure for Kids: A Guide for Parents and Children
coauthored with Elizabeth DuPont Spencer, LCSW-C
and Caroline M. DuPont, MD

Drug Testing in Drug Abuse Treatment

Drug Testing in Schools: Guidelines for Effective Use

Drug Testing in the Criminal Justice System

CHEMICAL SLAVERY
Understanding Addiction and Stopping the Drug Epidemic

ROBERT L. DUPONT, MD

Institute For Behavior and Health

ISBN: 1985750325
ISBN-13: 978-1985750326

Institute for Behavior and Health, Inc.
6191 Executive Boulevard, Rockville, Maryland, 20852, USA
www.IBHinc.org

Note: Some of the text in this book was adapted from *The Selfish Brain: Learning from Addiction* by Robert L. DuPont, MD published by the American Psychiatric Press, Inc. in 1997 and published by Hazelden in 2000. Chapter 7 is based on material from the book *A Bridge to Recovery: An Introduction to 12-Step Programs* by Robert L. DuPont, MD and John P. McGovern, MD published by the American Psychiatric Press in 1994.

ENDORSEMENTS

"This is a book that should be read by everyone whose life is impacted by addiction—and that includes each of us, whether it be through crime, loss of national economic competitiveness and jobs, weakened national security, higher taxes, or personal tragedy. In my own case, the latter included the death of a promising young cousin due to drug addiction. The author shares his knowledge gained from treating patients in the trenches to decision-making at the highest levels of government. In a very readable fashion, the book takes one from the biology of addiction to the promise of treatment—and, better yet, prevention. This is an important book. I couldn't put it down."

- Norman R. Augustine, Retired Chairman & CEO, Lockheed Martin; Former Under Secretary of the Army; Former Chairman of the American Red Cross

"Robert DuPont is a giant and progenitor in the effort to understand and defeat the epidemic of drug addiction. All of us who have worked in the field owe him an enormous debt of gratitude. We have all learned from him. Here, in this book *Chemical Slavery*, he puts together the personal and the scientific to help us understand and challenge what I believe is the worst illegal drug epidemic in our history. Few can bring his formidable credentials to the work he so well understands. He is a practicing psychiatrist, a scientist, a developer and advocate of sound policy, a devoted husband and father and a deeply engaged citizen. Here he brings his various roles and responsibilities together to help us find a way out of this chasm. He shows all of us how to be slaves no more. Read and learn."

- William J. Bennett, PhD, Former Director, Office of National Drug Control Policy

"*Chemical Slavery* is a must-read for every parent, student and politician. Dr. DuPont's analysis is clear and well-founded from a lifetime of experience with patients and government. No one understands our nation's drug problem better and Bob DuPont has the right answers as to what we must do."

- Peter Bensinger, Former Administrator, Drug Enforcement Administration (DEA)

"Dr. DuPont has been a prominent thought leader on addiction throughout his long and illustrious career. This book gives insights into his thoughts and new perspectives on the complex issues of addiction."

- Kelly J. Clark, MD, MBA, Chief Medical Officer, CleanSlate Centers

"Dr. DuPont combines 50 years of treating addiction with 50 years of understanding addiction to write this book which should be mandatory reading for anyone who is either trying to understand and/or treat addiction."

- Lee Dogoloff, Former Director, Special Action Office for Drug Abuse Prevention (SAODAP), Executive Office of the President

"This book brings together what Dr. DuPont has learned from the scientific literature, public policy, colleagues, patients and families. It is remarkable for its breadth, from single cells to AA. But, what I think is especially remarkable and even better than his classic *The Selfish Brain*, is the writing. It is clear, easy to understand, equally useful for families and patients and students and experts. He summarizes the entire field without the need for references or verbosity. It is professorial without professing and scholarly on the one hand and brilliantly insightful on the other, without ever reminding you how much he has done to enable him to know this much about addiction. You will know a great deal more about drugs, addiction, the selfish brain, and recovery regardless of whether you are concerned relative, friend, or family member or a student. As a professor and author of more than 1000 peer reviewed scientific papers and some professional books too, when I finished *Chemical Slavery*, I was grateful for Bob's work, career dedicated to helping others and our Society, and his mentorship. Also, long before you finish, you will have no doubt who the nation's addiction, treatment and prevention expert is."

- Mark S. Gold, MD, Chairman, Scientific Advisory Boards, RiverMend Health; 17th University of Florida Distinguished Alumni Professor; National Council, Institute for Public Health, Washington University in St Louis; Professor (Adjunct), Department of Psychiatry, Washington University in St Louis, School of Medicine

"This extremely ambitious book by Dr. DuPont is the first book that I know of by a leader in the drug abuse prevention and treatment field that has highlighted the message of Pope Francis: that engaging in drug taking for experiential purposes is tantamount to allowing oneself to become enslaved. No one would ever willingly accept such a fate. When one gives up one's will power, the theosophists say that one gives up one's soul power. The Dalai Lama has said that a person who uses drugs give up his or her authentic self. This book provides a range of significant roadmaps that have been used by a country, Sweden; and by institutions, treatment programs, families, and individual drug users and addicts, to safeguard or sustain and retain that authentic drug-free selfhood. By bringing to light in one place, many of these roadmaps, Dr. DuPont shares insights into how that authentic self can be safeguarded from the pitfalls of drug taking behavior. He shares insights into the steps that many have taken to retain or reclaim their authentic selves, initiative, will power, brain power, judgment, creativity, and essential humanity."

- Paula D. Gordon, PhD, GordonDrugAbusePrevention.com and Auburn University Outreach Drug Course Instructor

"In the field of substance use disorders, Dr. DuPont is a national treasure. For the past 50 years he has been a dedicated scholar, researcher, clinician and public policy advocate. He has drawn on the remarkable depth of his professional experience to produce the superb *Chemical Slavery*, soon to be a classic. It is clearly written in a way that will attract a wide audience from professionals to concerned parents. Thank you, Dr. DuPont."

- Howard A. Hoffman, MD, President and Medical Director, Foundation for Contemporary Mental Health, PIDARC/Next Step

"It is impossible to tell the story of drug addiction treatment and policy in the United States without giving prominent attention to the remarkable career of Dr. Robert DuPont. Treatment pioneer, policy adviser to Presidents, founding director of NIDA, and mentor to generations of scholars and clinicians, Bob epitomizes compassion for addicted people combined with hard-headed wisdom about treatment and recovery."

— Keith Humphreys, PhD, Esther Ting Memorial Professor, Stanford University, and Senior Career Research Scientist, Department of Veterans Affairs

"For 50 years, psychiatrist Robert DuPont has been at the forefront of society's efforts to cope with problems of alcohol and drug addiction. His accumulated knowledge, summarized in this book, has been influenced by his direct experience with patients and his years of leadership and consulting at the highest levels of the US government. In non-technical language he deals intelligently with issues such as personal responsibility versus behavior shaped by a brain disease; treating addiction versus prevention of use; harm reduction versus recovery; and the likely consequences of increasing use of cannabis. Several of Dr. DuPont's views differ from widely held beliefs and deserve serious consideration."

— Jerome H. Jaffe, MD, Adjunct Professor, Department of Mental Health, The Johns Hopkins Bloomberg School of Public Health, Baltimore, Maryland

"This is a book with unusually high concentration of knowledge, as well as wisdom. I like especially that in spite of this, it is easy to read. Anyone with some experience of longer texts can read the book and learn a ton. It is the ultimate educational book for young people studying to become social workers and physicians as well as police officers and lawyers—and of course everyone else—that want to understand the drug problem and get a grasp of what we can do to solve it."

— Per Johansson, Secretary General, National Association for a Drug-Free Society (RNS), Sweden

"Addiction is more prevalent and more costly than other chronic diseases of the brain. Among brain diseases, it is also the most preventable. This modern crisis has spawned countless pundits and authors issuing a wide range of opinions on drug policy. A few, rare writers have credibility, expertise, scholarship, perspective, and hands-on experience to inform policy solutions. Dr. Robert DuPont is among the rarest, for he has served in every meaningful capacity on the front lines of this national challenge—as the first NIDA Director, as the White House drug policy director, as a scientist, and a practicing addiction psychiatrist. From each of these experiences, he has gleaned critical principles, knowledge, lessons learned, and solutions. They are synthesized and shared in this comprehensive, vibrant and timely book. Its appeal is broad, its information objective, and its wisdom profound."

— Bertha K. Madras, PhD, Professor of Psychobiology, Department of Psychiatry, Harvard Medical School; Former Deputy Director for Demand Reduction, Office of National Drug Control Policy

"Dr. DuPont brings together his vast experience on drug policy (as the second White House Drug Czar and a valued consultant to each Presidential administration since 1973), his many years of clinical experience with patients and families afflicted with problems related to alcohol, opioids, cocaine and cannabis, his understanding of the translational science of addiction (from his years as Director of the National Institute on Drug Abuse and beyond), and his knowledge of the historical and cultural factors that have affected the prevalence of addictive disorders since ancient times. He brings this together in a highly readable book that should serve to inform families, physicians, policy makers, and individuals beginning to come to terms with their problem of addiction. A must read!"

- Roger E. Meyer, MD, Professor of Psychiatry, Penn State Hershey Medical Center; Former Executive Dean, George Washington University Medical Center

"Dr. Robert DuPont reflects upon and synthesizes decades of experience working in the field of addiction policy and treatment in *Chemical Slavery: Understanding Addiction and Stopping the Drug Epidemic*. Dr. DuPont has tackled addiction from all angles—as a clinician, policy advisor, thinker and advocate—and he now gifts us with a translation of both what he knows and that which he continues to grapple with. The result is comprehensive—a call to action, a history, a resource—and will become a trusted guide for the lay reader as well as for those in the field who want to make sure that policy and scientific understanding of substance use disorders are interconnected with the experiences of patients and families."

- Jessica Hulsey Nickel, President & CEO, Addiction Policy Forum

"One of the most powerful messages that Dr. DuPont conveys in this in-depth book is that 'Recovery Changes the Brain'. Our families and communities are ever changing because of the recovery movement. Dr. DuPont thoughtfully describes how changing social attitudes will positively affect prevention and recovery. As a professional in this field and a family member I am truly grateful for Dr. DuPont's dedication and scientific insight in the field of addiction."

- Nancy Rosen-Cohen, PhD, Executive Director, NCADD-Maryland

"Dr. DuPont has produced this century's seminal text on addiction. He somehow balances his lifelong, passionate desire to reduce drug use with a dispassionate analysis of the bold facts – all with the compassion of someone who cares deeply for the public health. If there is someone else living today in the addiction field with the knowledge, experience, breadth, integrity, and – most importantly, heart – to write such an ambitious, important book, I can't think of them."

- Kevin A. Sabet, PhD, three-time White House Drug Policy Advisor; Adjunct Professor, Yale University; President of SAM (Smart Approaches to Marijuana)

"Bob DuPont gets it. He possesses a keen understanding of not only the neurobiological tenets of addiction, but also the complexity and wreckage that it has caused in the lives of so many Americans and their families. From personal stories of recovery to public policies to address prevention, he presents a coherent strategy to help our nation navigate its way out of a public health crisis. As we move ahead, seeking to train the next generation of healthcare providers, Bob DuPont's resounding voice and wisdom will lead the way."

– Scott A. Teitelbaum, MD, FAAP, FASAM, Professor and Vice Chair, Department of Psychiatry; Professor, Department of Pediatrics, University of Florida, College of Medicine; Chief, Division of Addiction Medicine; Medical Director, Florida Recovery Center

"Dr. Robert DuPont, one of our nation's leading authorities on addiction and recovery—and one of my heroes—provides a thorough and easy to understand overview of addiction and recovery in his new book *Chemical Slavery: Understanding Addiction and Stopping the Drug Epidemic.* When someone so accomplished as a physician, scientist, and public policy expert authors a book that provides critical information for professionals in the field, government officials, and the lay person who is searching for answers for their family, it is remarkable literary genius. This is a must read for any family afflicted by addiction, as it will explain the disease, brain chemistry, and most importantly how to achieve recovery and a new way of life that is alcohol- and drug-free. Likewise, Dr. DuPont provides essential information that will benefit professionals in the field and those involved with public policy decisions and implementation. For all who read this book, you will readily be impressed with Dr. DuPont's breadth and depth of knowledge and his ability to relate to all of us. "

– Douglas Tieman, President and CEO, Caron Treatment Programs

"Dr. Robert DuPont has worked tirelessly to save the lives of individuals and to save our country from the destruction of substance abuse. His experience spans decades and his record of public service puts every American in his debt. Bob created much of the public policy now used to combat the drug problem and with *Chemical Slavery* he seeks to bring together individual experience and his recommendations for combating today's drug problem on the widest scale. Bob DuPont deserves our thanks and our attention."

– John P. Walters, Chief Operating Officer, Hudson Institute; Former Director, Office of National Drug Control Policy

"Individuals and families affected by addiction, addiction treatment specialists, allied service professionals, and drug policy leaders will find Dr. Robert DuPont's *Chemical Slavery* brimming with profound insight, practical proposals, and hope. This latest contribution will stir much needed discussion in the field."

– William L. White, Author, *Slaying the Dragon: The History of Addiction Treatment and Recovery in America*

DEDICATION

To all those hard working individuals in many professions who labor to prevent substance use and to those who work with people who are addicted to identify, treat and stay with them every step of the way until they reach the destination of abstinence and lasting recovery.

This book is also dedicated to two remarkable global leaders:

To His Holiness, Pope Francis, who has embraced the challenge of the global drug epidemic as a new kind of slavery, and has pledged himself to work for emancipation from it.

"Drugs have inflicted a deep wound on our society and ensnared many people in their web. Many victims have lost their freedom and have been enslaved to them; enslaved by an addiction we could call 'chemical'. This is undoubtedly a 'new form of slavery' alongside several others that afflict individuals and society in general today."

Remarks delivered November 24, 2016 by Pope Francis at
Narcotics: Problems and Solutions of this Global Issue at the
Pontifical Academy of Sciences, Vatican City

***

To Her Majesty Queen Silvia of Sweden, who, building on Sweden's unique and hard-won drug policy, has worked tirelessly for more than two decades to help youth all over the world grow up drug-free.

"Prevention of drug abuse among children and young people has been a primary focus of mine for over 20 years. In 1994, in cooperation with the WHO [World Health Organization], I founded Mentor International whose original vision still guides us today. It is to help build a world where children and young people are empowered to make healthy decisions and live free of drugs."

Remarks delivered November 23, 2016 by Queen Silvia at
Narcotics: Problems and Solutions of this Global Issue at the
Pontifical Academy of Sciences, Vatican City

CONTENTS

FOREWORD

Chemical Slavery: Understanding Addiction and Stopping the Drug Epidemic is an extremely important contribution to the field of dealing with drug and alcohol addiction. This powerful book is clearly written, comprehensive, and objective. It incorporates the most current scientific knowledge of how to deal with the human nightmare of compulsive drug abuse and the dishonesty and physical and spiritual destruction it causes. The life of an addict is sheer misery.

Dr. DuPont is a friend, a personal tutor on the addiction issue, a scientist, a Harvard-trained physician, and has been directly involved in the active treatment of addiction for over fifty years. He is also one of the most compassionate health professionals I have ever known. This book is informed and shaped not just by his broad scientific understanding of the medical and policy issues posed by addiction, but also by his lifelong engagement in the miracle of sustained recovery.

I was first appointed in 1996 to serve for over five years as the White House Director of National Drug Policy. Dr. DuPont was an immediate source of wisdom in helping me understand the complex and sometimes baffling nature of addiction. I had many expert and ongoing personal tutors over the years who deepened my understanding of these difficult issues of drug prevention and treatment: NIDA directors Dr. Nora Volkow and Dr. Alan Leshner; Dr. Sally Satel; Dr. Herb Kleber; Dr. Tom McLellan; Dr. David Musto; Dr. Westley Clark; DEA director Tom Constantine; and many others.

Bob DuPont was the most influential of my personal mentors by far. He was not exclusively a scientist or a treatment practitioner or a drug policy person. Bob DuPont had done all of it. He was the former White House drug policy director. He was the first director of NIDA (National Institute of Drug Abuse). Most important, he was the director of his own clinical addiction medicine practice with decades of hands-on involvement dealing with substance abuse. His first guidance to me was the most important I received in five years serving as Office of National Drug Control Policy (ONDCP) director. He said, "Barry, you will never understand this issue until you have attended a dozen open meetings of AA and NA." I did...and the experience changed my life. Since then I have understood that recovery is possible, in particular with the magic of the "Twelve Step Process."

The problems generated by addiction are staggering in magnitude. Roughly 21 million Americans are substance abusers, costing our society $442 billion a year. This slow-rolling epidemic killed 500,000 people in the past fifteen years. We have a massive criminal justice population of over 2 million behind bars and 5 million on parole or probation. The central problem driving this mass incarceration is that roughly 75 percent of this population has a chronic alcohol or illegal drug problem. They are not behind bars in any significant numbers because of possession of illegal drugs. They end up behind bars because they unravel their physical and moral health with dishonesty, loss of control, and a brain compulsion to remain high...or at least to feel normal.

This work by Dr. DuPont is important and a must-read reference for families, health professionals, law enforcement and religious leaders, coaches, educators, and business executives—all of whom must understand and respond to the terrible challenges posed by chronic drug and alcohol dependence. The health, criminal justice, legal, family, and social disasters that are clustered around addiction are at the heart of the most dismaying problems that face American families, communities, and businesses.

Fortunately, Dr. DuPont includes in a straightforward manner the consequences of not just illicit drugs, which are banned by a federal law, but also alcohol and cigarette abuse as well. In the past month, 66 million Americans were binge drinkers. Alcohol killed 88,000 Americans in 2015. The use by 55 million Americans of addictive tobacco nicotine products kills 480,000 Americans per year. That tobacco annual death rate is a number greater than American combat deaths in all of WWII.

This book you are about to read will have a powerful effect on your understanding of addiction. There are basically three parts to this work: the nature of addiction; the nature of addictive drugs and how they influence the brain; and, most important, addiction prevention, treatment, and recovery.

This is an optimistic book. First, sensible programs of education and prevention aimed at adolescents can dramatically reduce exposure to pot, smoking cigarettes, consumption of alcohol, and other drugs. Very good things happen to kids who reach the age of twenty-one with delayed or reduced exposure to drugs.

Second, if a loved one or employee or friend is being destroyed by the compulsive use of alcohol and drugs, detoxification, treatment recovery, relapse prevention, and long-term sobriety is without question very achievable. The recovery rates from addiction are immeasurably better than the cure rates of most cancers.

It is really an honor to endorse this splendid work by Dr. Bob DuPont. When I first read *The Selfish Brain: Learning from Addiction*, on which this powerful book is based, I asked Dr. DuPont to come to my White House office and autograph five copies—one copy to each of my adult children because they were parents, and one copy each to President Clinton and Vice President Gore.

Your better understanding of the issues involved with addiction will empower you to deal more successfully with this dreadful issue as you encounter it in your communities.

Barry R. McCaffrey
GENERAL USA RET
Director White House Office of National Drug Policy 1996–2001

PREFACE: WHERE THIS BOOK STARTED AND WHAT IS NEW TODAY

The development of this book began as a fully revised edition of *The Selfish Brain* which was first published in 1997 by the American Psychiatric Press and then published by Hazelden in 2000. That was a long time ago. Since then a number of changes have taken place that affect the field of addiction treatment and recovery: the drug-using population in the United States and in the entire world has grown and changed in ways that could not have been imagined just twenty years ago. Our understanding of the brain science of addiction has improved substantially. The illicit drug distribution system has become alarmingly more diverse, global, sophisticated, and effective. Finally, over these years, my understanding of the drug problem has become both clearer and simpler.

This new book, while rooted in the original text of *The Selfish Brain*, reflects new perspectives that take into account all of these changes in addiction research, prevention, treatment, and policy. The title of this book *Chemical Slavery: Understanding Addiction and Stopping the Drug Epidemic* reflects the way I have come to think about these things now. Drug policy, prevention, treatment and recovery are endlessly complicated and fascinating. Drug trafficking, sales, addiction and its resulting criminal fallout are always devastating. My current perspectives are woven into this book and the text has been revised significantly, reorganized and shortened to make it more accessible.

As with *The Selfish Brain*, this book features scientific and policy choices affecting the private tragedies and the political debates surrounding addiction. They have been at the center of my medical career for more than five decades. Both in the US and around the world, I have been engaged in high-level governmental and scientific public policy activities. At the same time, in the clinical practice of psychiatry, I have had the privilege of working with countless individuals and families dealing with addiction, in some cases for decades and over as many as three generations. Their struggles, their tragedies, and their triumphs have been my inspiration. My patients have been my most valuable teachers about addiction and recovery.

Only late in my career have I realized how interrelated these two domains of the drug problem are and how the lessons from one resonate with those from the other. That powerful interconnection—between public policy and scientific understanding on the one hand with the experiences of individuals and families on the other—is at the heart of this new volume.

To set the stage, addiction is both ancient and stunningly new. Addiction confounds understanding and humbles efforts to solve it. This book is my up-to-date report summarizing five decades spent trying to understand addiction and to figure out what to do about it.

You will not understand addiction unless you see clearly that addiction is modern, chemical slavery. Addiction is cruel and relentless. It devastates its victims—dominates and corrupts their lives. It is commonly fatal. And yet the victims of addiction pay cash to get into slavery and then as its grip tightens they spend even more money to hold onto this vicious slavery. More remarkable still, when emancipated from the slavery of addiction many victims return to it paying even higher prices—paying in suffering, yes, but also paying in cold, hard cash.

Think of it. In the US drug addicts pay about $100 billion a year for illegal drugs compared to about $34 billion a year spent each year on all addiction treatment, both public and private, for drug and alcohol addiction. That means that addicts themselves, with no help from the government or health insurance, could pay cash for the current levels of addiction treatment three times over. That $100 billion spent for illegal drugs comes not just from the rich but from some of our most economically disadvantaged citizens, mostly but not only the young. While addiction disproportionately affects the disadvantaged, the young and the mentally ill, addiction is widespread in every segment of the American society and all parts of the country: urban, suburban, and rural in towns and in cities of all sizes. The addiction epidemic is happening despite the fact that everyone in the US knows about this slavery and most Americans have had close contact with one or more of its victims. But for those without a personal experience with an addict, the modern media is chock full of the dreadful stories of the suffering and death of addicts.

You cannot begin to understand addiction unless you have this puzzling picture clearly in focus. You cannot understand how to prevent or treat addiction unless you see this relentless chemical slavery clearly for what it is, whether in your family and among your friends and neighbors or in the nation as a whole. Here is what Pope Francis had to say when I met with him at the Vatican in November 2016: "Addiction is not just awful. It is unimaginably degrading and dehumanizing. The current high-profile overdose death epidemic underscores the magnitude of the threat. There are good reasons to expect the addiction epidemic to increase in the future, worldwide. The level of addiction today is but a pale shadow of the potential."

This book is not only the story of this baffling modern slavery. I ask you to see not only this grim picture I want you also to see that addiction is not hopeless or inevitable. More than 20 million Americans have overcome addiction to alcohol and other drugs. The modern recovery movement is proof positive that addiction can be overcome. It is being overcome daily in every part of our country. Best of all the emancipated slaves, recovering addicts, show you and me how it can be overcome.

I am proud to be an American for many good reasons. One reason for my pride in our country stands out is the creation by two alcoholics in Akron, Ohio in 1935 of the modern miracle of Alcoholics Anonymous. Today there are more than 100 other Twelve Step programs including Narcotics Anonymous for those addicted to drugs other than alcohol and Al Anon for families and other affected by addiction. These are emancipation programs run by and for drug addicts, alcoholics and their families. This is a quintessentially American program. No government funding. No salaries. No regulations and no licenses. No degrees or certifications. The driver of this program is Step 12 – the commitment of addicts to help other addicts find their ways to recovery and to hold onto their emancipation one day at a time. This fellowship is not only found today in all parts of the US but it has spread all over the world. These recovery fellowship meetings are not cut out with a cookie cutter. Every meeting is different although all are inspired by the shared experiences of millions of recovering addicts. These fellowships adapt to every ethnic group, every language, every income and every educational level everywhere. Not everyone addicted needs the Twelve Steps. These fellowships do not constitute treatment but the Twelve Step fellowships do enhance all addiction treatments. If one meeting does not fit your needs, try others. For readers who are not addicts, find an open meeting near you and go to see for yourself this modern miracle in action.

The experiences, the testimony, of addicts both actively using and in recovery are the inspiration of this book. Let's get busy together understanding what is wrong and what to do about it when it comes to addiction to alcohol and other drugs.

INTRODUCTION:
WHAT WE CAN LEARN FROM ADDICTION

Humans have an appetite for drugs. Addiction is ancient. But the modern drug epidemic is as new as the Internet and is changing just as fast and as unpredictably. For example, once we would have thought it inconceivable that many of those who are addicted today ever would have tried an addictive substance. The breadth and reach of drug use today is unprecedented. The current prescription painkiller and heroin epidemic— including the controversies about its causes and how to stop it—is big news and is likely to remain so far into the future. In his 2016 landmark report on addiction to alcohol and other drugs, *Facing Addiction*, US Surgeon General Vivek Murthy called the current epidemic "a moral test for America."[1]

This challenge is a matter of life and death. Overdose is the leading cause of death among Americans under age fifty. In 2016, drug overdose deaths reached a new peak of 63,600 – an average of 174 deaths every day.[2] From 2015 to 2016 overdose deaths increased 21 percent. Overdose deaths have surpassed deaths from motor vehicle crashes (40,200) and firearms (38,440).[3]

---

[1] US Department of Health and Human Services (HHS), Office of the Surgeon General. (2016). *Facing Addiction in America: The Surgeon General's Report on Alcohol, Drugs, and Health.* Washington, DC: HHS. https://addiction.surgeongeneral.gov

[2] Hedegaard, M., Warner, M., & Minino, A. M. (2017, December). Overdose deaths in the United States, 1999-2016. NCHS Data Brief, 294. US Department of Health and Human Services, Centers for Disease Control and Prevention, National Center for Health Statistics. Available: https://www.cdc.gov/nchs/data/databriefs/db294.pdf

[3] Katz, J. (2017, October 27). You draw it: just how bad is the drug overdose epidemic? *The New York Times.*

No part of the country, no community, and no socioeconomic group is spared from the current drug epidemic—virtually every family in the country is affected in enduring and often deadly ways. In 2016, substance use disorders affected 20.1 million people in the US—and are estimated to cost $442 billion each year in health care, lost productivity, and criminal justice costs; yet, only one in ten people with substance use disorders receives treatment, and even fewer make their way into long-term recovery.[4]

As bad and as tragic as the drug epidemic is now, there is a potential for it to become far worse. We cannot ignore or wish away this epidemic. It demands our best efforts to understand it and to limit its damage. Stopping it will require that we work together.

How do we do that? To begin, we cannot stop something we don't fully understand. The first half of this book provides a comprehensive review of drug addiction—including how it develops, why drugs take hold of some lives but not others, and how our country came to this pernicious modern drug epidemic. The second half of the book is all about effecting change. It outlines the actions we can take individually and collectively to turn back the current epidemic and protect future generations from the ravages of drug abuse and addiction—namely through prevention policies, treatment, and recovery. We have much to learn from the tragedy of addiction, a powerful, pitiless, and ultimately effective teacher. It is time to compile those lessons, share them with as many people as possible, and then together take decisive action to change the deadly course we are on when it comes to drug abuse and addiction.

The book captures both my experiences for more than five decades as a practicing psychiatrist working with my own patients and my work as a leader on drug policy in the US and abroad. It is written for anyone interested in learning the lessons of addiction and how to put those lessons to good use. In particular, the book is designed for the following audiences: (1) professionals who work with substance use disorders (SUDs)—that is, addiction to alcohol and other drugs; (2) people dealing with SUDs in their own lives and in their families; and (3) people interested in the highly controversial area of drug policy. My goal in this new book is to bring sympathetic and optimistic understanding to all readers about the spreading global drug epidemic in its highly personal and often tragic dimensions and to outline personal and policy action steps we can take to stop this devastating epidemic.

---

[4] US Department of Health and Human Services (HHS), Office of the Surgeon General. (2016). *Facing Addiction in America: The Surgeon General's Report on Alcohol, Drugs, and Health.* Washington, DC: HHS. https://addiction.surgeongeneral.gov

We know that the biology of addiction is rooted in the human brain. Facing addiction, then, requires an understanding of brain science. But understanding the science of addiction is not enough to resolve or lessen this scourge on society and the lives of so many. We must also clarify who we are as individuals, families, and communities and how we can work together to make our lives and those of addicted people better—how we can get the individual addict into recovery and how we can put a stop to this drug epidemic.

In the larger social context, we need to carefully consider how we conceptualize the problem and its potential solution. We need a comprehensive view of the epidemic and then respond with widespread collaboration to stop it. From a policy perspective, viewing the challenge of the drug epidemic as a choice between prohibition and legalization is a mindless and dangerous oversimplification of the problem. Indeed, reducing this complex dilemma into competing bumper sticker slogans makes it more difficult to truly understand addiction and take productive action. We need to do more than settle for the false comfort of clichés. It is commonplace to observe that our nation cannot arrest our way out of the drug epidemic. What is seldom said, and what is equally important, is that we cannot treat our way out of the drug epidemic, including overdose deaths. We will have to do far more than arrest and treat. We will have to greatly improve youth prevention. I urge you to read in appendix C a commentary entitled, "Reducing Future Rates of Adult Addiction Must Begin with Youth Prevention." We will have to de-normalize recreational pharmacology, the underlying risk factor in the epidemic. We will have to mobilize families and communities as well as link the systems of criminal justice and health care. We must celebrate and learn from recovery.

I believe it is possible to create sensible and affordable public policies that discourage drug use, restrain illegal drug markets, and promote better treatment to support long-term recovery. These improved drug policies will require collaboration. We need the criminal justice system, treatment, and prevention programs to work together if we are to achieve significant and comprehensive goals—achievements that individual efforts cannot accomplish alone. Functioning at its best to discourage addictive drug use, this collaboration can reduce substance abuse while also decreasing incarceration and promoting recovery for those who do become addicted.

***

Throughout this book, three principles are related both to the struggles of the individual facing addiction and to the global community dealing with the modern drug epidemic. Each of the principles is rooted in social policy and scientific understanding as well as in common individual and family experiences. The three principles are:

1. The use of mood-altering chemicals for fun, or recreational pharmacology, is bad for health; it is potentially destructive to the individual, the family, and society as a whole. This principle is based on brain biology, which is the key to understanding why there is a drug addiction problem. Mood-altering drugs are chemicals that stimulate the natural brain reward system, the same reward system that drives sexual and eating behaviors. Drugs hijack this system by stimulating brain reward many times more powerfully than any natural reward. No animal in nature ever has had access to the type of the intense brain reward that is produced by sustained drug exposure. Even in human history, it's only relatively recently that great numbers of individuals have been exposed to so many drugs in quantities and by routes of administration that produce addiction. We cannot expect the human appetite for drugs to go away, because the reward mechanism is built into the brain. This innate biological system is highly influenced, for better and for worse, by drug availability, education and social norms, and by legal and regulatory actions related to both drug use and drug supply. The current epidemic of drug addiction shows clearly that using intensely rewarding chemicals for fun is a bad idea because of the power and the negative consequences of drug use to individuals, families, and communities.

2. The second principle of this book is more subtle and complex. It involves the responsibility of the family, the community, and the government for individual behaviors when it comes to drug use. The individual alone is often vulnerable to drug addiction, and not just for a short time—but often until death. Other people around addicts—including their physicians, counselors, teachers, friends, co-workers, and especially their families—have a central role to play in both the prevention and the treatment of addiction. Once the goal of reducing recreational pharmacology is accepted as valid and rational, then the roles and responsibilities of the family and society in helping to reduce this biologically driven and commonly destructive behavior can be identified and acted upon.

3. The last principle on which this book is based comes from the success built over the last eight decades of the recovery community. Springing from a small group of alcoholics in Akron, Ohio, in 1935 where the Twelve Steps of Alcoholics Anonymous

had its beginnings, this community continues to grow throughout the US and around the globe. These are people whose lives were damaged, often severely, and often for long periods of time, by their drug use. They have done the hard and sustained work necessary to stop using drugs and to build new and better lives. One of the most powerful lessons the recovery community has learned from painful experience is that stopping the chemical stimulation of brain reward by not using any addictive drug is required not only to stabilize and to improve their lives, but quite literally to save their lives. Everyone in recovery has a sobriety date, a date that is a major part of their identities. That is the date on which they last used any addictive drug. The wisdom of recovery is based on the experience of these millions of people.

This is one of the unexpected lessons or gifts of addiction—the near miraculous transformation that can result from the efforts to confront and overcome it. The millions of Americans now in recovery provide inspiration for a new generation of people providing and receiving prevention messages and addiction treatment. Those addiction heroes in recovery bear witness to the hope that recovery is possible. Their personal stories demonstrate how recovery is achieved. Recovery is a gift to addicts, to their families, and to many others touched by them.

I'll end this introduction by confirming my belief that, just as the most down and out addict can find recovery and build a new and rewarding life, together we have the potential to turn back this modern drug epidemic. Doing so will not be easy or fast, but I am sure it can be done. The crucial first step is recognizing that using chemicals to intensely and unnaturally stimulate brain reward is unhealthy and destructive.

PART 1: UNDERSTANDING ADDICTION

The two foundations of my work—my work with individual addicts and their families on the one hand and my work with government and public policy on the other—come together in this book. The wonder to me is the similarity of the trajectory of the two, beginning with initially ignoring and denying drug use and its consequences. Only when confronted by the mounting, unexpected and disturbing consequences of drug use is the challenge of drug use faced—often initially by families by offering understanding and sympathetic support, or in the policy realm by applying more of whatever is routinely being done. Reluctantly, as the costs of drug use continue to mount, and only after unmistakably serious consequences can no longer be ignored, is a more forceful and harder line taken that rejects continued drug use. In both cases it is not as if the early gentle responses do not work; sometimes for some people they do work and some drug problems are ameliorated by modest societal efforts. But there is a large group of drug users that resists these initial gentle responses. As this large group grows, it forces further understanding of the power of addiction to shape thinking and behavior not transiently but enduringly. These two similar trajectories—in families and communities but also in the country and the entire world—are explored in this book. Whether your interests lie primarily in one or the other of these domains, I encourage you to think of both because in the community and national dimension and the in family and personal dimension your understanding of addiction from prevention to treatment and ultimately to recovery will be enhanced by these notable, but seldom noticed, comparisons. Furthermore, once addiction is recognized to be an enduring part of living in communities and in families, rooted in biology and shaped by the characters of addicts interacting with their specific environments, including their unique families, can the real understanding of addiction occur. Drug addiction is a deadly but fascinating and distinctly human disorder that threatens to grow far more widespread and destructive in coming years, not just in the US but all over the world.

Only with this broad perspective is it possible to grasp the progression of addiction, its treatment and the hard-won miracle of recovery from addiction for individuals, communities and nations.

1. ADDICTION TO ALCOHOL AND OTHER DRUGS

An estimated 8 to 10 percent of Americans suffer from addiction to alcohol or other drugs. The use of alcohol, tobacco (nicotine), prescription painkillers, and illicit drugs has become one of the leading causes of death in the US with more than 500,000 people dying from overdose between the years 2000 and 2016. Addiction is the largest preventable health problem in the US.[1]

Substance abuse costs the nation hundreds of millions of dollars per year, including legal, medical, and treatment costs. This is an involuntary tax resulting from the use of drugs. No part of the nation and few extended families have been spared the deadly, overwhelming, and confusing grip of addiction. Every major social and community institution has been hit by substance abuse and addiction, although many continue to ignore it, treating it as if it were an uncommon problem experienced only by a small number of troubled people. And yet, in 2016 28.5 million people said they had used illegal drugs or misused prescription drugs, and more than 65 million reported binge drinking in the previous month.[2] Substance misuse, including addiction, affects people of all ages and in all walks of life. It is an equal opportunity destroyer that places particularly severe burdens on the disadvantaged and the young.

Defining Addiction

What makes a chemical a drug? In one context, chemicals used to treat any illness are drugs as in the term "drug store." But for our purposes, drugs have an entirely different and far more specific meaning—we are

---

[1] The National Center on Addiction and Substance Abuse. (2015). *Guide for Policymakers: Prevention, Early Intervention and Treatment of Risky Substance Use and Addiction.* New York, NY: Author.
[2] Center for Behavioral Health Statistics and Quality. (2017). Results from the 2016 National Survey on Drug Use and Health: Detailed Tables. Rockville, MD: Substance Abuse and Mental Health Services Administration.

referring to those chemicals that, in their ability to stimulate pleasure and suppress physical and emotional pain, can take control of the brain and cause addiction. There are many chemicals that affect the brain that are not addictive. For example, antidepressants such as Prozac are chemicals that affect the brain in powerful ways but they aren't addictive.

In the Twelve Step fellowships of Alcoholics Anonymous and Narcotics Anonymous, the definition of alcoholism and other drug addiction is left to each member of these organizations of which the only requirement for membership is the desire to stop drinking or using other drugs. There is general agreement, however, that alcoholism and other drug addictions are a disease. In the first of the Twelve Steps, addicts must admit powerlessness over their use and that drinking and using the drugs have made their lives unmanageable.

For professionals in the addiction field, the current official definition of drug problems is described in the Diagnostic Statistical Manual of Mental Disorders, Fifth Edition (DSM-V), published by the American Psychiatric Association (APA). The overall diagnostic category is substance use disorder (SUD), which is judged to be mild, moderate, or severe. This diagnostic framework replaced the differentiation of substance abuse from substance dependence that was made in the DSM-IV.

Further, in the DSM-V, the diagnosis is substance-specific, for example, opioid use disorder, marijuana use disorder, or alcohol use disorder. It is generally recognized among treatment professionals and among people in recovery that to overcome a substance use disorder, no matter which drug is involved, it is necessary to abstain from the use of any addicting chemical. The DSM-V includes a list of specific criteria commonly seen in SUDs, such as continued use despite persistent or recurring problems (health, social, interpersonal, work, school, and so on), tolerance (that is, more of the drug is required to achieve the same effect), craving, inability to quit or cut down on use, withdrawal, and using more of a drug than intended. A person can be officially diagnosed with an SUD only if at least two of the eleven criteria are met over the past year. When two to three criteria are met, the SUD is considered to be mild; when four to five are met, it is considered moderate; and with six or more met criteria, the diagnosis is severe.

Terminology in This Book

There is a robust and useful discussion now occurring in addiction medicine about the most appropriate words to describe the health problems related to the use of alcohol and other drugs. The older terms addict, alcoholic, and drug abuse increasingly are seen as stigmatizing.

The newer, less stigmatizing, terms include substance use disorder, drug misuse, and nonmedical drug use. In this book, I use all of these terms more or less interchangeably. In most cases, I use the term addiction when referring to a high-moderate to severe substance use disorder (a person meets the criteria for loss of control over addictive chemicals), alcoholic when the person is addicted specifically to alcohol, and addict when someone is addicted to alcohol and/or other drugs. I will also use the term abuse when referring to any problem-causing drug use, whether the person is addicted or not, because this term has become a generally accepted term for using alcohol or other drugs in harmful ways. I choose to use the older of the terms not to disparage the individuals caught in the web of addiction but rather to frankly acknowledge the stigma on the addictive use of alcohol and drugs—a stigma that I consider to be justified and needed. To be clear, I am not for stigmatizing addicted people just their addictive behavior. That is the crucial issue in this overall discussion: the person with a substance use disorder is responsible for the physical, mental, legal, and social consequences of his or her disorder and the addicted person has control over the continued use of the substance.

When I refer to drugs, unless I specify a particular substance, I am writing about all addictive substances, including marijuana, methamphetamine, heroin, and a wide variety of synthetic chemicals, from PCP to fentanyl. Use of any one or a mix of these chemicals can result in an addiction—the cunning, baffling, and powerful, as well as the fascinating and frustrating, human condition that is the addicted or selfish brain.

The National Institute on Drug Abuse (NIDA) provides the most succinct definition of substance abuse and addiction that sums up both the APA criteria and the condition of powerlessness described in the first of the Twelve Steps:

"People use substances for a variety of reasons. It becomes drug abuse when people use illegal drugs or use legal drugs inappropriately. This includes the repeated use of drugs to produce pleasure, alleviate stress, and/or alter or avoid reality. It also includes using prescription drugs in ways other than prescribed or using someone else's prescription. Addiction occurs when a person cannot control the impulse to use drugs even when there are negative consequences—the defining characteristic of addiction. These behavioral changes are also accompanied by changes in brain functioning, especially in the brain's natural inhibition and reward centers."[3]

Sometimes, including in this book, addiction is characterized by the loss of control over drug use. The addicted brain is said to be "hijacked" by the addictive use of alcohol and other drugs. I do not believe this means that addicted people are unable to exert control over their drug-using behaviors. It is my opinion, which may be controversial with many in the addiction field, that they control their behavior at all stages of the disorder. What I mean by this is that an addict's brain—and so their thinking and judgment—is so distorted by their repeated drug use that they choose to continue to use their addictive substances despite the negative consequences. Their addictive behavior is commonly contrary to their own interests and it is in this sense that I see the addict's drug use as being out of control.

Most professionals will agree that people who abuse alcohol and other drugs and aren't addicted—that is, they don't demonstrate the substance use disorder criteria for loss of control of their use (such as being unable to quit despite the desire to do so, craving, or using larger amounts or longer than intended)—are responsible for stopping once they realize the negative consequences of their use. In short, I believe that if people who abuse substances have demonstrated the ability to make decisions about their use, then they are responsible for managing their substance use disorder—which means stopping use altogether if the drugs are illegal (or if the drug is the nicotine in tobacco) and either abstaining from drinking (the safest) or drinking only socially but not to intoxication. Similarly, people taking prescribed addictive medications will take only the amount prescribed and never use the drug to get high.

However, some people have brain chemistries that predispose them to impaired control of their use along with meeting the other criteria for a moderate to severe substance use disorder. I consider this a defining feature of addiction, which as we'll see in the next chapter. Their brains have been changed by their drug use so that they commonly deny to themselves and to others many of the negative consequences of their drug use. Cigarette smokers are responsible for smoking cigarettes. But are they also responsible for the lung cancer that afflicts some smokers but not others? In my view, the answer is "yes." That does not mean cigarette smokers with cancer are bad people or do not deserve compassion and treatment. So it is with alcohol and drug users and the disease of addiction, which also afflicts some drinkers and drug users and not others.

---

[3] National Institute on Drug Abuse (NIDA). (2016). The science of drug abuse and addiction: the basics. https://www.drugabuse.gov/publications/media-guide/science-drug-abuse-addiction-basics

What is less controversial for most people in the addiction field is that we need to hold people suffering from any substance use disorder, including addiction, responsible for the negative consequences of their use, whether legal, medical, or social, including the harms to their loved ones. This was recognized by the founders of Alcoholics Anonymous (AA) in the four of the Twelve Steps that include alcoholics admitting their wrongs (Steps 4 and 5) and making restitution for the harm they caused (Steps 8 and 9). We can certainly hold nicotine addicts responsible for developing lung cancer with all the warnings that are available, just as we must hold methamphetamine or heroin addicts responsible for not only the resulting damage to their minds and bodies, but also for any crimes they committed and the financial and psychological devastation experienced by their families connected to their drug use. Similarly, people with even one DWI, whether they drink too much only on occasion or are true alcoholics, are accountable for the damages resulting from their alcohol abuse. Just as we hold people responsible for injuries to themselves and others in car crashes that occur when they run a red light or text while driving, we hold drug abusers accountable for the harm they cause while using.

People with an addiction commonly do not stop using until they hit bottom and confront their out-of-control behavior. They may also finally face the end of enabling by loved ones. "Enabling" is others, often family, taking actions that mitigate or protect drug users from some of the negative consequences of their drug use. Enabling perpetuates the drug use and delays the drug user's recognition that continued drug use means a continued rain of negative consequences that, over time, gets worse until the drug user "surrenders" which means accepting the unmanageability and the pain of life with continued drug use. Whatever path to the bottom, these individuals have my sympathy and my offer of help. Those who have the courage and persistence to do the hard work to recover from their disease have my deepest respect.

We especially need to help young people avoid any addictive substance use and, when substance abuse is already taking place, all of us—professionals, families, and community members—need to provide the help people need to stop using, including providing quality treatment for those who are addicted. In fact, helping people not develop substance use disorders and helping people recover from addiction, are the two central goals of this book.

Social Disapproval as a Public Health Strategy

Social disapproval can be very useful as a public health strategy—helpful in supporting both prevention and treatment and in promoting recovery. But holding people responsible for their use is different from stigmatizing people with addictions. What is and should be stigmatized is the willful abuse of all addictive substances, the use of any illegal drugs by adults, and the use of all drugs of abuse by youth. On the other hand, it is wrong and counterproductive to stigmatize the alcoholic or other drug addict as a person, even as we hold that individual responsible for any harmful behavior resulting from that use. His Holiness Pope Francis, in discussing how to think about people suffering from the use of alcohol and other drugs, said "The most needy of our brothers and sisters, who seemingly have nothing to give, offer us a treasure—the face of God, which speaks to us and challenges us."

The removal of the stigma of the alcoholic and the drug addict had its beginnings with its recognition as a disease with the publication of *Alcoholics Anonymous* in 1939 and by the New York Medical Society in 1954. This has been confirmed since then with the advances in brain research resulting in the designation of addiction as a brain disease. Social disapproval is not "stigmatization." It is possible to socially disapprove of not wearing seat belts, including making it illegal, without "stigmatizing" or even disrespecting the person who drives without a seat belt. For this reason, I believe that families and society should disapprove strongly of the use of illegal drugs. Moreover, they should strongly disapprove of the use of any addictive drugs—including alcohol, tobacco, and marijuana—by young people, the group most vulnerable to addiction.

The Role of Biology

Mood-altering drugs are chemicals that trick the brain's natural control system. Through this control system, people experience feelings of pleasure and pain. These brain mechanisms are designed to manage fundamental behaviors such as aggression, feeding, and reproduction.

Biology is just one factor in behavior. Human behavior is also guided by relatively changeable and adaptive cultures, even though the brain mechanisms that underlie behavior remain essentially the same, albeit with variations in brain functioning from person to person. Communities have learned techniques for managing anger, fear, eating, and sex over thousands of years of cultural evolution. Individuals learn during their lifetimes how to manage their own feelings from the wisdom and values of their families and communities. People generally manage their behaviors based on their values, their experiences, their knowledge, and the behaviors they see around them. When it comes to behaviors rooted in strong feelings, the family and the community are the principal sources of the hard-won, culturally based behavior management expertise.

When the brain's reward or pleasure centers are stimulated, the brain sends out powerful signals to repeat the pleasure-producing behaviors. With respect to aggression, fear, feeding, and sexuality, the brain knows only "more" and "no more" or, in computer language, "on" and "off." These basic, primitive mechanisms, which are common to animals, do not consider future consequences or values. They do not stop to consider other people's feelings or needs or know the importance of delayed gratification. It wants what it wants right now. The primitive brain directs the person to relieve distress and to promote pleasure. Fortunately, in addition to cultural expectations that restrict some human behaviors, when it comes to many natural pleasures, our brains have built-in protections. The brain has powerful feedback systems to say "enough" when it comes to natural behaviors, including aggression, feeding, and sex.

Addiction begins when the brain chemistry of this selfish brain is changed by an addictive substance such as alcohol or other drugs. Without this interaction of the reinforcing chemicals in the brain's pleasure centers, addiction would not be possible. That is why prevention techniques that discourage exposure to addicting drugs, outside of rigidly controlled traditional medical and religious contexts, are powerful and effective in preventing addiction to the extent that they can prevent the abuse of alcohol and other drugs.

People who have never been addicted to alcohol or other drugs find the behaviors of addicts to be incomprehensible: "Why would anyone pay thousands of dollars every year for a powder to sniff up their noses?" "Why would anyone want to regularly get drunk and out of control?" "I cannot imagine wanting to put a needle in my veins five or six times a day, every day of my life." "It is such an awful feeling to have your brain poisoned by alcohol or drugs!"

The explanation for these seemingly irrational behaviors can be found in the sensations and emotions these addictive substances produce in some people. The feelings experienced by addicts are intense and compelling. In the end, these feelings—misleadingly called "pleasure" because that word is too mild—take over the whole self of addicts including the addicts' thinking. It is this sense that addictive drugs "hijack" the addict's brain, because the drug use changes the addict's thinking to promote continued drug use and to discount people and events that would discourage use. What starts as attempts to repeat the pleasurable feelings produced by mood-altering substances becomes an obsession with finding and using these substances despite the harmful consequences for the addicts and the people around them. For this reason, members of Alcoholics Anonymous call addiction "cunning, baffling, and powerful."

What Causes Addiction: Learning from Animals

So why do otherwise intelligent addicted people repeatedly do things that cause themselves and those they love such pain? The biologically rooted power of addiction can be seen in experiments with laboratory rats that had electrodes placed in the pleasure centers of their brains. When their pleasure centers were stimulated, these rats repeated behaviors controlled by the researchers to produce more sensations of pleasure.

Rats find even mild electric shocks to their feet to be extremely unpleasant. In one experiment, laboratory rats were placed in a cage that had an electric grid down the middle that the rats had to cross to get various rewards. The electric shocks to their feet were not strong enough to cause them harm, but they were sufficiently unpleasant to the rats so that they would not cross the electrified grid even to have sex or to get food or water. They would die of dehydration and starvation rather than cross that grid. But these same rats walked across that electrified grid as if it were not there to get drugs of abuse—the pleasure centers of their brains were so rewarded by drugs of abuse that they willingly endured electric shock.

In other experiments, research scientists gave monkeys cocaine only when the monkeys worked hard enough to complete difficult problem-solving tasks. The monkeys were also given access to sex, food, and water as alternative rewards after long periods of deprivation. The researchers measured how much work the monkeys would do to get each of these rewards, all of which produced stimulation of the brain's pleasure centers. They found that the monkeys worked harder for cocaine than for any other stimulation, including sex or food. In fact, when the monkeys were permitted to use as much cocaine as they wanted, they used the drug until they died of convulsions and heart failure.

These laboratory experiments with animals make clear that the stimulation of the brain's pleasure centers by drugs or by direct electrical stimulation is far more rewarding and controlling of behavior than when these same brain mechanisms are stimulated by natural means, including by food or sex. This same happening is repeated thousands of times a day by addicted people who put alcohol and other drug use first in their lives. This comparison is not meant to minimize the power of food and sex in controlling human or animal behavior. Clearly, the stimulations of food and sex are often as powerful as drugs and are sometimes even overwhelming. However, they usually pale in comparison to the potency of addiction to alcohol and other drugs to stimulate behavior.

With few exceptions, such as a bird or primate occasionally eating a fermented fruit, animals in natural states do not encounter or use drugs of abuse. Some students of addiction have discovered that animals in the wild occasionally do encounter plants that have mood-altering effects and that the animals do become intoxicated when they eat these plants. Three conclusions can be reached about these observations of alcohol and other drug use in natural populations of animals. First, these natural exposures to intoxicants are distinctly unusual experiences. Second, the experience of intoxication is dangerous for animals (as it is for humans), often leading to the animals becoming victims of predators that they would have avoided if sober. Third, no wild animals have daily access to intoxicating drugs as do human addicts nor, unlike human addicts, are they likely to seek them out to the detriment of their health.

An experiment sheds light on why it is useful to plants to produce intoxicating chemicals. Scientists noticed that the coca bush in South America, containing small concentrations of cocaine, was seldom subject to insect predators, as were other nearby plants. Even young coca leaves rarely show evidence of insect damage. To understand how this worked, botanists sprayed cocaine-containing dust on tender tomato plants before releasing insects known to love tomato plants. After a few minutes of exposure to the plants dusted with cocaine, the insects acted bizarrely and stopped eating, dying within a day or two. The scientists found that the cocaine boosted the effects of the neurotransmitter octopamine in the insects' nerves, hopelessly scrambling their messages. This experiment left little doubt as to why wild animals, including insects, generally do not eat coca leaves. The same set of factors applies to nicotine in the leaves of the tobacco plant, which protects the plants from insect infestations. Nicotine has been used as an insect poison because of its effect on brain neurotransmitters.

In contrast to animals, it is harder to understand addictive behavior in humans because there are so many complex factors shaping a person's actions. Each act of an individual has many possible explanations. Some observers of human addiction have explained it as a form of slow-motion suicide; as an expression of anger toward spouses or parents; as an economic, racial, political, or ethnic protest; or as an expression of a deep psychological disorder.

All of these factors can play into the unique dynamics of the addictive process for each individual, but the fundamental explanation for addiction common to all addicts is far more simple, as seen in laboratory experiments: Human addicts use alcohol and other drugs for the same reasons that laboratory animals do—for the feelings of pleasure that the substances produce in their brains. In these animal experiments, it is unmistakably clear that using addicting drugs produces rewards more powerful than other natural stimulations and that this experience is the far more dominant factor than the complex psychological, historical, or economic factors that may enter into the progression of this disease. Addiction to alcohol and other drugs is above all a universal biological process run amok. That's why it's becoming more common to hear addiction called a "brain disease." There is one more lesson from animal experiments with addicting drugs that has a powerful message for those who set our drug policy. It is not just young rats, unhappy rats, or rats with a certain genetic makeup that are subject to addiction to these drugs. While certain animals are more or less vulnerable to addiction, all the rats become addicted to the same drugs to which humans do if they continue to use the drugs until their brains are trained to the drug experience.

Tolerance, Withdrawal and Dependence

The more the brain is exposed to a chemical over time, the less the brain responds to a particular dose of that chemical. This is the definition of "tolerance," which is one of the criteria of addiction, and it means that more of a drug is required to produce the same effect when the drug is used frequently and at high doses. However, even for addicts there is a ceiling to how much they can tolerate: Cigarette smokers do not commonly smoke more than forty cigarettes (two packs) a day, and alcoholics seldom drink more than about ten ounces of pure alcohol (eighteen beers or a fifth of distilled liquor) a day, no matter how long they use these substances. The fact that people who are addicted to alcohol and other drugs do not use even more of these substances over time demonstrates the limits of drug tolerance. Most nonusers are impressed by how much drug use tolerance permits. They cannot imagine liking the feelings produced by smoking one much less forty cigarettes a day or drinking twenty-six ounces of vodka a day.

Along with tolerance, withdrawal is one of the characteristics of physical dependence. Withdrawal symptoms generally occur after everyday use of a drug for prolonged periods of time, when the drug use is abruptly stopped (sometimes called stopping "cold turkey" because "goose bumps" is a common symptom of withdrawal). Both tolerance and withdrawal occur when the brain adapts to the regular presence of a chemical. Even though these two phenomena are common in many people who abuse drugs, they do not necessarily indicate addiction, as is commonly thought. There is enormous confusion when the defining feature of addiction is equated with drug withdrawal. In this view, addicts continue to use drugs because when they stop they have painful withdrawal symptoms. This is the image of the man with the golden arm, the addict who is hooked on drugs because he fears the suffering of withdrawal. There are two simple and common experiences that disprove the central role of withdrawal in drug addiction. Addicts everywhere have many episodes of stopping drug use, mostly involuntary—because they don't have the money for their drugs, because they are hospitalized or incarcerated, or for dozens of other reasons that are quite distinct from wanting to stop using drugs. If withdrawal was the major problem preventing addicts from becoming drug-free, then when they were forced not to use drugs for a week or two, or even for many months or years, they would celebrate their liberation from addiction. They would certainly never go back to the bondage of drug use. But return they do, often again and again. Addicts relapse to drug use, even after long periods of abstinence, with a regularity that makes relapse to use after being drug-free a defining characteristic of addiction. Withdrawal is very painful. Addicts work hard to avoid withdrawal. But withdrawal is not the core problem of addiction.

Both tolerance and withdrawal, as symptoms of physical dependence, occur in response to most mood-altering chemicals that affect the brain, whether they produce addiction or not. They reflect the brain's adaptation to a new chemical environment, one that includes the continuous presence, often at a high concentration, of a particular chemical. This traditional pharmacological definition of physical dependence is quite different from the use of the word "dependence" traditionally used in the context of addiction. The narrower and older indicator of dependence focused on the presence of withdrawal symptoms when the substance was removed. The broader and more accurate definition of addiction reflects the fact that addicts depend on the use of self-destructive, pleasure-causing drugs to conduct their lives. Tolerance and withdrawal symptoms often indicate that people are physically dependent on a drug, but alone they do not necessarily mean users have developed the complex disease of addiction.

In this book, I distinguish between physical dependence and addiction by using the term "physical dependence" as the simple cellular adaptation of the body, especially the neurons in the brain, to the continued presence of a chemical that influences brain function. In contrast, "addiction," while often including physical dependence, is a complex, lifelong brain disease affecting the entire self—body, mind, and spirit.

Risk Factors for Addiction

Over thousands of years, human beings in all cultures have developed reasonably effective guidelines to deal with pleasure and pain and with associated common behaviors. Cultures define when and how aggression, fear, feeding, sexuality, and many more complex but equally important feelings are expressed by human beings living in communities that share many values. Human communities permit and even encourage aggressive behavior in contests and sports, often imposing elaborate rules on the most intensely aggressive behaviors. Exposure to and mastery of fear is managed by common rituals. Culturally based rules are established in human societies for feeding and sexual activity. No human community could exist with unbridled expression of these powerful feelings by each individual community member. The survival of the community itself, as well as the survival of the individuals in the community, depends on the adherence to the community's social contracts governing aggression, fear, feeding, and sex.

Within any community there is a high level of diversity, both cultural and biological. Some people are tall and some are short; some are thin and some are fat; some are quick-tempered and others are calm. Like physical characteristics, habitual behaviors also show great diversity in human (and animal) populations. Some people instinctively court danger and excitement, whereas others strenuously avoid both. Similarly, some people conform to community norms governing pleasure-driven behavior and some do not. Nature has seen to it that biological and cultural diversity is maintained because diverse populations are best able to adapt to changing environments and to take advantage of changing opportunities. Diversity is as important for adaptations of populations when it comes to values as it is for physical characteristics as height and weight.

Cultural and character diversity means that within any community there are widely different personal values managing the experiences of not only aggression, fear, feeding, and sexuality, but also the use of addictive drugs. This diversity translates into differences in the risk of addiction to alcohol and other drugs. Some personal values are relatively protective of individuals and the community, and others are less protective when it comes to addiction. The most consequential variation in risk of addiction in a community is the willingness repeatedly to use addictive drugs outside of medical supervision and social and legal norms for fun and often with peers who use the same drugs. Every day we see the results of this inescapable diversity of addiction risk in families, communities, and nations. In a family with three or four children, it is common to see that one child has a drug or alcohol problem whereas the others do not. Similarly, some segments of communities have larger problems with self-destructive behaviors like addiction, and others have smaller problems. Age, gender, and, of course, genetics (more about this later) are also major factors in the rates of problem behaviors, including addiction. No culture or set of shared values either guarantees addiction in a person or erases the risk entirely because all human brains are susceptible to the varying degrees of pleasure caused by drugs of abuse.

Values and Drug Use in Traditional Cultures

Humans living in many relatively homogeneous traditional cultures in all parts of the world did not encounter drugs and did not have to worry about controlling alcohol or other drug intoxication. For these reasons, the human brain's hardware developed without built-in protections from drug-caused risks. It was only when these drugs were introduced into these cultures from outside that humans had the opportunity to use intoxicating drugs repeatedly, and only in recent times have people learned how to use purified, highly potent brain-stimulating drugs by powerful routes of administration.

Drugs defy the brain's built-in control mechanisms for dangerous behaviors like fear of predators and fear of heights that have developed over millions of years. Traditional values acted to limit exposure to alcohol and other drugs as they were experienced in pre-modern cultures. Traditional values of human societies prohibited the use of intoxicating drugs outside medical and religious ceremonies. Drug use, in all stable pre-modern cultures, was controlled not by the individual but by the community's medical or religious leaders.

Early human communities were relatively small, isolated, and culturally homogeneous. The diversity of these communities was limited as the community shared values about how to manage aggression, fear, sex, and feeding. Traditional cultures permitted relatively few different roles and comparatively limited personal choice of behavior. The shared values within these cultures served to inhibit the use of alcohol and other drugs in communities that had any exposure to these substances.

Values and Drug Use in Modern Cultures

In modern times, with the assimilation and, in many cases, the destruction of these traditional cultures and values, (such as with Native Americans and the Australian Aborigines), a new challenge regarding addiction has emerged as large segments of the population, especially youth in the US, have been exposed to dozens of addicting drugs in settings that permit or even encourage drug use. Modern values emphasizing personal control of one's life and simultaneous increases in the social tolerance for alternative lifestyles have provided a fertile ground for the contemporary drug abuse epidemic. These values have been increasingly prominent in the US and other countries throughout the world, especially for youth, in the last five decades.

Modern countries with great cultural diversity have large numbers of people living in complex and interdependent communities. Not only are these modern communities much more diverse with respect to values that determine the risk of addiction, but individuals in them function with far more anonymity and independence than was true in pre-modern cultures.

Modern communities have many advantages over earlier village-based cultures, permitting, for example, a wider range of lifestyles and greater personal control by each person over his or her own life. However, one result of the new, more diverse, larger, and more anonymous communities is an increased risk of addiction. A major challenge for the future in all parts of the world is to fit effective prevention and treatment for addiction into this modern value system. The challenge is great, as the conflict of values found throughout this book demonstrates.

All people are not equally vulnerable to addiction to alcohol and other drugs. Genetic and environmental factors, in particular, heighten vulnerability. People whose parents and other family members are addicted and people who live in environments that are relatively accepting of alcohol and other drug use are at increased risk of addiction. People who are oriented to immediate reward rather than to delayed gratification, people with mental health disorders, those without a strong family or community support system, and people who lack moral values are all at higher risk of addiction. Relative risk of addiction is affected by many other factors as well, including availability of intoxicating substances, gender, and age—for example, addictions to alcohol and other drugs are more common among males and among people ages fifteen to thirty. Adolescence is a uniquely vulnerable age because the adolescent brain is especially susceptible to drug effects and because the frontal lobes of the brain, which put the brakes on risky behaviors, are not fully developed until the mid or late twenties. This is the reason the vast majority of drug use begins in adolescence and, when it does, can persist for years and even decades.

Genetic predisposition to alcoholism and drug addiction is real, important, and increasingly the subject of scientific study. But both nonhuman animal studies and human studies show that genetics is not the only factor influencing addiction. Most children of alcoholics or drug addicts do not themselves become alcoholics or drug addicts. Many addicted people do not have parents or siblings who were addicted to alcohol or other drugs. Genetics can raise or lower the risk of addiction but it does not alone control it. The development of addiction requires many forces, including those that are environmental and experiential.

The substance being used also affects the risk of addiction. For example, cocaine and heroin are far more likely to produce addiction than marijuana or psychedelic drugs, given the same level of use, genetic vulnerability, and social tolerance. Routes of administration—for example, injecting versus oral use—are also important in a person's relative risk of addiction. While these factors, and many others, govern relative risk of addiction, all people are vulnerable to addiction with some people having more of a predisposition for addiction than others.

To the extent that people, especially young people, are exposed to nonmedical drug use in relatively permissive environments, the drug problem worsens.

Exposure to alcohol and other drugs, especially for teenagers who are in peer groups without the presence of responsible adults, poses an especially high risk of addiction.

The human experience of getting high is more than the biology of the brain interacting with the drug. The setting in which the drug is taken influences the drug-taking experience. Similarly, the drug user's mind-set (a term used for the expectation that the drug user has when the drug use takes place) affects the drug experience as well.

The most high-risk picture for the development of addiction is not difficult to define. When a person with a high genetic vulnerability (such as having parents or siblings who are addicted to alcohol and other drugs), a "co-occurring mental health disorder," and/or impulsive character traits is exposed to a highly addictive drug taken by a high-risk route of administration (smoking or injecting) in a setting that promotes drug intoxication with an expectation of getting good feelings (the setting and the mind-set), the gun of addiction is loaded, it is aimed at the center of the brain, and the trigger is pulled. Addiction does not require all these high-risk factors to be present, but surprisingly often, especially in the most deadly cases of addiction, they are all or almost all lined up in just this way.

Personal and Genetic Factors That Raise the Risk of Addiction

- Having parents or siblings who are addicted to alcohol and other drugs
- Being impulsive and focused on immediate gratification rather than being willing to delay gratification
- Having personal values that revolve around one's own feelings of pleasure rather than on concern for others, and having no moral center
- Being immature
- Having a mental health disorder

Environmental Factors That Raise the Risk of Addiction

- Being exposed frequently to alcohol and other addicting drugs
- Living in a family that tolerates drug use and/or excessive alcohol use
- Having a community that tolerates addiction and its consequences
- Having friends who use alcohol and drugs addictively

Not Blaming the Victim, While Holding Addicts Responsible

As a physician, I am committed to the disease concept of addiction. Yet, at the same time, I believe in holding addicts responsible. How can a sick person be held responsible for having a disease? Is this not blaming the victim? We do not hold people with many illnesses responsible for their disease, so how can a compassionate person hold alcoholics or other drug addicts responsible for their disease?

Although addicted people, like other sick people, are not responsible for their diseases, they are fully responsible for their behaviors during every stage of the disease. The addicted person's disease is a heightened vulnerability to drug-induced rewarding experiences, which has both biological and environmental elements. Still, addicts' behaviors are entirely their responsibility, including the harm they do to others because of their drinking or drugging and whether or not they take advantage of the various treatment and recovery options available, such as Alcoholics Anonymous and Narcotics Anonymous.

Putting addiction into a medical context (always a good idea) is helpful in thinking about the question of personal responsibility for the disease of addiction. As described earlier, there are two distinct dimensions of personal responsibility for substance use disorders and other diseases. The first is the responsibility for having contracted the disease. The second is responsibility for managing the disease once it has taken hold. It is not only lung cancer among smokers where the patient has a major role in getting the disease as well as managing it. In a very large percentage of diseases there is an element of responsibility for developing the disease by ignoring health risks and an even larger number of diseases that require the patient to take personal responsibility for managing the disease.

Recovery is thwarted when we excuse alcoholics and drug addicts for their behavior while drinking or using, because excusing removes socially imposed consequences of their use. Tough antidrug sanctions, in the family and in the community at large, are key factors in influencing people not to use alcohol and other drugs to begin with or to stop using these substances if they are misusing them but not addicted. These sanctions are vital to successful prevention and treatment of addiction. Do addicted people need to hit bottom to recover? The distorted thinking that denies the role of substance use in the problems in the addict's life makes it difficult for the addict to see the problem and the solution to that problem. Something needs to happen to break through that denial, to make clear the path to recovery. What is that "something"? Sometimes it is as little as physicians saying to patients that they have an illness and that this requires them to stop their use of alcohol and other drugs, or a spouse or other family member's admonition. At other times it is time in jail or the loss of a job. The disease progresses until the denial is overcome, often with a sense of desperation that leads to a new, positive direction, or until death occurs.

Think about how a family or a society could function if it excused alcoholics for their behaviors when drunk, behaviors that include inflicting injury on others and committing other crimes. Is a drunk driver personally and legally responsible for killing an innocent pedestrian? In making the determination of personal responsibility for the drunk driving crash, does it matter whether the driver was an active alcoholic or merely a social drinker who had one too many drinks before taking the wheel? Think what a society would be like if it excused heroin addicts of their responsibility for robbing to get money to pay for their drugs, or cocaine addicts of their responsibility for selling drugs to others. It does not take deep thought to realize that excuses for addicts' behaviors can cause society great harm and do immeasurable harm to addicts themselves.

Characteristics of Addiction

- Addiction means continued use despite repeated, serious problems because of that use.
- Addiction involves loss of control (unmanageability) and dishonesty (denial). It both feeds on and causes self-centeredness, sensitivity to criticism, and dishonesty.
- Addicts develop tolerance—more of a drug is required to produce the same effect when the drug is used frequently and at high doses.
- Addicts are not responsible for having their disease, but they are responsible for choosing to use drugs that are well-known to cause addiction and they are responsible for all of the harms they cause because of their use of addictive drugs. They are also responsible for what they do about their disease once they hit bottom and confront their loss of control.
- Addiction is a family disease—family members commonly suffer from codependence, where they protect the addict, enable addictive behaviors, and contribute to the progression of the disease.

This excusing is yet another well-meaning but misguided form of enabling. It is a principal environmental cause of substance abuse. It prevents people from getting help for their addiction. Enabling is the ultimate form of both irresponsibility and uncaring. When it comes to addiction, enabling is love turned cruel, not by its intentions but by its inescapable consequences. Holding addicts responsible for all of their behaviors, for their personal choices, means not blaming or controlling; it is simply being realistic. Recognition of the disease concept of addiction does not label addicts as "victims" who are not responsible for their actions; rather, it offers both addicts and non-addicted people a practical, understandable way to approach the otherwise bizarre and confusing behaviors of addicts and those around them.

Many well-meaning people seek to soften the edges in dealing with addicted people by avoiding words such as "alcoholic," or "addict" and by ignoring character defects when referring to the negative personality traits that addicts display. They find such blunt words dated, prejudicial, and offensive. It is no accident that the Twelve Step programs and many of the best addiction treatment programs use this direct and clear language. By not being direct, denial of the active phase of this deadly disease of addiction is prolonged. By using these strong words without apology or ambiguity, denial is stripped away and the real work of getting well from addiction can go forward. I use strong words in this book because I have learned to use them from my work with recovering people. Recovering people use these words to describe themselves and their behaviors when they were actively addicted to alcohol and other drugs. The addicted people in recovery with whom I have worked have characterized their lives when they were using alcohol and other drugs as filled with deceit and dishonesty when it came to the chemicals they loved to use. None has objected to my characterization of addiction, which focuses on two central features: the loss of control over the use of alcohol and other drugs and dishonesty.

Busting Denial with Drug Testing

Drug users do not choose addiction, illness, or death. Virtually no one intends to become addicted. They simply choose to use alcohol and other drugs to get high. They start out believing they can do it safely. Some do; many do not. Is the use of currently illegal drugs a more protected privacy right than speeding or driving without a seat belt? Are drug-using behaviors less likely to harm others? Is it less intrusive to ask all air travelers to go through a metal detector than to ask all employees, or all schoolchildren, to take a drug test if substance abuse is evident? I do not think so, but some people, equally well informed and sincere, disagree with me.

People use drugs because of the effects the drugs have on their brains' pleasure centers. Drugs, however, do not just go to the users' brains. Drugs are found in every part of the body after drug use. Drugs are detectable in blood, urine, sweat, and saliva. Drugs are detectable in hair as well as in fingernails and toenails. Drugs can be found in every organ of the body from the skin to the liver and from the brain to muscles. Drug testing gives us a way to determine if a person is using drugs in the face of their denial and to hold them accountable.

Drugs are dream busters. Drugs rob individuals, families, and communities of their hopes, making life unmanageable for everyone. Drug tests are denial busters, exposing the nonmedical drug user to the healing forces of family and community life and giving good, immediate reasons to say no to illicit drug use.

Drug Policy and the Social Contract for Drug Use

The "social contract for drug use," which forms the foundation of my thinking about drug policies, can be simply stated: Self-controlled use, as well as sale, of illegal addictive drugs such as heroin, cocaine, meth, or marijuana (in most states and countries) for fun is prohibited. I call this behavior "recreational pharmacology." However, when science judges one of these same drugs, or drugs similar to them, to be useful in the treatment of an illness or disease other than addiction, then its use as part of medical treatment, controlled by an informed prescribing physician, is legal. Medical use of a potentially addicting medicine is not self-controlled. The proper use of medicines is not characterized by deceit and dishonesty. Medicines are not taken whenever one feels like it. Medicines are not taken to a party or with other drugs of abuse. Real medicines are used as they are prescribed for the medical conditions for which they are prescribed and with all the facts about the patient's drug use openly reported to the prescribing physician.

Many dangerous and potentially abused drugs have legitimate medical uses. Morphine, codeine, and opioid painkillers, and more recently, some of the chemicals found in cannabis, are good examples. Use of potentially addicting drugs within controlled medical practice is appropriate for medical purposes, as long as the illness being treated is not addiction itself and as long as the supply of the potentially addicting medicine is restricted to the patient and does not find its way into other hands. Sadly, beginning in the late 1990s, overprescription of opioid painkillers, such as OxyContin and Vicodin, along with a newly effective supply on the streets of highly pure heroin and fentanyl, and a myriad of synthetic analogues, launched an epidemic of addiction and overdoses to these drugs that grew to devastating epidemic proportions. By the time policy makers and the medical community finally started to address this problem, overdose deaths had passed fatalities from motor vehicle crashes and gun violence. The problems of excessive medically prescribed opioids are not limited to their diversion into the illegal drug market as some "patients" sold their drugs, or to the problems of addiction among the pain patients; we also have growing evidence that when taken for many years at high doses, these medicines lose their effectiveness at pain control and are often associated with unproductive lifestyles.

In the US, the nonmedical use of alcohol and tobacco (and as of this writing, in an increasing number of states, marijuana) is legally accepted for adults. In fact, until recently most people did not consider alcohol and nicotine to be drugs. Even today international treaties do not consider them to be drugs. On the other hand, the use of these substances by youth is legally prohibited, unlike all other consumer products, underlining just how different alcohol and nicotine (and marijuana) are from chocolate and blue jeans. Many formal and informal rules of conduct restrict the use of alcohol and nicotine by adults, making clear that these are not routine commercial products.

Whether the sale and use of a particular drug is legal or not makes no difference when it comes to its effects on the brain, including addiction. Its legal status also has no effect on the best way to treat someone who has developed a substance use disorder to the drug. However, making a drug legal significantly increases both its availability and its social acceptability. Legality of a drug also unleashes powerful commercial promotion of its use, as can be seen with both alcohol and nicotine and increasingly with marijuana.

This social contract makes recreational pharmacology culturally unacceptable and prohibited legally for all but a small number of exempt drugs, especially alcohol and nicotine. And for those exempt drugs, it sets specific strong cultural and legal boundaries on both sale and use. This is called a "restrictive drug policy" because it treats the chemicals that produce brain reward and drug abuse as a special case separate from other commercial products. This is a public health strategy because it limits use of these chemicals for reasons of health and safety.

What is a "Drug Policy"?

A policy is a shared way of dealing with an issue or behavior. It can be a law or a commonly-held way of thinking about a behavior.

A national drug policy is the way a country handles drug use as a global drug policy is the way many countries handle drugs. Families and communities also have shared approaches. Today there are vigorous battles over drug policy including the legalization of marijuana for medical or recreational purposes and over the ease of access to medically prescribed addictive drugs as well as over the use of criminal laws dealing with drug sales and use.

Proposals to Modify the Social Contract and Restrictive Drug Policy

Some people would like to change this basic social contract for drug use, for example by making recreational use of marijuana legal for adults, as has happened in many states although at this writing it remains illegal in all states under federal law. This legalization approach has been proposed for all drugs of abuse, from hallucinogens to cocaine, methamphetamine and heroin. These modifications in the social contract deserve wide public debate. My view is that we should strengthen the prohibition of all currently illegal drugs and increase the social and legal restrictions on the use of alcohol and nicotine, especially for youth under the age of twenty-one.

Whatever a person's views of these laws, unless the US drug laws are changed, every citizen has a duty to respect the contract on drug use as it is now in force. The laws are subject to change by the will of the people. Today, drug laws are under spirited debate with the future quite uncertain.

Political disagreement with this social contract for drug use is inescapable and, to some extent, even desirable. Nevertheless, I believe that the use of illegal drugs outside the current contract is unhealthy and that legal sanctions should continue to be in place. The full force of informal and legal punishments needs to be imposed on people who violate this basic social contract. This policy, developed over the last hundred years, is internationally imposed on virtually all of the nations in the world through formal treaty obligations.

There now is a vigorous debate about the consequences of violations of the laws against drug use and drug sale. This debate also is appropriate and desirable. Illegal drug sale is a serious crime and deserves serious punishment. Illegal drug use also deserves legal consequences aimed primarily at stopping the drug use. There is a growing body of experience in using the criminal justice system to promote recovery for the five million Americans on parole and probation, about 75 percent of whom have serious problems with alcohol and other drug use. In general, long prison sentences are undesirable except in the context of repeated serious crime and particularly grievous crimes such as murder.

This book focuses on prevention, treatment, and recovery. All of these important goals are the same for legal and illegal drugs because they are about brain stimulation by addicting drugs and because this powerful brain biology has nothing to do with the legality of particular drugs.

Defining Recovery

Some people use drugs, sometimes a lot of drugs, for a long period of time, and then stop for many reasons, sometimes for the rest of their lives, without ever being in treatment or in recovery support. Simply stopping drug use is not the same as being in recovery. Stopping use is common in nicotine addiction as well as with alcohol and other drugs. The people who need addiction treatment and long-term recovery support are those for whom simply stopping does not work or does not last. Treatment and sustained recovery are the more visible part of the drug and alcohol addiction picture. It is a commitment to abstinence—intentionally stopping for good, committing to and doing the hard work needed to maintain abstinence as well as the character development, one day at a time—that makes recovery possible. The ideal progression is completing an addiction treatment program followed by continuing recovery support. In my practice, I sadly see many addicted patients who try in vain to moderate or limit their alcohol and drug use or who try to simply stop on their own only to fail over and over again. Trying that option makes sense, once or twice. But when it fails, over and over again, it is time do something more. When stopping on your own or when using in moderation fails, it is not the failure of the addict. It is the tenacity of the disease of addiction, the "fault" of the selfish brain, the addicted brain, not the "fault" of the individual. Addiction is not just sometimes fatal; it is often fatal. Addiction is not something that only happens to weak or failed people. Addiction regularly takes down the strongest, the smartest and the best people.

Treatment is an often essential step toward recovery. Chapter 6 addresses intervention and treatment, and while my focus is primarily on the programs that have grown from Minnesota Model that combined recovery support with health care, I address the use of medicines to treat addictions to alcohol and other drugs which is growing.

As you will see in later sections of this book, I strongly support abstinence-based treatment models and the Twelve Step programs such as Alcoholics Anonymous, Narcotics Anonymous, and others. This support is based on my personal and professional experience with addiction and recovery. Although I am not a member of these fellowships, I have watched the miracle of recovery hundreds, if not thousands, of times. I started my medical career with methadone treatment of heroin addiction in the public sector. I remain supportive of using medicines in the treatment of addiction; however, I suggest that medication assisted treatments, and all other addiction treatments, be evaluated on their ability to produce long-term recovery. That includes no use of alcohol or other drugs and long-term involvement in recovery support to reduce the enduring threat of relapse and to improve the quality of life of addicted people.

The recovery support groups, discussed at length in chapter 7, are predominantly Twelve Step programs that use the same Twelve Steps to recovery that form the foundation of the program of Alcoholics Anonymous. Whether you're an addicted person or a family member, at the meetings of any Twelve Step program you see the deadly disease of addiction and the inspiring process of recovery. These meetings are easily accessible to virtually everyone in the US today.

If my book does nothing more than to let you know that these Twelve Step meetings are the places to find in-depth, real-life expertise about addiction, and if the book helps you find your way to meetings, I will be fully satisfied in my efforts. I must add, however, that recovery support is by no means limited to the Twelve Steps. There are a growing number of other useful recovery support groups that do not use the Twelve Steps. People sometimes ask me why there are so many Twelve Step meetings and relatively so few alternatives. My answer is simple. The community support meetings are not paid for by the government or by health insurance. They are run by and for people recovering from addiction. Thus the scale of the each of the alternative community support groups reflects the size and motivation of the population that is helped by these alternative approaches.

The word "recovery" describes the near-miraculous release of the addict from the grip of addiction. Recovery is emancipation from the chemical slavery of addiction. Since continued drug use despite problems and dishonesty are the hallmarks of addiction, the hallmarks of recovery are not using any alcohol or other drugs (from alcohol and marijuana to cocaine and heroin) and honesty. A patient told me years ago there is more honesty in a meeting of recovering addicts than there is in a psychiatrist's office. Recovery does not happen suddenly and it does not occur spontaneously. Recovery is an ongoing process that takes both time and hard work. It is an unending process. People say they that are "in recovery" rather than saying that they are "recovered" for good reason. Recovery is about building character and living a good life that is not dominated by self-centeredness and selfishness. Recovery replaces the resentments typical of addiction with gratitude. Recovery is the biological and the spiritual healing of the selfish brain.

2. A SHORT HISTORY OF DRUG USE AND THE MODERN DRUG EPIDEMIC

While human drug use is old the current drug epidemic is new. The drug overdose epidemic did not just suddenly appear in the past decade or two and this is not the first time that drug use has been at the top of the nation's agenda. It is impossible to understand today's addiction crisis without recognizing how we got here, where it came from and how it is both similar and different from what has gone before. The human brain has not changed over thousands of years but the drug problem has changed dramatically because the drugs have changed, the exposure to drugs has changed and the culture has changed in dealing with drug use. These changes are rapidly dramatically. When it comes to understanding addiction the past matters to the present.

In traditional or pre-modern cultures, drugs were generally not used for pleasure in environments of high availability. There was not the high tolerance for drug use and the low community control over socially disapproved behaviors that exist today in the modern world, especially in the US and other developed nations.

This chapter will review, in brief, how drug use has evolved, changed, and grown throughout history. This information will help to explain the origins of the latest drug epidemic facing our nation as well as problems plaguing youth today and the forecast for the future.

Drug Use in Traditional Cultures

Pre-modern cultures generally lacked the ability to supply drugs or to purify the few addicting drugs to which they had access. Even more important, traditional societies had high levels of social control over the behaviors of community members. Usually people lived in small villages where everyone knew everyone else. If anyone's behavior, because of drug use or for any other reason, was a problem to the community, then direct, personal, and effective action was taken to address the offending behavior. In many cases if the offending behavior did not stop, that individual was cast out of the community.

> ### Drug Use in Traditional Societies
> - Use of addicting drugs was restricted to low-potency materials.
> - Routes of administration were low risk.
> - Use of addictive substances was reserved for religious or medicinal purposes, not for recreation.
> - There was tight social control over all personal behavior.

Traditional communities lacked not only today's diversity but also most of the opportunities for deceit and anonymity that characterize modern life. Lying was harder when everyone knew each other's every step throughout the day. In primitive cultures, being banished from the community meant certain death at the hands of hostile neighboring human communities or in the mouths of hungry carnivores. A solitary human being was helpless.

When drugs were used in these cultures they were of low potency and were commonly used only for ceremonial or medicinal purposes, which made the physical and psychological health problems from repeated, compulsive drug use characteristic of addiction unlikely to arise.

For example, Native Americans used tobacco without suffering from emphysema or lung cancer because their tobacco use prior to contact with Europeans was limited to uncommon ceremonial occasions. Native Americans did not have readily available mass produced cigarettes, which maximized the addicting properties of tobacco. They typically used tobacco in clay pipes smoked in community rituals. The easily understood contrast between socially controlled traditional Native American ceremonial smoking of tobacco pipes and personally controlled modern cigarette smoking captures the distinction between pre-modern non-addictive drug use and modern addictive drug use.

The use of opium and marijuana in Asia in pre-modern times was similar to Native Americans' use of tobacco. Opium and marijuana use was commonly limited to an oral route of administration, usually in teas, which were used infrequently at low doses as medicines.

Early Alcohol Use

Alcohol use was a more complex story before the modern era because as soon as beer and wine could be produced, which happened in many cultures thousands of years ago, drug-induced intoxication was possible. For traditional cultures, the unavailability due to relatively high cost of producing alcohol in large quantities kept its use limited, as did formal and informal social controls over behaviors associated with the abuse of alcohol. Even when pre-modern societies permitted sufficient use of alcohol or another drug to produce intoxication, this use was infrequent and managed in families and communities.

One of the sad paradoxes of modern times is that traditional cultures, which had achieved a safe equilibrium with the use of drugs as long as they remained isolated and were able to retain their values, languages, and spiritual practices, have proven to be tragically vulnerable to today's alcohol and other drug problems. To see Native Americans and other indigenous peoples, such as Australia's aborigines, suffer from the use of alcohol, cigarettes, inhalants, and other modern drugs, is to face the painful reality that traditional cultures are not prepared to withstand exposure to modern drugs and to tolerant values governing drug-taking behaviors. Traditional communities lack the limited but valuable cultural immunity to the abuse of alcohol and other drugs mainly due to the loss of their lands, languages, and spiritual practices to colonialization.

Drug Use in the Shrinking Globe

The second phase of world drug history, the beginning of the world's first drug problems, was linked to the distillation of alcohol and the dissemination of drug habits as part of the Age of Discovery. These two milestones were modestly disruptive and would have remained fairly rare had they not occurred at the time of the population migration to cities and the breakdown of the village culture that took place in the pre-industrial world with the advent of the agrarian revolution. This marked a period of rapid transition from traditional cultures to the modern era.

When Europeans discovered distillation—heating beer and wine so that the alcohol vaporized before the water did, and then condensing the alcohol to separate it from the water, thereby dramatically raising the concentration of alcohol—the world experience with alcohol changed forever. Rum was made from sugar cane, vodka from potatoes, whiskey from grains, and brandy from wine, all using simple distillation. The social impact of cheap distilled alcohol on an increasingly urban Europe was sudden and devastating.

When distilled liquor later was exported, the new threat of this more potent form of alcohol became global. Rum, for example, was part of the triangle trade of slaves from Africa to the Caribbean, molasses from the Caribbean to New England and Europe, and surplus rum from North America and Europe to Africa. Farmers from the American Midwest who grew grains in the early 1800s found that they could ship the value of their crops more economically across the Appalachian Mountains or down the Mississippi River as whiskey rather than as corn or wheat. Taxes on whiskey became an important part of the new nation's political and economic history, reflecting the relative importance of alcohol in the cash economy.

Alcohol and the Emergence of Protestantism

It is no accident that in Western Europe the Protestant Reformation was closely tied to anti-alcohol sentiments. The Reformation took place in the fifteenth and sixteenth centuries in northern Europe. When distillation of alcohol became widespread in these countries, the newly emerging urban communities, in particular, suffered intensely from an epidemic of drunkenness. Communities in northern and western Europe were the breeding ground for the religious Reformation partly because of the social disruption caused by the escalating use of distilled spirits.

It seems likely that Muhammad's prohibition against the use of alcohol, which has served to protect hundreds of millions of Muslims from alcoholism, was related to the early discoveries of distillation of alcohol, in that the discovery by the Muslim chemists did not lead to profound social harm. This harm was prevalent in Europe, however, where there was no similarly effective religiously based prohibition against alcohol use to protect the population before the Reformation.

Tobacco, which had been used for ceremonial purposes by Native Americans, rapidly entered international trade as the habit of smoking became global within two decades of the initial European exploration of the Western Hemisphere. The properties of tobacco leading to physical dependence were observed quickly, leading to initial hostile societal reactions to tobacco use throughout the world. Initially tobacco was available only leaf form that was dried, crumbled and smoked in a pipe. It was only the introduction of the cigarette, and then then cigarette rolling machine in the early twentieth century that made tobacco a major global health threat.

Alcohol and Other Drug Use Since 1900

Although alcohol problems were severe in some cultures after the Reformation, there were relatively few problems with other drugs until the last 100 years or so. In addition to tobacco, there also was a modest spread of the use of some traditional drugs outside old boundaries as a result of new travel and trade. Opium smoking came into wider use in Asia. Coca leaf chewing, which previously was limited to traditional, religious uses in the Andes, was exploited by the Spanish conquerors in a cynical manipulation of native culture. The Spanish found that they could pay the tin miners in Bolivia with coca leaves, which was less costly than giving them food, housing, clothing, or money. Older medical and religious restrictions on drug use began to break down for marijuana, coca, and opium throughout the world after the sixteenth century, as colonialism disrupted traditional cultures, while the introduction of tobacco as a substitute for local Native Americans encouraged the practice of smoking. This route of administration spread to all parts of the world as a new and far more dangerous form of drug taking, especially for marijuana and opium. Opium was smoked widely only after the introduction of tobacco smoking. This change in the route of administration dramatically increased the addictive potential of opium. A similar change occurred for marijuana. When smoking replaced oral ingestion of marijuana, the scene changed as cannabis intoxication and addiction became commonplace for the first time.

Modernization of Drug Abuse

Cannabis and opium use in the Middle East had a history similar to the experience of smoking tobacco in North America, with most traditional use of cannabis being restricted to oral, primarily medicinal use until European imperialism introduced smoking which was a superior route of administration, thus disrupting the traditional social controls over the use of these drugs. Only then did the abuse of cannabis and opium become serious social and health problems in the Middle East. As the societies of the Middle East reasserted control over their own people at the end of the colonial era, the use of cannabis, opium, and other drugs, sometimes mistakenly called "traditional," was increasingly stigmatized and restricted to the lowest social classes.

No nationalist, anti-imperialist government anywhere in the world had ever promoted open use of opium, cannabis, or other so-called traditional drugs. In fact, the opposite had been the pattern with the breakup of colonial rule all over the world. China's hostility to the use of opiates at the time of the opium wars was a good example. A century later Iran followed suit with a tough crackdown on drug use after the Islamic Revolution in 1979. These experiences also showed how difficult it was to extinguish drug habits when use evolved toward modern attitudes about drugs that resulted in increased addiction. Iran and China continued to have serious problems with increasingly modern and global patterns of addiction.

Coca leaf chewing did not spread worldwide at the start of the modern era, as did opium and marijuana smoking, because the coca leaves lost much of their psychoactive potential shortly after being picked. When the early explorers brought coca leaves back home, the Europeans were unable to understand what the South American natives found so attractive about chewing the leaves of the coca bush. Because cocaine was available only when the leaves were fresh, coca chewing did not spread far from the Andes Mountains where the coca bushes grew.

Despite the disturbing changes as alcohol and drug use became global, especially in large port cities, the worldwide drug scene 150 years ago was, by contemporary standards, not menacing. It bore a striking resemblance to the earlier era of traditional cultures. The relatively high costs of the drugs, their difficult transportation, and their low potency led to a relatively low availability of drugs and low rates of drug-caused problems throughout the world. Most people in all parts of the world continued to have little access to alcohol and other addicting drugs until the twentieth century.

During the nineteenth century, the industrial and scientific revolutions that led to the creation of large, impersonal cities produced an unforeseen side effect. The new urban environments that promoted more personal choice and less restriction, in contrast to earlier traditional behaviors and values, also gave rise to the modern drug problem. The pursuit of personal happiness, regardless of its effect on the community, increasingly became a quest for modern individuals. For millions of people, this increased license and emphasis on personal pleasure opened the door for the self-managed use of alcohol and other drugs—the use of drugs for pleasure and fun.

In the middle of the nineteenth century, cocaine was identified as the psychoactive component of coca leaves. It was purified so users far from the slopes of the Andes Mountains could have access to this powerful drug in a chemically pure form for the first time. Pure morphine and codeine were first extracted from the sap of the opium poppy at about the same time. Also, the hypodermic needle was invented in the middle of the nineteenth century, thereby allowing addicting drugs to be injected directly under the skin. As with the introduction of smoking, this was a new route of administration of drugs with threatening implications for the entire world. Old drugs became more addictive as a result of purification and of changes in their routes of administration. Smoking and injecting drugs of abuse posed serious new risks.

Drugs and Deviant Behavior: The Shift to Modern Values

In the twentieth century, the ages-old short list of abused drugs was expanded to a virtually infinite number as modern chemists found molecule after molecule that produced reward in the brain's pleasure centers. Alcohol was joined by the barbiturates, cocaine by the amphetamines and methamphetamine, and cannabis by a whole new array of synthetic hallucinogenic drugs from LSD (lysergic acid diethylamide) to PCP (phencyclidine) and MDMA (methylenedioxymethamphetamine). The range of synthetic and semisynthetic narcotics was equally long, from methadone and hydromorphone (Dilaudid) to meperidine, opioid painkillers, such as hydrocodone and fentanyl, and heroin.

Modern travel and communication ensured that drugs were available in every part of the world. Drugs were, like spices 500 years earlier, the perfect product for the growing global trade because of their high value and light weight. The rise in the wealth of individuals in all parts of the world as a result of the Industrial Revolution meant that more people had the means to buy drugs in the rapidly expanding world market of alcohol and other drugs. The twentieth-century trade in cigarettes, a global mega-business, bore little resemblance to the tobacco trade in the nineteenth century in terms of size and health consequences. Similar changes took place in the alcohol trade and, more recently and more dramatically, in the illegal global drug trade of marijuana, cocaine, and heroin.

Drug Use in Modern Societies

- People are widely exposed to multiple addictive substances.
- Highly potent drugs and routes of administration are available.
- Communities allow for greater anonymity and behavioral diversity.
- Communities are often impersonal and tolerant of deviance.
- Low social controls are in place over individual behavior.
- The criminal justice system is charged with reducing drug supply and drug use.
- Opioid painkillers are overprescribed.
- Rates of use and severe drug-related problems are high.

More troubling than the explosive growth in the number, potency, and availability of drugs is the shift of values that has taken place in all parts of the world over the last 200 years. In earlier and simpler times, most people were born, lived, and died in close-knit, relatively stable, and isolated communities. They shared values and shunned outsiders who sought entrance to their communities. Modern police and criminal justice systems are far less effective in controlling deviant behavior than was the old-fashioned village social system. In the twentieth century, the relatively inefficient and expensive modern social control systems became the major guardians of the public health when it came to nonmedical drug use.

A Short History of Drug Abuse in the United States

The US, a nation of immigrants from all parts of the globe, has had more than its share of addiction problems since its earliest years as a nation. The rampant alcohol consumption per person in the country peaked in the early years of the nineteenth century and then slowly declined with the progressive impact of anti-alcohol sentiment. In the course of the nineteenth century there were three massive, grassroots progressive movements that changed the nation: emancipation from slavery, women's suffrage, and the prohibition of alcohol sale and use. All three had similar political support as improvements in the culture and the lives of US citizens. In many ways they defined American aspirations.

The Church of Jesus Christ of Latter-day Saints (Mormons), the Seventh-Day Adventists, and many other American Protestant denominations featured prohibition of alcohol as central to their faiths. In 1846, Maine became the first state to prohibit the sale and use of alcohol. Over the next seventy-four years, prohibition spread state by state until national prohibition was established in 1920 with the Eighteenth Amendment to the constitution. The Nineteenth Amendment was almost simultaneous, granting of the vote to women. Both were central features of the progressive era.

At the end of nineteenth century, the US experienced a massive patent medicine epidemic. Cocaine was an ingredient of Coca-Cola (hence the name "Coke") along with flavoring from the kola nut, thus Coca-Cola. Cocaine was altogether discontinued as in ingredient in 1903, though the amount of it was insignificant. Then as now it was the non-cocaine flavoring from the coca leaf that was essential to the unique flavor of Coke. At the start of the twentieth century, heroin was sold to any willing buyer as a soothing syrup for babies and even as a treatment for alcoholism. Initially it was sold as a cough medicine for which it was very effective and rapidly spread as a patent medicine that became a particularly popular remedy with women in the last years of the nineteenth century and the dawn of the next. The federal response from Congress came in the form of the Pure Food and Drug Act of 1906 and the Harrison Narcotics Act of 1914. The consequence of the widespread and destructive use of these drugs in the US was their prohibition. Prohibition was a response to a serious drug problem; it was not the cause of the drug problem and at that time it did not lead to the widespread use of alcohol or other drugs.

Later, the prohibition of alcohol and other drugs (including cocaine and heroin), led to dramatic reductions in the use of these substances and to reduced social costs and negative health effects. The cocaine and heroin problems that were severe at the turn of the century all but disappeared in the US by the mid-1900s. Alcohol problems fell sharply during the fourteen years of national prohibition, which ended with the repeal of Prohibition in 1933. After the start of Prohibition, cirrhosis deaths, a good independent measure of excessive use of alcohol, declined sharply as did arrests for public drunkenness and disorderly conduct. Violent crime, often attributed to the prohibition of alcohol by opponents of the measure, did not rise in the US during those years. Nor did homicides increase during that period, despite the wide publicity given to gang, such as the Al Capone gang in Chicago.

There were negative consequences of the prohibition of alcohol and other drugs, however. Because the use of these substances was now a criminal act, Prohibition created the economic incentive for an illegal alcohol supply system, one that was rapidly taken over by organized crime. As health care costs fell under Prohibition, criminal justice costs rose, although the net effect of Prohibition was to lower the overall societal costs of the substances that were prohibited.

With the repeal of Prohibition, the consumption of alcohol began to rise slowly but steadily in the US from less than one gallon per person per year during Prohibition (when illegal alcohol or "moonshine" was used by some people) to about two gallons per person at the end of World War II. Average annual alcohol consumption then rose further to a peak of slightly less than three gallons per person in 1985, a point still below the per person annual alcohol consumption in the US 150 years earlier. After 1985 the long-term fall in per capita consumption, which had characterized the nation's experience with alcohol for 100 years before Prohibition's repeal, was resumed, albeit at a slow rate of decline.

Notable in the youth drinking scene over the last several decades is the emergence of widespread binge drinking. While social drinking is generally limited to one to three drinks in a drinking event among adults, among youth from about ages fifteen to twenty-five who drink, the pattern is to drink five to fifteen drinks in a drinking session. When I asked a teenage patient to limit his drinking to one or two drinks in an evening, he laughed at me, "That is not even drinking! I might as well not drink if I'm going to do that." He explained that the intoxicating, or brain poisoning, is precisely the goal of his drinking. Absent that intoxication he saw no reason to drink alcohol. Binge drinking is uncommon and generally shunned in adult society, but it has become widespread and socially accepted in many youth peer groups.

The most important development in the history of the US response to the problem of addiction to alcohol and other drugs occurred in 1935, when Alcoholics Anonymous (AA) was started in Akron, Ohio. In later years, the US developed the largest national response in world history to the problems of addiction, including research, prevention, and treatment programs.

The Modern Drug Epidemic

From the nineteenth century to the present, the US has stood at the forefront of worldwide changes in the use of alcohol and other drugs. The US was the world's first modern democratic society and became the world leader in new behaviors from fashion and music to drugs. This was also the first society to experience widespread use of the products of modern science that were not derived from natural materials. David Musto, the distinguished Yale historian of drug abuse, has called modern drug addiction "the American disease."

The American experience with illicit drugs was changed forever in the 1960s when the use of marijuana, cocaine, amphetamines, heroin, and other drugs—including psychedelics such as LSD, mescaline, and psilocybin—became increasingly common. In 1962, before the modern drug epidemic, 4 million Americans had used an illicit drug at any time in their lives. Thirty years later that figure had risen nearly twentyfold to 77 million, or slightly more than one-third of all Americans over the age of twelve. Those figures reflect the dramatic rise of the US drug epidemic, the world's first modern drug epidemic. The onset of this drug epidemic occurred when the Baby Boomers hit adolescence and it continues to the present day.

The drug epidemic at the end of the nineteenth and the beginning of the twentieth centuries was triggered by two drugs: cocaine and heroin. Early in the twenty-first century they are again making headlines with new epidemics. It is striking that while the past one hundred years has seen an explosive increase in the number of drugs of abuse and entirely new patterns of drug supply and use that these two very old drugs still are at the top of public health and media attention.

The Modern Drug Epidemic—Part 1, Hallucinogens, Heroin, and Marijuana

Many modern drugs of addiction were developed in laboratories with the intention of providing solutions to the stress and psychological problems that plagued modern Americans. They often were legal at first and, if not available on the street, were prescribed by physicians who were unaware of their addictive qualities.

For example, amphetamine was first synthesized in 1919 and was considered harmless for years, even to the extent that Benzedrine and Dexedrine tablets were handed out to troops in World War II to give them energy and "courage" in battle. In the 1950s they were widely prescribed to housewives as diet pills and antidepressants (called "mother's little helper") and were soon being taken for their mood-altering effects, leading to abuse and for many, addiction. This resulted in new restrictions, including removing the drug from nasal inhalers, which had been bought by addicts who ingested the drug-soaked filters.

When Valium (diazepam), the first of the benzodiazepines (which also include Xanax, Klonopin, and Ativan) to be introduced in 1963, came on the market, it was seen as a panacea for anxiety and stress, but soon proved to be highly addictive for many users. Users found themselves taking larger and larger doses to experience the high on which they had become dependent. Eventually, when abuse turned into addiction, taking the drug became necessary to stave off the discomfort of withdrawal. Barbiturates, such as phenobarbital, also were prescribed as sedatives for years but never achieved the widespread addictive use of the benzodiazepines, although they were a leading cause of death from suicide.

The modern drug epidemic began in the early 1960s when a few risk-taking, intellectual, anti-establishment leaders promoted what they called the consciousness expansion of hallucinogenic drugs, chemicals that disrupt thinking so profoundly that psychosis sometimes developed. Psilocybin and mescaline, naturally occurring chemicals found in certain mushrooms and cacti, respectively, were the initial hallucinogenic substances used. Their use often produced discomfort, nausea, and dizziness, which limited their appeal. Lysergic acid diethylamide (LSD) was introduced to the public by Harvard psychologist Timothy Leary and Richard Albert in 1963 and sparked an increase in experimentation with various psychedelics. The natural hallucinogens were quickly displaced by LSD, a powerful and purely synthetic hallucinogen free of these troublesome side effects. Although hallucinogens were among the first drugs of abuse in the modern drug epidemic, public attention rapidly left these drugs and turned to heroin, marijuana, and, later, cocaine. This shift of public attention did not mean that hallucinogens were no longer used.

The late 1960s saw a rapid increase of heroin addiction in major cities, particularly among inner-city minority young men. The heroin epidemic of this period was measured in the rate of serious crimes and overdose deaths, both of which were rising rapidly to alarming levels. At the same time marijuana use emerged as a polarizing political issue caught up in the youth culture driven by the front edge of the Baby Boom generation, then in their teens and early twenties, along with their opposition to the Vietnam War and support for the Civil Rights Movement. The heroin epidemic sparked the creation of methadone treatment and significant efforts to reduce heroin supply, including ending opium cultivation in Turkey and the French Connection that brought heroin from Turkey to the US, especially to large cities with New York and California in the center of the problem.

Prior to the early 1960s, marijuana was vilified by mainstream society, most infamously by the 1936 film *Reefer Madness*, with use mostly limited to non-conformist subcultures, such as artists, musicians, writers, and self-styled hipsters. In the 1960s marijuana use became more commonplace with about one in nine American high school seniors reporting daily or near-daily marijuana use in 1978, the peak of youth marijuana use in the US. All of these drugs from the decade of the 1960s caused negative psychological experiences, including psychotic breaks, in some users.

Policy Responses to the Modern Drug Epidemic—Part 1

The explosion of drug use in the 1960s did not go unnoticed by public health officials and the US government. This era, roughly 1968 to 1978, was the first time drug use was seen as a major national issue, with the focus on heroin and marijuana. In response, the first White House drug czar was appointed with great media attention on June 17, 1971. The National Institute on Drug Abuse (NIDA) was launched in September of 1973, the same year that the Drug Enforcement Administration (DEA) was created. At this point, there was an effort to "decriminalize" (remove criminal penalties from use—but conspicuously not to legalize—marijuana by the National Commission on Marihuana and Drug Abuse in its 1973 report *Drug Use in America: Problem in Perspective*. While this report was rejected by President Nixon, who had established the Commission in 1969, the decriminalization movement took hold and by 1978, ten states had decriminalized marijuana.

American drug policy took a sharp turn focused on the rapid increase in marijuana use by youth with the creation in 1977 and 1978 of the Parents' Movement, which in 1981 was adopted by Nancy Reagan in her "Just Say No" campaign. The use of marijuana by youth soon plummeted after a meteoric rise: Among school seniors, past month marijuana use dropped a remarkable 68 percent between 1978 and 1992. The earlier substantial support for marijuana decimalization and marijuana use all but disappeared from the political and media scene in the US during those fourteen years. This dramatic shift was powerful evidence that youth drug use rates could change dramatically over relatively short periods of time. In this same time period, heroin all but vanished from the nation's agenda as Mexico and Columbia replaced Turkey and France as major heroin suppliers to the US. The Drug Enforcement Administration (DEA) subsequently sponsored an opioid aerial eradication program in Mexico, complemented by targeted city drug arrests of key trafficking leaders which led to significant reductions in heroin overdose deaths from 2000 per year in 1976 to 800 in 1980.[1]

The Modern Drug Epidemic—Part 2, Crack Cocaine and Meth

Cocaine use rose rapidly in the US in the late 1970s and early 1980s among affluent drug users, most of whom were previously heavy users of alcohol and marijuana. But it was the emergence of crack cocaine in the mid-1980s that reignited the drug issue, taking the political focus away from both heroin and marijuana as American cities were decimated by the sudden epidemic of smoked cocaine. Prior to this dramatic and unprecedented development, cocaine was mostly sniffed up the nose and was widely thought of as almost as harmless as marijuana appeared to be. One high-level US government official then observed "the risk of cocaine use is less than the risk of downhill skiing."

In US cities, the problems of crack cocaine use and crime became

---

[1] Bensinger, P. (2016, March 22). Reducing heroin use and abuse: lessons learned, 1976-1981. Presented at DEA Museum Lecture Series, *The Heroin Epidemic: Then and Now – Lessons Learned*, Washington, DC.

thoroughly and disastrously intertwined, not only because crack users stole property and sold drugs to buy their crack, but because cocaine use itself made people aggressive and paranoid. In the late 1980s the crack epidemic was accompanied by an explosive increase in crime, including murder. Crack cocaine impacted individuals, families, and whole communities with a ferocity never before seen with any other drug habit.

Policy Responses to the Modern Drug Epidemic—Part 2

The crack epidemic was the second time that drug policy hit the top of the nation's agenda. Crack cocaine effectively dashed any hope of drug proponents peddling their permissive ideas to the American public about illicit drugs. The question that drug legalizers could not answer became "What about crack? How would you handle that drug if illicit drugs were made legal?" They could not answer because this drug was so disastrous to virtually everyone using crack and to those around them.

The US entered a presidential election season in early 1988 as the crack epidemic put an exclamation point to the news that cocaine use was not benign. This added a political dimension to the public reaction, as representatives of both parties tried to outdo each other in their responses to the epidemic of rising drug abuse and serious and violent crime.

There was an important subtext to the crack story. Most of the powdered cocaine use was by whites while much crack use was by blacks, and certainly the images of urban crime and violence were primarily black. The move to reduce the very serious crime epidemic in the late 1980s and through the mid-1990s was focused on two targets: "career criminals," those arrested for three or more felonies, and drug dealers, especially crack dealers. The penalties for crack were more severe than for the same amount of powdered cocaine, prompting concern that this tough response to crime was racially motivated. At the time, the support for these tough laws dealing with crack was bipartisan and included prominent black legislators.

A Turning Point in the Drug Epidemic

The crack cocaine epidemic experienced a turning point with the 1986 death of Len Bias, the University of Maryland basketball superstar, who died of an overdose the morning after signing a multimillion-dollar professional contract with the Boston Celtics. This single, dramatic event changed many people's view that cocaine was the safe champagne of abused drugs. America's amnesia about cocaine's dangers, which were widely understood in the early decades of the twentieth century, ended overnight when Len Bias died.

This was the most public drug abuse death up to that time. Bias's death produced a massive reaction, whereas earlier deaths of such media figures as Elvis Presley, Jimmy Hendrix, and John Belushi did not, in part because all of them were seen as jaded by their celebrity. In addition, Bias's death occurred when crack cocaine first hit North America like a destructive hurricane. Unlike a hurricane, however, the crack epidemic in America's inner cities grew for several years as it exploded with crime and violence.

Crack: The Ultimate Addiction

Cocaine hydrochloride was the standard form of cocaine from the end of the nineteenth century until crack appeared. It could be snorted or injected, a pattern of use that was also seen with heroin over the same period of time. In the 1980s, first in Bolivia and Columbia, a new technique for using cocaine as it was being purified was developed. This evolved into what was called freebase, a chemical form of cocaine that was more fat soluble than the hydrochloride and that had a lower vaporization temperature, which permitted smoking. At first, freebase cocaine had to be made with ether extraction from the powdered cocaine hydrochloride, a process that was dangerous because the ether is explosive. But in the mid-1980s, a new technique was developed to manufacture freebase: baking soda and water were used to make gray "cracks" or "rocks" of cocaine freebase. This was an easier and safer technique to create a smokable form of cocaine.

The rapid acceptance of crack cocaine by novice and veteran drug abusers can be attributed to several factors. Cocaine is a highly addictive drug. The first rush after using cocaine produces such a strong sense of pleasure that many first-time users are strongly motivated to recapture those feelings. Smoking drugs was an acceptable activity for many people. Especially with the media attention to the dangers of intravenous drug use, even many dedicated drug abusers became wary of needles and injected drugs. Thus, those seeking intense drug highs, caused by rapidly rising high brain levels of abused drugs, were attracted to drug smoking.

Marketing tactics of drug dealers also influenced the spread of crack cocaine. Distributors packaged crack in relatively small units, making the purchase more attractive and affordable to adolescents and those with lower incomes. Buying powdered cocaine once meant spending several hundred dollars at a time, but buying crack after 1985 meant coming up with only $5 to $10.

Bias's death not only changed the nation's thinking about cocaine, but it also dispelled many lingering myths about drug abuse. For two decades, so-called drug experts had told the public that people use drugs because they suffer from low self-esteem or from some mental disturbance. Others claimed that drug use reflected failures in family life or economic disadvantage. Len Bias was not depressed. He was certainly not financially or educationally disadvantaged. The one aspect of his story that did reinforce a stereotypical—and wrong—view of addiction was that Bias was black. About 65 percent of illicit drug users in the US are white.

This very public drug death was and still is a useful standard against which to gauge any theory of why people use illegal drugs. The simple answer, repeated throughout this book, is that most users like the feelings that drugs produce, and they believe they can get away with that use, that chemical high.

After Len Bias's death, many Americans reassessed their opinion about cocaine, finding it to be much more addictive and dangerous than originally thought. In fact, cocaine's popular image shifted almost overnight from "soft," like marijuana, to "the most addictive" of all drugs, "worse than heroin." Most of the media coverage of cocaine, which had been accepting if not approving before 1986, turned unrelentingly hostile to cocaine use in subsequent years. Prevention and intervention efforts aimed at cocaine use targeted an audience that previously had dismissed the incipient dangers of cocaine use, especially youth who were frequent users of alcohol and marijuana.

The 1980s also saw the beginnings of an epidemic of methamphetamine abuse and addiction, which exploded in the 1990s with the spread of meth labs across the country where the drug could be manufactured cheaply with household chemicals. It took a major crackdown on these labs and restriction of the quantities of the some of the ingredients to stem the tide as treatment centers and law enforcement struggled to handle the flood of addicts, many of whom didn't respond to traditional treatment methods and had high relapse rates.

The Modern Drug Epidemic—Part 3, Medical and Recreational Marijuana

Although marijuana was not the first drug in the modern drug epidemic, by 1968 marijuana had become the central drug in the epidemic. Because marijuana did not produce respiratory depression or other acute effects associated with overdose death (as did heroin, barbiturates, and even alcohol), and because withdrawal was not observed when chronic marijuana users refrained from use for a few days, marijuana had the reputation of being a safe high.

Marijuana, a product of the cannabis sativa plant, has a long history.

Like the other four most commonly abused drugs in the world—alcohol, tobacco (nicotine), cocaine, and heroin—marijuana is agriculturally produced. The drug is usually smoked, although it can also be swallowed. Unlike alcohol, cocaine, and heroin, marijuana is not a specific single chemical. Rather, marijuana is a crude drug, a complex chemical slush.

The cause of the high from using marijuana is delta-9-tetrahydrocannabinol (THC), which is found in relatively high concentrations in today's marijuana. Thirty or forty years ago, typical THC levels in smoked marijuana were 2 to 6 percent. Now the marijuana plant has been modified to produce concentrations of 15 to 20 percent THC and the concentrates are up to 95 percent THC.

Marijuana is also called cannabis. The term "marijuana" in the US reflects the origin of the drug entering the country from Mexico in the early decades of the twentieth century, but as the marijuana issue has become global, the term "cannabis" has replaced it in international policy discussions. In this book, both terms are used.

Marijuana and the Law

Dating back to the beginning of the modern drug abuse epidemic in the 1960s, there has been a movement to remove criminal penalties from marijuana use in the US. While at the federal level, marijuana currently remains a Schedule I drug (drugs designated as likely to be abused and having no federally approved medical use), legalization of the sale and recreational use at the state level has occurred in nine states and the District of Columbia, with more states undoubtedly yet to follow. Separate from the issue of legalizing recreational or medical use of marijuana is the movement to lower the penalty for simple use and possession of small amounts of marijuana—from a felony to a misdemeanor, and in some cases to a simple infraction—to help reduce overcrowding in US prisons. Under United Nations treaties it is not acceptable for any country that has signed the treaties to legalize marijuana. However, countries can eliminate the use of jail or prison sentences as a penalty for violating marijuana laws and still be consistent with these treaties. In the US, many arrests are still made for marijuana possession, but imprisonment is rare and mostly limited to situations involving other offenses. It is possible to support such legal changes regarding punishments while not legalizing the recreational use of marijuana and experiencing the commercial promotion of marijuana use. In fact, that was the conclusion of the National Commission on Marihuana and Drug Abuse, better known as the Shafer Commission, appointed by President Nixon, in 1973.

Accompanying the move to decriminalize marijuana possession and use was a strong movement to promote marijuana as a medicine for just about every disease. This effort was originally halted in 1978 when the Parents'

Movement emerged with a focus on preventing youth marijuana use. During the next twelve years there was little interest in either marijuana decriminalization or use of marijuana as a medicine.

The movement to a more permissive marijuana policy in the US resumed in the early 1990s. It achieved a dramatic success with the legalization of marijuana as a medicine beginning in California in 1996. The first ballot initiative to approve recreational marijuana was put forward to voters in California in 2010. While this initiative lost narrowly, it was followed by successful ballot initiatives for recreational marijuana in the states of Washington and Colorado in 2012. As of early 2018, twenty-nine states and the District of Columbia have approved medical marijuana and eight states—including California—and the District of Columbia have approved recreational marijuana. More states are expected to join in both categories in coming years. Organizations like Smart Approaches to Marijuana (SAM) have since begun documenting the effects of these state policies, ranging from increases in marijuana-related poison control calls and emergency room visits to increases in marijuana-related motor vehicle crashes, to increases in marijuana-related crimes, to a flourishing marijuana black market.[2]

With the advent of legal marijuana, a large new industry has developed to extend beyond the early smoked marijuana cigarette, or "joint," to produce products with greater potency and that can be consumed orally, known as "edibles," which include cookies, candy, soda, and alcohol-like drinks. Smoking has evolved to use hash oil to produce a far more intense and impairing high. Vaping has been used to consume cannabis oils.

Drug Policy: No Use Versus Harm Reduction

The drug policy debate is between those who promote the drug-free, no-use standard for both drug use prevention and drug treatment and those who seek to reduce some of the harmful effects of drug use without stopping the drug use.

Drug-free policies define the goal of prevention as no use of illegal drugs. For youth, the health objective is to protect the adolescent brain from the destructive impact of all drugs, including the three gateway drugs (alcohol, nicotine and marijuana), and from the associated mental health social and economic consequences. Adults dealing with substance use disorder also are encouraged to stop completely. Drug-free treatment aims to end any use of alcohol and other drugs of abuse and to promote "recovery" which includes not only no use of all drugs but also significant character improvement.

2 Smart Approaches to Marijuana. (2018, March). Lessons Learned from Marijuana Legalization in Four US States and D.C. Alexandria, VA: Author. http://learnaboutsam.org

Recovery-oriented treatment includes a "sobriety date" – the last day on which the person used alcohol or other drugs. Harm-reduction efforts, in contrast, seek to prevent teens from driving drunk but not to stop them from drinking. The fundamental drug policy vision of harm reduction is to treat illegal drugs, starting but not ending with marijuana, as we now treat alcohol and tobacco with a "tax and regulate" system of drug supply coupled with a public education campaign about the potential harms of drug use and treatment for those who need and want it.

Other prominent examples of harm reduction include giving intravenous drug users clean needles and places to inject drugs, including heroin, "safely" and legalizing marijuana. Harm reduction blurs the line separating medical drug use from nonmedical drug use, labels recreational drug use "self-medication," and claims medical benefits for many abused currently illegal drugs. The harm reduction movement shifts the primary goal of addiction treatment from recovery to reducing some of the harm from drug use while tolerating continued drug use. Efforts to legalize marijuana, first for medical uses and subsequently for recreational uses, is another part of the harm reduction movement to tolerate – but tame – continued drug use.

In addiction treatment there is a crucial drug policy issue about the use of medicines as prescribed, including potentially abused medicines such as buprenorphine and methadone. An addict patient taking these medicines is considered to be in recovery if that patient no longer uses alcohol, marijuana and other drugs of abuse. But the many people using buprenorphine and methadone who continue to use marijuana and other drugs cannot be considered to be in recovery. In my opinion, perhaps some of the harm reduction agenda could be compatible with a drug-free objective if it were implemented as a state on the road to a drug-free status of recovery. It is difficult for me to see how harm reduction can be useful in youth prevention.

While drug-free and harm-reduction policies and programs are often presented at battling alternatives there is a better way to see them as both reasonable and even as synergistic. The goal of prevention is not use and the goal of treatment is recovery including no use of alcohol or other drugs. On the path to those goals are harm-reduction options. If harm-reduction efforts are judged not just on keeping the drug users alive for another day but primarily on their ability to achieve stable long-term recovery then the two waring dug policies factions can be united.

Marijuana as Medicine

Marijuana, with its over 420 chemicals—let alone marijuana smoke, with over 2,000 chemicals, many of which are known to be harmful to the user's health—has not, as of this writing, been definitively established as a safe medicine. Nevertheless, some specific chemicals in marijuana have powerful effects on the brain and other parts of the body. Modern biomedical research of these chemicals has identified many effects, some of which may have therapeutic potentials to treat specific illnesses.

Several years ago, dronabinol (Marinol), a synthetic THC, was approved by the Food and Drug Administration (FDA) as a medicine in both capsule and suppository forms to treat the severe nausea and vomiting sometimes caused by cancer chemotherapy.

The discovery that THC reduces nausea and vomiting for these cancer patients led to strong political pressure from the pro-marijuana lobby to approve marijuana (which, again, contains a natural form of THC) for medical treatment as a compassionate response to the suffering of cancer patients. Marijuana, or even purified THC, was not and never has been proposed as a treatment for cancer. The only proposed use for marijuana or THC in the treatment of cancer patients is to reduce the nausea and vomiting associated with chemotherapy.

Oncologists, the medical specialists who treat cancer, studied THC and found that it was helpful for some patients but that it had many unwanted side effects, including making it unsafe to drive a car and sometimes causing psychosis. Most cancer patients who were not previously drug addicted found the effects of THC to be extremely unpleasant. Oncologists did not want to use smoked crude marijuana as a medicine because it contained so many chemicals, some of which actually caused cancer and suppressed the immune system, and because the dose of THC reaching the patient could not be controlled accurately with smoking. In recent years, new synthetic medicines, unrelated to THC or marijuana, have been developed that have made THC obsolete in the medical treatment of nausea and vomiting from chemotherapy. Ondansetron (Zofran) is one example of these more effective, far safer, and more powerful anti-nausea medicines.

Marijuana has been proposed as a treatment for a number of other diseases and ailments:

- The wasting (loss of appetite and loss of weight, which can be life threatening) in AIDS. This proposal comes from marijuana's well-known tendency to produce "the munchies," or the desire to eat high-calorie foods. Not only is there no solid scientific evidence that marijuana or THC helps AIDS patients, but marijuana's well-known ability to depress the immune system and to cause cancer makes it extremely unattractive as a medicine for AIDS sufferers, who are literally dying from damaged immune systems. The fact that marijuana can cause some AIDS sufferers to feel high and therefore less upset is no more a reason to use marijuana as medicine for these sick patients than it is to give them alcohol or cocaine.

- Asthma. Although THC does dilate the bronchi (which are closed down by asthma attacks) in the short run, the irritants in marijuana smoke actually cause lung problems, including long-term bronchial constriction, after prolonged use. Therefore, marijuana is not likely to gain favor as an asthma treatment.

- Glaucoma. THC does reduce the pressure in the eye for a few hours, as do many other substances, including alcohol. However, glaucoma is a twenty-four-hour-a-day disease, so treating a person for glaucoma with marijuana would require the person to smoke marijuana or take THC pills around the clock. Worse still, marijuana and THC are weak in their effects on pressure in the eyeball, so the person with glaucoma would not only have to use marijuana smoke or THC 24/7 but also take routine glaucoma medicines. No controlled scientific studies have shown that THC or marijuana add anything useful to the other medicines routinely used in the treatment of glaucoma, all of which last longer, produce fewer unwanted side effects, and are more effective in reducing eye pressure than is marijuana, or THC.

- The spasticity of multiple sclerosis (MS). No controlled studies have been conducted to show that THC helps with this serious problem, although cannabidiol (CBD), a non-psychotropic cannabinoid found in marijuana, may prove effective. Sativex®, an oral administration spray of equal parts THC and CBD, has been approved for use in the United Kingdom and several other European countries to treat spasticity of MS. It is presently undergoing clinical trials in the US for the treatment of cancer pain.

In 1997 the Institute of Medicine (IOM) was asked by the Office of National Drug Control Policy to "review the scientific evidence to assess the potential health benefits and risks of marijuana and its constituent cannabinoids" which culminated in a report released in 1999.[3] Among the IOM's conclusions: "If there is any future for marijuana as a medicine, it lies in its isolated components, the cannabinoids and their synthetic derivatives. Isolated cannabinoids will provide more reliable effects than crude plant mixtures. Therefore, the purpose of clinical trials of smoked marijuana would not be to develop marijuana as a licensed drug but rather to serve as a first step toward the development of non-smoked rapid-onset

---

[3] Joy, J. E., Watson, S. J., & Benson, Jr., J. A. (Eds). (1999). *Marijuana and Medicine: Assessing the Science Base.* Washington, DC: National Academies Press, p.vii.

cannabinoid delivery systems."[4] The IOM noted that the use of agricultural products in medicine had a distinguished history. Morphine, for example, derived from the opium poppy plant, had been used since it was first purified in the middle of the nineteenth century. In the twentieth century, morphine was largely replaced by semisynthetic drugs like oxycodone and hydromorphone and by purely synthetic drugs such as methadone and fentanyl. The IOM foresaw a similar evolution with marijuana—from the crude plant to purified cannabinoids and then to purely synthetic analogues.

None of the medical uses for marijuana proposed so far met even the minimal standards of safety and efficacy required of a proposed medicine. Thus, although THC capsules and suppositories remain available to doctors treating cancer patients for nausea and vomiting, there is no other FDA-approved use for THC, and there is no FDA-approved use for smoked marijuana as a medicine to treat any illness. When THC and marijuana have been used in experimental settings to treat various illnesses, doctors have found that the psychoactive effects—the high and the mental clouding—are unpleasant to most patients, except those who were previously drug abusers. Marijuana and THC are poorly tolerated and exceedingly unattractive to most medical patients.

Meanwhile, the pro-marijuana lobby has not been satisfied with the approval of purified, synthetic THC because its objective is to focus on very sick patients using smoked marijuana, the crude drug, as medicine. They want the public to see smoked marijuana as medicine—as a way of emphasizing the positive image of marijuana. Many pro-marijuana apologists insist on the use of crude, smoked marijuana, not THC or other purified chemicals for medical treatments. The marijuana-as-medicine controversy has become a political issue in the US.

The FDA and the National Institutes of Health oppose such proposals, as do the National Institute on Drug Abuse and the Drug Enforcement Administration. Virtually all of the medical organizations that speak up for the welfare of patients in each of the proposed areas in which marijuana might be used are also opposed to marijuana as medicine. Most of the proponents of marijuana as medicine have been, until recently, the same people who want to normalize and/or legalize illicit drugs, especially marijuana. With the growing list of states approving the medical use of marijuana, there are those in the medical community who are taking a closer look at the viability and safety of synthetic oral cannabinoid medications that don't include high-producing THC. Anecdotal evidence is growing that for some people, these new drugs offer relief from pain and a

---

[4] Joy, J. E., Watson, S. J., & Benson, Jr., J. A. (Eds). (1999). *Marijuana and Medicine: Assessing the Science Base.* Washington, DC: National Academies Press, p.175.

number of chronic disorders that haven't responded to traditional treatments and this has inspired new research to find a scientific basis for these claims.

It is helpful to remember that all abused drugs have powerful effects on the body. Someday we may discover that one or more individual chemicals in some of the commonly abused drugs, including marijuana, will play a uniquely useful role in the medical treatments of some illnesses. Today's biomedical research on the effects of abused drugs may identify important therapeutic effects of some of these specific chemicals.

Even the most anti-drug activist needs to recall the nature of the modern social contract for drug use. It specifies that, under the careful supervision of a physician, abused drugs will be available in medical treatments of illnesses other than addiction. Thus, medical use of the chemicals in abused drugs, including marijuana, is not an enemy of drug abuse prevention—as long as the medical use of potentially addictive medicines meets the standards set for other medicines and as long as the use is properly controlled to protect both the patient and the community from potential harm when such medicines leak out of the medical care system.

To this contract for medical treatments with abused drugs, I add one additional element: Substances that are of high abuse potential and substances that are currently widely used nonmedically should be required to meet a higher standard than substances not widely abused. Not only should they be shown as safe and effective in specific medical applications—the standard that any medicine must meet—but they should also meet the standard that they provide a significant benefit not currently available from non-abused or less abused medicines.

In short, before marijuana or opioids, two widely abused substances, are introduced as medicines, they should be shown to offer specific benefits not available with less socially risky substances. Although it is possible that in the future some of the chemicals in abused drugs will meet this higher standard, none does so today. Certainly, smoked marijuana would never be approved by the FDA as a medicine, any more than smoked tobacco or, for that matter, alcohol, will be approved as an acceptable modern medicine.

The marijuana-as-medicine advocates have several advantages in the current political debates over medical use. The pro-drug lobby is large and powerful in the US, and it has concentrated on this issue because it had proved powerless in its earlier, more frontal assault on the prohibition against marijuana. To sharpen their attacks on prohibition and to gain supporters, pro-marijuana advocates focused on the most feared illnesses that induce the greatest sympathy for their sufferers, such as terminal cancer, AIDS, and multiple sclerosis. They have exploited the widespread belief that government agencies that control the approval of medicines are too slow and too tradition-bound to approve many medicines that can help suffering patients with these illnesses, especially potential medicines that are controversial because they are abused drugs.

Finally, this lobby has capitalized on the interest in traditional medicines and on alternatives to modern scientific medicines, both of which have enjoyed a new vogue in recent years. Folk medicines have an appeal to many Americans who fear modern science. Thus, marijuana's history as a folk medicine is perceived, in this highly romanticized interpretation, as evidence that it should be available today as a prescribed or an over-the-counter remedy.

Recall that prior to the establishment of the FDA, in the free-for-all days at the end of the nineteenth century, patent medicines did contain abused drugs. Although the pro-marijuana lobby can score some points today by talking about folk medicines in ancient China, the patent medicine debacle of a hundred years ago not only is closer to home but virtually impossible to romanticize. It was a total disaster. We do not need to repeat that experiment at the beginning of the twenty-first century.

Many chemicals found in marijuana or related to chemicals found in marijuana smoke are currently being investigated by pharmaceutical companies in all parts of the world. The normal profit motive will reinforce the desire of these companies to find more effective medicines for serious illnesses. It is possible that someday, perhaps soon, one or more of these chemicals will become widely useful in the modern treatment of a disease. If so, we can all be grateful for one more benefit from the modern scientific study of abused drugs.

The quest for better drugs is intense. The pharmaceutical industry has great incentives to develop cannabinoids and synthetic analogues. The fact that this has not occurred in the past forty years does not mean it will not happen in the future, but it does underline the difficulties scientists have had in having chemicals in marijuana, let alone synthetic analogues, meet the routine tests all medicines must face of safety, effectiveness, and purity.

Among the three fundamental standard requirements for any medicine to be approved by the FDA, it is perhaps clearest that marijuana itself could never be approved because every crude marijuana product is different in its composition and freedom from contaminants. The FDA approves products, not plants. Further, the FDA standard of consistent stable doses of products cannot be met by a crude whole plant. It can be met by the cannabinoids as is shown by the widespread availability of THC and forthcoming cannabis-based medicine (such as Subsys® and Epidiolex®).

At a personal level, I am strongly in favor of studying the effects of cannabinoids and their synthetic analogues including their uses as medicines. I am delighted with the current approval of two THC products, the imminent FDA approval of CBD products, and products that are a mix of THC and CBD. It may well be that additional cannabinoids will prove to be useful medicines. No one will be more enthusiastic about the use of safe, effective, and pure cannabinoid medicines approved by the FDA than me.

But when it comes to smoking marijuana and calling it medicine, that makes no sense. How many medicines are smoked? None. Smoking is an inherently unhealthy delivery system. The "medical marijuana" debate really is that simple. Vaping, edibles and other ways of using the marijuana plant all have the same problem. Physicians do not prescribe medical marijuana, even in states where medical marijuana is legal. Physicians can "recommend" it but unlike real prescribed medicines for marijuana there is no specific product, quantity, dose or duration of use. How many medicines are "recommended" by physicians who provide cards to patients to buy whatever product they want, as much as they want, for use whenever they want for a year-long period? Then these "patients" come back to the recommending physician for another card the next year. That is how medical marijuana works in many states. It surely does not appear medical to me.

Modern Drug Epidemic—Part 4, Opioid Painkillers, Heroin, and Synthetic Drugs

Beginning about the same time as the California voter approval of medical marijuana in 1996, there was a dramatic change in the practice of medicine as a movement to actively treat pain with high doses of opioid drugs. Prior to that time, opioid drugs were used for a few days to treat acute pain, like a heart attack or post-surgical pain and for the treatment of terminally ill patients with short life expectancies. These drugs included morphine which, like codeine, is derived from opium and a wide range of semisynthetic opioid analgesics including hydrocodone, hydromorphone, oxycodone, and fentanyl. Then in 1997 oxycodone was marketed in a long-acting high-dose preparation called OxyContin with much publicity to physicians for the long-standing "under-treatment" of pain. Thus began the current epidemic of overprescribing opioids.

Today, there are twelve million Americans taking pain medicines on a daily basis and about two to three million using prescription pain medicines nonmedically—meaning they either do not have their own prescription for these medicines or they are using them at doses or in ways not intended by their prescribing physicians (often by snorting or injecting them).

The explosive medical use of opioids fueled the widespread nonmedical use of these highly abusable drugs and a dramatic and sustained increase in opioid overdose deaths that led the US Centers for Disease Control and Prevention (CDC) in 2012 to describe drug overdose deaths as an epidemic. In 2016, there were 63,600 drug overdoses deaths, or 174 overdose deaths a day, of which about 116 deaths a day were from opioids—including both prescription opioids and heroin. Of the 42,249 opioid overdose deaths, about 15,469 were from heroin, 14,487 from natural and semisynthetic opioids, 19,413 from other synthetic opioids, 3,373 from methadone.[5] This epidemic produced a counter-reaction by physicians treating pain that raised questions about the effectiveness of long-term high-dose opioid use to treat pain and led to a dramatic effort to rein in the overprescribing of these medicines.

Figure 2–1 Age-adjusted drug overdose rates, by opioid category: United States, 1999-2016[6]

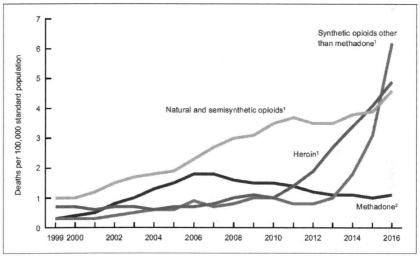

[1]Significant increasing trend from 1999 to 2016 with different rates of change over time, p<0.05.
[2]Significant increasing trend from 1999 to 2016, then decreasing trend from 2006 to 2016, p<0.05.
NOTES: Deaths are classified using the *International Classification of Diseases, Tenth Revision*. Drug-poisoning (overdose) deaths are identified using underlying cause-of-death codes X40-X44, X60-X64, X85, and Y10-Y14. Drug overdose deaths involving selected drug categories are identified by specific multiple-cause-of-death codes: heroin, T40.; natural and semisynthetic opioids, T40-2; methadone, T40.3; and synthetic opioids and other methadone, T40.4, percentage of drug overdose deaths that identified the specific drugs involved varied by year, with ranges of 75%-79% from 1999 to 2013; and 81%-85% from 2014 to 2016. Access data table for Figure 4 at: https://www.cdc.gov/nchs/data/databriefs/db294_table.pdf#4
SOURCE:NCHS, National Vital Statistics System, Mortality

There is a widespread misunderstanding that the prescription opioid

---

[5] Thielking, M. (2017, December 21). Life expectancy in the US is falling – and drug overdose deaths are soaring. *STAT*. The opioids most commonly involved in overdose deaths. Data from National Center for Health Statistics

[6] Hedegaard, M., Warner, M., & Minino, A. M. (2017, December). Overdose deaths in the United States, 1999-2016. NCHS Data Brief, 294. US Department of Health and Human Services, Centers for Disease Control and Prevention, National Center for Health Statistics. Available: https://www.cdc.gov/nchs/data/databriefs/db294.pdf

epidemic seeded the heroin epidemic, which began in about 2010, with some observers claiming that the more recent clampdown on prescribing opioids drove addicts of pain medicines to heroin. While this was a factor in the rise of heroin addiction and overdose deaths, it is far from the main factor in the epidemic. Less than 4 percent of people who use prescription painkillers nonmedically progress to heroin use in the course of five years after initiating that use.[7] The vast majority of the nonmedical users of prescription opioids use many drugs, usually dating back to their adolescence. It is much less likely that they are drug-naïve when they started to use prescription opioids. The people who switch from prescription opioids to heroin are even more likely to have been heavy drug users from youth than those who do not migrate to heroin from nonmedical use of prescription opioids.

Heroin and Opioids

Heroin is a white powder that may be injected intravenously, taken by mouth, or smoked (like crack cocaine). While previously heroin was widely feared by most potential drug users and its use by intravenous injection was seen as a mark of depravity, this perception has been changing with the recent heroin epidemic as more people who have become addicted to opioid prescription painkillers have turned to the more readily available cheap, pure heroin on the streets as their supply of pills is cut off.

Heroin and other opioids are natural or chemically modified extracts of the opium poppy. There are natural opioids (formerly called "opiates"), like morphine and codeine. Morphine is one of a large number of related chemicals called alkaloids found in the sap extracted from the opium poppy; codeine is another closely related natural alkaloid found in opium. There are also synthetic and semi-synthetic opioids that have similar effects, such as methadone, and prescription painkillers like hydrocodone, oxycodone, and fentanyl. For practical purposes, this entire class of drugs—natural and synthetic—can be considered opioids.

The big news in the US as this book is written is the shift in the heroin market. In the revived heroin epidemic, the first since the early 1970s, heroin is now coming to the US mostly from Mexico and it is more potent

---

[7] Muhuri, P. K., Gfoerer, J. C., & Davies, M. C. (2013). Associations of nonmedical pain reliever use and initiation of heroin use in the United States. *CBHSQ Data Review*. Rockville, MD: Substance Abuse and Mental Health Services Association Center for Behavioral Health Statistics and Quality.

and less expensive than in any previous period. It is marketed in new ways and to new populations of drug users. Equally important, new strategies of distribution are being used, including delivery to the users at home, like ordering a pizza, and they have focused not on inner-city minority communities but rather rural and suburban areas where there is less violence and much less police presence. These new drug dealers are clever businesspeople, eager to increase their lucrative market. They go where the money is and the police are not. No longer is heroin an inner-city drug used by minority young, male criminals. Instead the heroin epidemic is most severe in rural and suburban areas with high percentages of women as users. The deaths are, however, concentrated on the young—mostly in their twenties and thirties.

From a law enforcement and prevention perspective, there are important differences between the challenges of nonmedical prescription opioid use and heroin use. But from a treatment perspective, these are all opioids that affect the brain in the same way, whether they are clandestinely manufactured or diverted from medical practice.

In this new modern drug epidemic, along with marijuana, prescription opioids, and heroin, an entirely new class of drugs has become widely available. New psychoactive substances (NPS) are synthetic drugs that mimic some of the effects of older, often agriculturally produced, drugs including synthetic marijuana known as "K2" and "spice," and synthetic cathinones known as "bath salts." NPS are inexpensive and instead of being sold by typical drug dealers, or through legal channels as alcohol and tobacco—and increasingly marijuana—are sold are commonly sold in convenience stores and gas stations in attractive packages. Although they are labeled as incense, plant food, or bath salts prominently marked "not for human consumption," their uses are clear to drug-abusing consumers. These new synthetics are also often sold over the Internet and distributed anonymously using widely available public pathways like the mail and package delivery services, bringing drugs directly to the homes of drug users.

The ongoing development of new synthetic drugs of abuse is the story of hijacking of solid scientific study receptor-focused chemistry for nefarious purposes. Clandestine chemists have simply read the scientific literature, including suggested synthetic pathways, to produce these drugs. These new, novel drugs are among those called "designer drugs" because they are "designed" to evade the law and conventional drug tests.

As of December 2015, the United Nations had registered 643 separate new synthetic drugs in the United Nations Office of Drugs and Crime Early Warning Advisory on New Psychoactive Substances. In that year alone, seventy-five entirely new synthetic drugs were reported for the first time.

The newer synthetic drugs are generally inexpensive highs, often with the drug chemicals sprayed onto leaves and packaged in attractive plastic packages to be smoked like marijuana in pipes or self-rolled cigarettes. They are often sold for $1 a dose, making them barely more expensive than tobacco cigarettes. This low price makes them especially attractive to youth and to poor drug users. The use of these cheap synthetic drugs has been particularly prominent among the homeless.

In 2016, 3.5 percent of twelfth-graders, 3.3 percent of tenth-graders, and 2.7 percent of eighth-graders reported using synthetic marijuana in the past year.[8] The same year, 0.8 percent of twelfth-graders, 0.8 percent of tenth-graders, and 0.9 percent of eighth-graders used synthetic cathinones in the past year.

What is most important about these new synthetic drugs? It is not their toxicity, since so many drugs of abuse are quite toxic, but the fact that they are entirely synthetic. No crop needs to be grown and harvested to produce these drugs, unlike heroin, cocaine, and marijuana. The laboratories that produce these drugs are small and mobile, making them very difficult to find and to permanently shut down. The highly mobile synthetic drug creation and distribution system is the future of a large part of the drug abuse market. The changes in the supply of drugs pose a significant new threat to the public and will likely increase drug availability and drug diversity, thereby increasing the human toll of addiction. There are virtually unlimited chemicals to synthesize and sell in this truly global drug supply system. This is the future of drug abuse in the world. What's more, NPS are virtually invisible on most drug tests, including those used in safety sensitive jobs and in highway safety as well as in drug treatment.

The Global Sweep of Addiction

With the exception of alcohol, tobacco, and opioid painkillers, most of the drugs causing addiction today are not native to the US nor are the brains of Americans uniquely vulnerable to the effects of alcohol or other drugs. One key factor that makes the US the center of drug abuse in the world is its role as the breeding ground for the modern freewheeling consumer culture. The US experience with drugs offers important lessons to the rest of world, lessons that need to be shared more than ever today, as the problems that were once thought to be uniquely American are increasingly understood to be global and, at root, human problems.

Although addiction is uniquely human and its pervasiveness a modern phenomenon, the brain's vulnerability to alcohol and other drugs is

---

[8] Miech, R. A., Johnston, L. D., O'Malley, P. M., Bachman, J. G., Schulenberg, J. E., & Patrick, M. E. (2017). Monitoring the Future national survey results on drug use, 1975–2016: Volume I, Secondary school students. Ann Arbor: Institute for Social Research, The University of Michigan.

nothing new. Problems have been caused by the use of alcohol and other drugs for thousands of years in all parts of the world. What is modern is not the interaction of the brain with specific addicting chemicals. What is new in the world is the exposure of large segments of communities to a wide range of addicting substances by high-risk routes of administration in environments that permit and even encourage the use of these chemicals.

People in all parts of the world share today's drug problem. Alcohol and other drug abuse will not disappear from any society or culture in the foreseeable future. Addiction is as inevitable as poverty and crime and as inescapable as sickness and death. Addiction is deeply rooted in biology and in human societies, especially modern consumer-oriented democracies. Saying that the problems of drug abuse are inescapable does not mean we are helpless and that individuals, families, or countries should take on a passive approach. As with other inescapable human problems, the rates at which drug problems occur are highly influenced by many factors over which individuals, families, communities, and nations have substantial control. Because the personal anguish and social costs suffered as a result of drug problems are so great, it is vitally important that drug problems be understood clearly and that balanced, practical policies be found to minimize drug use in the form of recreational pharmacology. Drug policies must be consistent with the resources and values of each family, each community, and each nation. There is a major international dimension to drug prevention policies. Alcohol and other drug problems underline the increasingly interdependent relationships of all people on the planet. Today, both drug-using behaviors and drug supply are global. They command our best thinking and best efforts. They are matters of life and death.

Drug Policy: An Effective and Humane Model

A successful model of an effective and humane restrictive drug policy exists. It can be adopted worldwide. It shows the way to strongly discourage recreational drug use, to effectively promote both drug prevention and treatment, and to sharply limit the use of incarceration. It is a strategy that was developed in response to an epidemic of intravenous drug use in Stockholm, Sweden, in the late 1960s. At first the Swedes tried what we now call harm reduction. They encouraged physicians to prescribe amphetamines and opiates to addicted patients to wean them off illegal drugs and to keep them away from criminal drug dealers. A psychiatrist working with the Stockholm police, professor Nils Bejerot, observed what happened next.

The addicts, provided drugs by their physicians, did not stop using drugs. Worse yet, they sold many of the drugs that were prescribed to them to other drug users. In other words, they used their prescribed drugs to spread the drug epidemic.

Professor Bejerot, in response to what he saw happening, conceived a new way of responding to the drug problem. He observed that Sweden could never treat its way out of this epidemic. This phrase has an eerie resonance with today's common mantra that countries cannot incarcerate or arrest their way out of the epidemic. In truth, both are correct. Sweden's response was to develop over many decades a program of active discouragement of recreational drug use backed by a criminal justice system that promotes treatment and insists on abstinence. This approach is at the core of the Swedish drug policy. It is widely supported across the broad range of Swedish politics. This drug policy results in low levels of youth drug use and low levels of incarceration. It has a strong drug-free foundation. It uses health care and the criminal justice system working together to emphasize both drug prevention and drug treatment while limiting the use of incarceration for drug use.

3. ADDICTION AND THE BRAIN

One of the most promising aspects of brain research is the study of addiction. To understand how drugs work in the brain is to understand how the brain works. Drugs of abuse, as well as brain-altering medicines, produce their effects by traveling through the bloodstream to the brain where they enter the brain cells. Each drug or medicine modifies the function of specific brain cells in unique ways. Nonmedical drug use distorts healthy brain functions, impairing the workings of the marvelous and fragile brain. A clear and sober brain thinks best. A brain high on alcohol and other drugs is a brain that is dysfunctional. Many of the ill effects of drug abuse on the brain persist, in some cases for a lifetime.

In the last five decades, the US has invested billions of dollars in the fight against illegal drugs. Most of the money has gone to law enforcement and treatment, but billions have been spent on research aimed at understanding how drugs work, from the physiology of the brain to the sociology of addiction. The study of abused drugs produces benefits beyond dealing with addiction, enhancing the understanding of how useful medicines, such as antianxiety and antidepressant medicines, work.

Of course, useful medicines are also at the heart of our current drug epidemic. Opioids such as morphine, oxycodone, hydrocodone, and codeine can be effective in the medical treatment of pain when used judiciously, but when overprescribed or used illicitly, they are a plague, showing that the way a drug is used is as important as its biology. To understand how these drugs affect the brain and why I call the addicted brain "selfish," let's explore how the brain is constructed and how it works.

The Human Brain
The human brain is a three-pound gelatinous gray mass covered with deep wrinkles and connected to the rest of the body through the spinal cord and string-like nerves that extend in an intricate web to every part of the body. Brain cells operate in a chemical bath maintained by the blood

passing through and around them. Because the brain is exquisitely vulnerable to changes in this bath, the blood is separated from the brain by the blood-brain barrier, a filtering system that limits the movement of chemicals from the blood vessels into the brain.

The brain's principal fuels are oxygen, taken from the air by the lungs, and glucose, the sugar used by all of life as the most basic currency of energy, which comes from the food we eat. If our brain's supply of either oxygen or glucose is interrupted, even for a few seconds, we lose consciousness and in a few minutes our brain dies. Unlike other parts of the body, the brain does not regrow after injury. No other organ in the body is as sensitive to such brief interruptions in the supply of fuel. In addition to oxygen and glucose, some other chemicals pass from the blood to the brain through the blood-brain barrier, including abused drugs.

The brain produces neurotransmitters that affect adjacent nerve cells and neurohormones that enter the blood supply and affect distant parts of the brain and other parts of the body. The brain is closely linked with the endocrine system, which produces hormones that control most bodily functions, and with the immune system, which protects the body against infection. The three integrated systems—the nervous, endocrine, and immune systems—are the principal guardians of the body's well-being and its ability to adapt to changing internal and external environments.

The Neuron—The Basic Cell of the Brain

The brain, the organ of the mind, is composed of billions of cells. Neuroscientists believe that a single human brain contains between 100 billion and 1 trillion neurons. The fundamental cells in the brain were discovered just over 100 years ago. The neuron is the basic building block of the network of nervous tissue in the brain and the nerves. It has three major parts: the cell body, the axon, and the dendrites (see figure 3–1.). The cell body contains genetic information in its nucleus as well as the metabolic engine for the neuron. The axon is the extension of the neuron that reaches out to make contact with other neurons to send messages. The dendrites are extensions of the neuron that receive messages from other nerve cells.

Chemical Messengers

Neurons send messages to each other across a minute space between the sending axon and the receiving dendrite. This tiny space is called the synapse. When a message leaves a neuron, the swelling at the end of the axon releases chemicals into the synapse. These chemicals are stored in the axon in packets, called synaptic vesicles. For a signal/message to pass from one neuron to another in the brain, the sending axon must release chemicals into the synapse and the receiving dendrite must receive these specific neurotransmitters. The nerve impulse, received from another neuron, is sent along the dendrite through the cell body to the axon on to the next neuron in a continuous integrated electrochemical flow of messages. The neurons conserve energy by recycling the neurotransmitters released by their axons into the synapses. The neurotransmitters, having sent their messages, are taken back (reuptake) into the axon to be recycled again and again (see figure 3–2).

Figure 3–1 The neuron.

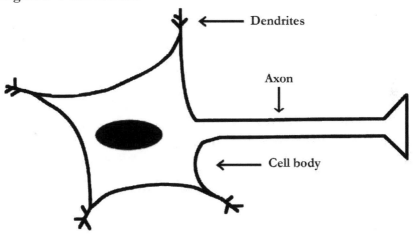

Figure 3–2 Synaptic transmission.

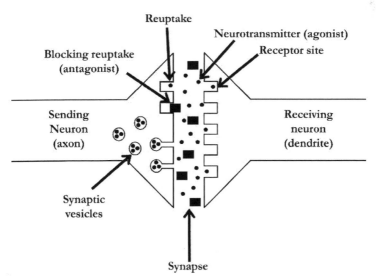

Locks and Keys

A message can be sent only if the axon's neurotransmitter fits into the highly specific receptor site on the dendrite, much like a key fits into a lock. In this scenario, the neurotransmitters are the keys. The locks, called receptor sites, are on the dendrites of the message-receiving nerve cells. The identification of this lock-and-key relationship, unique for each separate neurotransmitter in the brain, has been the central discovery of neuroscience over the last four decades. The study of drug abuse has played an important role in this rapidly evolving science. Most drugs work by influencing specific lock-and-key complexes in the brain's synapses.

Each neurotransmitter in the brain is associated with specific brain areas or brain functions. Some neurotransmitters are relatively common in the brain and found in many areas, and others are more localized. Most synapses contain more than one neurotransmitter (key) and more than one type of receptor site (lock). The message is transmitted from the receiving dendrite through the nerve cell body to the sending axon as an electrochemical impulse, and this action depends on the integrity of the entire nerve cell. Drugs that interfere with the cell membrane—as phencyclidine (PCP or angle dust), alcohol, and inhalants do—influence nerve cell transmission by a mechanism separate from drugs that affect the synapse.

Nerve cells affect each other in many, often subtle ways, in complex networks, with some cells modifying the transmission from one neuron to another. Neurons primarily take on either excitatory or inhibitory roles in the brain. Drugs of abuse fit both categories. Some, called stimulants, such as amphetamines and cocaine, are mainly excitatory, whereas others, called depressants, such as alcohol and opiates, are mainly inhibitory. Drug abusers can experience reward, or pleasure from both stimulation and inhibition of neurons in the brain.

The nervous system works as a balance of inhibitory and stimulant forces. Stimulating one side of the balance usually inhibits the other side. When it comes to drug abuse, the brain acts as if it seeks change, many changes in feeling are experienced as desirable by drug abusers. Non-abusers of drugs do not like these extreme changes of feeling. For example, social drinkers may enjoy the slight buzz from a drink or two, and even occasionally becoming intoxicated at a party, but they don't seek these feelings on as a regular basis or in the extreme way that alcohol abusers do—and many people find the effects of alcohol, especially in high doses, intensely unpleasant. Cigarette smoke makes nonsmokers sick, but smokers pay billions of dollars a year for the feelings nicotine produces.

Local and Long-Distance Messengers

Neurotransmitters work in the synapse in which they are produced. The brain also manufactures chemicals that carry messages to remote parts of the brain or to other parts of the body. Neurotransmitters are local messengers, moving across a single synapse to produce their effects. Hormones are long-distance messengers that are carried by the blood to act at distant sites in the body on organs other than the brain. The midbrain controls the functioning of the pituitary gland, the master gland located in the center of the head at the base of the brain. Hormones are sent out from the pituitary gland to manage vital body functions such as metabolism, sex, and reactions to stress through their effects on the thyroid, sex, and adrenal glands. This complex in the center of the brain is where pleasure and pain are handled, where hormones are managed by the pituitary gland, and where the brain controls all behavior. This is the final common pathway for all drugs of abuse.

Neurotransmitters are called agonists because they activate transmission across the synapse. The effects of specific neurotransmitters can be blocked by equally specific antagonists, chemicals that block the receptor sites on the dendrites (see figure 3–1). When the receptor site is occupied by an antagonist, the agonist (the external chemical stimulus or natural neurotransmitter activating that receptor site) cannot trigger the nerve cell to transmit a message. Antagonists essentially block the lock in the receiving dendrite, preventing the sending nerve cell's messenger, the neurotransmitter, from going through and producing an effect. Scientists now use hundreds of agonists and antagonists, introduced into the blood or directly into specific parts of the brain, to study the brain in both health and disease.

When a particular neurotransmitter system is excessively stimulated over a long period, the brain partially reestablishes equilibrium by reducing its sensitivity to the particular neuro-receptors or by decreasing the number of these specific neuro-receptors. This is called down-regulation. There are limits to this process of adaptation, which is one mechanism of tolerance. As I explained in chapter 1, tolerance means that with repeated exposure to a chemical affecting a neurotransmitter, the brain becomes less able to respond to that particular dose of the chemical and more is needed to achieve the desired effect. Tolerance is a sign of physical dependence on the substance, as is withdrawal.

Both tolerance and withdrawal are caused by the brain becoming adapted to the regular presence of a chemical. This simplified explanation of how neurons work in the brain focuses on the synapse, the tiny but continuously active space between neurons, one sending signals and the other receiving them. The activity in the synapse is affected by both abused drugs and brain-affecting medicines. These chemicals enter the bloodstream, pass the blood-brain barrier, and become part of the chemical bath reaching all the synapses in the brain. Drugs influence a synapse in many ways. Psychoactive externally supplied chemicals facilitate or inhibit transmission between particular groups of axons and dendrites. Some chemicals act by blocking the reuptake or recycling of chemical messengers (neurotransmitters) from the synapse back to the sending axon. This is called reuptake inhibition. It facilitates transmission by prolonging the period the neurotransmitter stays in the synapse. Other drugs directly mimic neurotransmitters. They are agonists sending messages by themselves, fitting the lock on the dendrite in the synapse. Other drugs act as antagonists, blocking the effects of natural neurotransmitters or drug agonists. Many abused drugs produce their effects by acting on the brain in more than one way.

The Roles of Different Parts of the Brain

Many neuron cell bodies, often dark gray, are located on the brain surface, making up the gray matter. The axons of these neurons, covered by white myelin, extend in pathways to connect with other groups of neurons throughout the central nervous system. These interlacing pathways are the white matter underlying the covering gray matter of the brain. The white pathways connect with other groups of gray cell bodies in various parts of the brain. Each of these separate collections of neuron cell bodies, dark spots in the white matter of the brain, fulfills a specific role.

The cerebellum at the back of the brain manages the body's movement and equilibrium, whereas the gray matter above the temples manages most voluntary muscle movement and speech. The central part of the brain has several areas with many cell bodies, or nuclei, managing the response to stress and pain and the experience of pleasure. These central gray areas are closely connected to the endocrine and immune systems.

Specific nuclei in the brain and their principal pathways are often served primarily by specific neurotransmitters. For example, the neurotransmitter dopamine is particularly important in the production of pleasure, including feeling high from nonmedical drug use. Central gray areas at the base of the brain that manage the experience of pleasure are the nucleus accumbens and the ventral tegmental area. They are connected by pathways responding to dopamine. The brain reward or pleasure centers are closely connected to the pathways and the nuclei that manage pain, memory, and emotions as well as appetite, sex, fear, and anger. They are part of the brain's control center for behavior, so they are connected to the centers that manage movement and to the frontal cortex, the part of the brain that manages conscious thoughts (see figure 3–3).

Figure 3–3 A cross section of the human brain showing the projection from the ventral tegmental area (in the midbrain) to the nucleus accumbens and the frontal cortex. Addictive drugs produce their rewarding actions by increasing dopamine in the nucleus accumbens and ventral tegmental area.

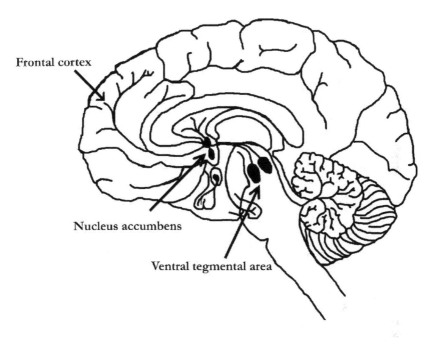

The brain areas that control brain reward or pleasure are a major focus of this book and are the locations of the brain mechanisms of addiction. Addiction, and other behaviors associated with appetites (such as feeding and sexual behavior), are primarily associated with the limbic system, the neuron network in the brain that manages feelings and emotions.

Neurotransmitters and the Selfish Brain

The first neurotransmitter was identified only fifty years ago. Today, scientists have identified over sixty neurotransmitters and speculate that there are three hundred or more naturally occurring chemicals used to send messages from one neuron to another. The first specific receptor identified was the opioid receptor, discovered in 1972. Shortly thereafter, the benzodiazepine receptor—the target of medicines such as Valium (diazepam) and Xanax (alprazolam)—was identified. Brain cells are affected by everything that happens to the body: actions, thoughts, experiences, and the fabulous range of chemicals in the blood as well as the chemicals produced by the brain itself.

Three Major Neurotransmitters

This review focuses on three of the relatively well-understood neurotransmitters, each of which has an important role in drug abuse: norepinephrine (NE), dopamine (DA), and the endorphins.

The catecholamines are a family of related chemicals based on the amino acid tyrosine, one of the fundamental building blocks of proteins. NE and DA, members of the catecholamine family, are major brain neurotransmitters. DA is the chemical that brings gusto to the brain. It plays a role in the control of appetite and pleasure, including eating and sex. DA blockers are useful medicines in the treatment of schizophrenia, a major mental illness thought to be the result of excessive DA in certain brain areas. Parkinson's disease is associated with depletion of DA in the midbrain nucleus that controls fine movements and muscle tone. General DA depletion throughout the brain contributes to severe depression. Notice the range of brain activities associated with this single neurotransmitter, DA, from Parkinson's to schizophrenia and from depression to drug abuse.

Three Major Neurotransmitters

- **Norepinephrine**: Messenger for anger and fear, the flight-or-fight responses
- **Dopamine**: Messenger for pleasure
- **Endorphins**: Messenger for pain and stress

Norepinephrine (NE) and Fear

NE is the neurotransmitter that governs the sympathetic nervous system, which is composed of the nerves not subject to voluntary control. These nerves manage the "flight-or-fight" response associated with the feelings of fear and anger. Fear stimulates the sympathetic nervous system; we see this happening in increased heart rate, elevated blood pressure, and shutting down of the blood supply to the intestines so that blood flows to the muscles preparing for emergency action.

The NE neurotransmitter system that controls the sympathetic nervous system is found in all parts of the brain but in only 1 percent of the brain's synapses. More than half of the NE system is concentrated in two small areas associated with the alarm function of the brain, including the locus coeruleus, the central gray matter associated with panic attacks in agoraphobia. Some antidepressant medicines influence the NE system, with some of these medicines blocking the reuptake of NE in the synapse. These medicines also block the panic attacks associated with agoraphobia, an anxiety disorder linked with the fear of certain places or situations. Because depression is associated with NE deficiency, some chemicals that raise the level of NE in the synapse are effective antidepressants.

The Punch of Dopamine (DA)

Chemicals that influence the DA neurotransmitter system not surprisingly have many brain effects. Each chemical that affects the DA system does so in unique ways. For example, although cocaine and Thorazine (chlorpromazine), a medicine used to treat schizophrenia, both affect the brain's DA system, they do so in entirely different ways. Cocaine, which raises DA levels in the synapse, usually worsens the symptoms of schizophrenia. Thorazine, which reduces DA, is not a substitute for cocaine in the lives of drug abusers, and they, like most other people, find the drug unpleasant. On the other hand, people with schizophrenia, thought to suffer from DA excess, are seldom happy people. This observation highlights the important point that the DA system is not simple or uniform; it is made up of a wide range of subsystems of neurotransmitters and neuroreceptors. For this same reason, although most antianxiety medicines affect a single receptor complex, these medicines are not interchangeable any more than painkillers or antidepressants are interchangeable, even though many of them affect the same basic receptor complexes in the brain.

Endorphins—Nature's Heroin

The third highlighted neurotransmitter is different from the closely related NE and DA, both of which are small chemicals called "amines." In the 1970s, as scientists sought to understand how heroin affected the brain, they discovered the specific brain receptor for morphine, the core of the heroin molecule. Having found the opiate receptor lock in the brain, they searched for the natural neurotransmitter key that fits this lock in the synapses of the pleasure centers in the brain and elsewhere in the body. This neurotransmitter turned out to be not a simple chemical, like NE and DA, but a series of relatively long chains of protein building blocks, or peptides. This family of natural neurotransmitters is now known collectively as endogenous opioid peptides, or endorphins.

The three broad classes of endorphins are the brain's own morphine-like substances, the natural neurotransmitters that fit the receptor lock for morphine. The endorphin brain system reduces pain, promotes pleasure, and manages reactions to stress. Today, more than a dozen natural endorphins are known, and at least five different types of opioid receptors have been identified in the mammalian brain. Scientists have recently discovered additional neuropeptides that are also neurotransmitters, some of which do not involve the opioid receptors. Endorphins act not only as neurotransmitters but also as neurohormones (affecting nerve functioning at more distant brain sites to which they are carried by the blood) and as neuromodulators (natural chemicals modifying the workings of other neurotransmitters).

Endorphin receptors are found not only in the brain but in other parts of the body as well. This helps to explain why, although drugs of abuse are used by addicts for the way they affect the pleasure centers of the brain, these drugs also produce effects on many other parts of the body. For example, opioid receptors are prominent in the intestine, so opiates not only cause addiction but also cause the gut to become quiet. For this reason, opioid drugs are used in the treatment of diarrhea as well as in the treatment of severe pain.

Drugs and the Brain

The effects of chemicals on the brain are determined by how much of the chemical reaches the brain. This is called the dose response. The brain doesn't respond to very low levels of any drug. As the level of the chemical rises, the brain's responses not only increase but change—that is, low levels of a drug produce one response and high levels produce different responses. The brain, continuously active and functioning as a single integrated unit, is influenced by all of the chemicals taken into the body that pass the blood-brain barrier. The rapidly changing concentrations of drug chemicals in the synapse are governed by the chemicals' concentration in the blood and by the body's ability to metabolize and eliminate them.

Roadways to the Brain

Drug users take drugs by one of several routes of administration. This includes taking drugs by mouth (the drugs enter the body through the gastrointestinal tract) and by smoking (the drugs enter the body through the lungs). Drugs can also be injected with a hypodermic needle under the skin or directly into the bloodstream. Drugs may be absorbed through the nasal membranes directly into the blood, a route of administration that is similar to injection under the skin but that does not require a needle and syringe. When drugs enter the body by smoking, they reach the brain within eight seconds without first passing through the liver. This route of administration produces effects that are similar to injection of drugs into the vein (intravenous use) and intranasal use, which produces initial brain effects in about sixteen seconds.

The most intensely rewarding drug experience comes when the brain is hit by a high and rapidly rising level of drug chemicals. When chemicals are used for medical reasons—not to get high—they are usually taken orally to avoid the rapid rise and fall of blood levels, an experience that drug abusers avidly seek. A few medical psychoactive chemicals are taken by injection rather than by mouth, because these particular medicines are not absorbed efficiently from the gastrointestinal tract or are quickly metabolized by the liver. With few exceptions, psychoactive medicines, unlike abused drugs, are taken by mouth. When brain-affecting medicines are injected in medical treatments, they are injected into muscles or under the skin. When drug abusers inject drugs, they often inject into the vein.

Most psychoactive nonmedical drug use is by intravenous injection or smoking to get the most rapid rise to the highest level of the drug in the brain. This rapid rise is highly reinforcing because it is particularly effective in stimulating the brain's pleasure centers. This is why smoking and intravenous injection are the routes of administration chosen by addicted people and why these routes of administration are so much more addicting than is oral use of the same drug.

Alcohol: An Unusual Drug

Alcohol at first appears to be an exception to the general rule that addicted people take drugs by smoking or injection. But a closer look at drinking suggests this exception is more apparent than real. Alcohol is quickly and completely absorbed from the gastrointestinal tract, rapidly passing the blood-brain barrier. Even when taken by mouth, alcohol is relatively fast-acting, especially when taken on an empty stomach, compared with other orally consumed brain-affecting chemicals. Nonalcoholic drinkers consume low doses of alcohol, often with food, which slows the absorption of the alcohol out of the intestines and into the bloodstream. This pattern of drinking produces a relatively slow rise to low brain levels of alcohol. Nonalcoholic drinkers purposefully consume alcohol in ways that avoid the increased "buzz" produced by rapid rises to high levels of alcohol in their blood. Alcoholics, in contrast, are more likely to consume large amounts of alcohol on an empty stomach, drinking fast to achieve the rapidly rising, high brain levels typically sought by addicted people. The faster the rise of drugs in the blood, and consequently in the brain, the more reinforcing the drug use.

Searching for the Root of Addiction

Addiction to alcohol and other drugs involves the use of a drug nonmedically to produce a high, leading to loss of control and denial. Alcoholics and drug addicts use "alcoholically" or "addictively," meaning they use alcohol and other drugs in the ways that some lovers behave: recklessly, irrationally, and impulsively. Often when people think about the roots of addiction, they think of social or economic factors such as family dysfunction or poverty, but, while these can contribute to drug abuse, the root of addiction lies far deeper than just demographic characteristics. The root of addiction is in the human brain.

In the 1950s, Robert Heath, a brilliant researcher at Tulane University, sought to understand the brain mechanisms underlying the commonly observed lethargy of many people with chronic schizophrenia. He implanted electrodes into the brains of disturbed patients. To his surprise, he found that patients reported feelings of pleasure following stimulation of certain clusters of neurons at the base of the brain. This finding was particularly remarkable because the brain itself has no sensory nerve endings and cannot feel in the way other parts of the body do. Non-schizophrenic people reported the same experiences when stimulated in these specific brain areas, a discovery which led Heath to shift his study to brain-stimulated pleasure rather than schizophrenia.

Shortly thereafter, other researchers found that centers in the brain, located close to these pleasure centers, produced sensations of intense pain. When the pain centers, also deep in the midbrain, were stimulated by electrodes, experimental animals became disturbed. They would do almost anything to avoid stimulation of these particular areas of their brains. Both the pleasure and pain centers are collections of gray matter, clumps of neuron cell bodies, at the base of the brain in the center of the head.

Two researchers in Canada, James Olds and Peter Milner, found that rats with electrodes in their brains would work hard to get electrical stimulation of their pleasure centers. They worked just as hard to avoid electrical stimulation of their closely related pain centers. The rats hooked up to the electrical stimulation pressed the bars that sent them pleasurable shocks to the point of exhaustion, in preference to water, food, or even sex. When these experiments were extended to human subjects, they reported that electrical stimulation of the pleasure centers not only produced good feelings but changed their moods, creating a sense of well-being and euphoria. This experimental, direct stimulation of pleasure centers in their brains also reduced the sensitivity to pain and minimized the effects of abused drugs.

The line of research just described confirmed the observation made over half a century earlier by Sigmund Freud that "our entire psychical activity is bent upon procuring pleasure and avoiding pain." Freud extended this observation by noting that human beings, who could think about probable consequences of their behaviors over a long period of time, did not simply act to seek immediate pleasure and avoid immediate pain—they actively pursued long-term goals of maximizing pleasure and minimizing pain. He described this longer view as delayed gratification and attributed it to the mental mechanisms that manage human behavior, which he called the ego.

Addicts appear to be prominent exceptions to this rule. Addicted people act, with respect to their alcohol and other drug use, as if they were enslaved to immediate pleasure, despite the prospect of even catastrophic long-term negative consequences of their drug use. This finding led some Freudian psychoanalysts to describe addiction as an ego defect, a defect in self-care. Because addicts often lose their moral sense, psychoanalysts also described a deficit in addicts' consciences, labeled superego defects.

Scientists today use chemical probes of the brain, rather than electrical wires as were used by Heath and Olds, to stimulate or inhibit specific brain areas. The pleasure and pain centers in the brains of all animals, including human beings, are governed by the neurotransmitters that powerfully influence behavior. All the abused drugs, working in remarkably different ways, affect the midbrain pleasure centers.

This final common pathway explains why addicts use seemingly diverse drugs. In a wide variety of ways, all abused drugs stimulate the pleasure centers of the brain and inhibit the brain's pain centers. It is this pleasure, and the reciprocal suppression of pain and distress, that addicts strive to experience. They are not too picky about the precise pharmacology of how they get this effect, although, like all consumers, they are governed by habit, fashion, and price. In some cases, people can't control their drinking but can take or leave other drugs; it's the same for those whose principal drug of choice is heroin, meth, or marijuana. However, when addicts change from one drug to another, such ordinary influences on consumer behaviors—like habit, fashion, and price—are usually the cause for the change, not pharmacology.

The Brain's Reward Mechanisms

In the last few decades, the work on the brain's reward mechanisms has become one of the most productive areas of neurophysiological study. There are three areas of the brain with dopamine (DA)-containing neurons. The first brain area includes the ventral tegmental area and the nucleus accumbens, the principal pleasure centers. The second area is the substantia nigra, the largest cluster of DA-containing neurons in the brain. The substantia nigra manages movements. Depletion of the cells in the substantia nigra produces Parkinson's, a disease associated with muscular rigidity. The third DA-containing area of the brain, the arcuate nucleus, is a major pathway to the pituitary gland and the management of the body's hormonal balances and immune system.

The study of drugs of abuse has zeroed in on the first of these areas, the ventral tegmental area and the nucleus accumbens. These cells beat in unison, releasing DA in rhythmic pulses. Scientists have discovered that all drugs of abuse cause the neurons in this area of the brain to release relatively large amounts of DA into their synapses. Each drug of abuse does this in a different way. Nicotine causes the same release of DA from the same cells of the ventral tegmental area and the nucleus accumbens as is caused by drugs as diverse as heroin, alcohol, and cocaine, although it does so by an entirely unique mechanism. More important, nicotine stimulates these cells without producing intoxication or impairment, as the drugs of abuse typically do.

Animal studies of brain mechanisms also have shown that if the axons connecting the ventral tegmental area with the nucleus accumbens are cut, an animal stops working to get drugs. If the animal is physically dependent on alcohol or another drug, the animal will show withdrawal symptoms, even with those particular nerve fibers cut. These experiments made clear that the animal's drug-using behavior is shaped primarily by reward—by the release of DA in the ventral tegmental area and the nucleus accumbens— not by withdrawal symptoms, because the animals stopped using drugs when the drugs did not produce reward even though stopping caused withdrawal symptoms.

Neurophysiologists wondered if these cells were stimulated by non-drug pleasures. Three dogs with probes in their nucleus accumbens were given meat bones, one of the most intense pleasure experiences for a dog. As expected, the dogs were excited and happy, but surprisingly researchers found no release of DA in the dogs' nucleus accumbens. Worried that they had failed to tap the correct spots in the dogs' brains, the researchers prepared three more dogs and repeated the experiment, using all six dogs.

The scientists were even more surprised to find that after giving juicy meat bones to all six dogs, the first three dogs now showed release of DA from the nucleus accumbens, but the three dogs added to the experiment did not. Repeated experiments helped explain what was happening, showing that there was learning in the brain following pleasure stimulation. Only after repeating the experience of intense pleasure did these particular brain cells release DA.

The brain pleasure centers had to learn to fire in response to particular stimuli. Even more remarkable, the scientists discovered that much of the DA release occurred before the dog actually began to chew on the meaty bone. As soon as the dog knew it was getting the bone, or even anticipated getting the bone based on prior rewarding experiences, the nucleus accumbens cells released pulses of DA. These experiments showed that reward centers required training by repeated experience and were highly influenced by anticipation. These centers in the brain were appetite centers, producing strong feelings of pleasure based on past rewarding, stimulating experiences.

This line of research is profoundly important to understanding the working of the addicted brain. The specific part of the brain that responded to all addictive behaviors was turned on by a wide variety of drugs and by many nondrug rewards. The ventral tegmental area and the nucleus accumbens required repeated experience to trigger the pulsing release of DA. The anticipation of rewarding experiences, based on prior brain stimulation, was itself powerfully rewarding. Finally, these experiments showed that reward shaped addictive behavior, not withdrawal as had long been thought.

This research explains why most drug abusers easily switch from one drug to another and why withdrawal is an inconstant feature of addiction rather than a crucial aspect of addiction. The different drugs use different mechanisms to produce the same basic brain reward. Behavior is shaped by the reward of drug use, not by the pain of withdrawal symptoms. These experiments also show why addictive behavior tends to be repetitive behavior and why anticipation of pleasure (the set, or the expectation of the drug user) is such an important part of the drug experience.

This important research into the brain's pleasure centers has not yet explained why some people are at higher risk of addiction or why different substances or behaviors influence the risk level of addiction for particular individuals. Some people are more likely to have food addictions; others are more likely to have alcohol or other drug addictions. It is not as if a person had a single addictive risk, although some people do appear to be especially vulnerable to many addictive substances or behaviors.

Addiction reflects the DA-based pleasure/reward mechanisms of the brain as people (and other animals) repeat experiences that they find intensely pleasurable. There are many doors into the reward control room in the brain. Food and sex are natural doors, whereas alcohol and other drugs are chemical doors. For each person, I imagine that some particular doors to the control room are larger than other doors. This is the reason that some people use alcohol and like it and others use alcohol and do not. The first group has big alcohol doors to their pleasure centers, and the second group has small alcohol doors. The size of each hypothetical door, and the ease with which it is opened, is partly determined by genetic factors. Groups with large doors and groups with small doors both can be addicted to alcohol use and other addicting behaviors if they repeat the rewarding experience often enough. There are some ways to stimulate this part of the brain that are relatively safe and other ways that are inherently unsafe. The substance and the route of administration play major roles in determining relative risk for drugs of abuse.

In specific synapses of the brain, scientists at last discovered the behavior control room and began to explore how it works and what goes wrong in addiction. The new neurophysiology resonated with the new clinical understanding of the experience of addiction, offering important insights for both the prevention and the treatment of addiction. The biology of addiction has been found to be a central reality shaping the experience of addiction. The brain says yes to pleasure/reward. That experience of pleasure is rooted in the DA-containing neurons in the brain's ventral tegmental area and in the nucleus accumbens.

How important are the feelings produced by the brain's DA-containing pleasure centers when it comes to everyday behavior? Sex and eating are the models for all pleasure-driven behaviors. What happens to sexual behavior when a person feels no reward from sex? It stops. I have seen this many times in my practice of psychiatry. When a person does not feel sexual pleasure, even with an intense effort of willpower, that person's sexual behavior stops. The same phenomenon takes place with eating. People who are profoundly depressed lose their capacity to experience pleasure. They often stop sexual behavior and eating. People who have exhausted their brain's pleasure system by abusing drugs also reduce both sex and eating. Often, they lose the ability to experience pleasure from anything at all, which is one reason that chronic addicts are so miserable. Many behaviors are driven by this same process of seeking good feelings and avoiding bad feelings. Feelings of reward not only add depth and color to life but are absolutely necessary to life itself. It is no accident that the mechanisms of reward are universal and powerful in all animal species. That is why these mechanisms are hardwired into our brains.

Paths to the Pleasure Centers

Abused drugs directly affect the synapses in the pleasure centers. Many other activities and substances have an impact on the firing of the pleasure-producing neurons. These centers and the brain mechanisms involving pleasure and pain play a vital role in the everyday life of all animals. Food and sex are obvious stimuli for these centers in humans, but so are more mundane activities, from exercising and watching television to reading a good book or buying new clothes.

Understanding the biological basis of addiction requires looking at the uncommon and often mysterious experiences of addiction to alcohol and other drugs from a different perspective. Begin by thinking about nonchemical pleasures. Assuming that nonchemical pleasures are inherently safe is clearly wrong. Far too much human misery is caused by nondrug pleasurable experiences, such as eating and sex, to permit such a simple assumption.

That's why I've concluded that addiction involves the two key factors of loss of control (unmanageability) and dishonesty (denial). Addicts have such strong and highly valued experiences with particular pleasurable activities that they put those sensations, those experiences, above everyday responsibilities and risk serious harm to themselves and others by pursuing their addictive pleasures. Addicts also lie about their behavior; they cover up what they are doing and they deceive others—they deny they have a problem.

Experiences That Shape Behavior

- Positive reinforcement produces pleasure to encourage a certain behavior.
- Negative reinforcement relieves pain to encourage behavior.
- Punishment, or aversive control, uses painful stimulation to discourage a certain behavior.

Reinforcement and Punishment

New brain research has involved the work of not only chemists and anatomists, but psychologists as well. As previously noted, addiction is more than a chemical reaction in the brain. Psychologists describe three types of behavior-affecting stimuli: positive reinforcement, negative reinforcement, and punishment. A good feeling is positive reinforcement. When a hungry laboratory rat is given a food pellet after a specific behavior, this is positive reinforcement. Relief of a painful experience is a negative reinforcement. When a painful shock stops when a rat presses a bar, the rat has received a negative reinforcement. Both positive and negative reinforcement are rewarding; they lead the animal (or the human) to repeat the experience. Both types of reinforcement need to be distinguished from aversive control or punishment. For example, when a rat receives a painful stimulus, such as an electrical shock after a particular behavior, this is punishment. It discourages the behavior with which it is associated.

All three behavior-shaping experiences are common for both animals and humans. They each have direct application to the experience of addiction. The pairing of pleasure and pain is mirrored in the brain's structure. Pleasure and pain centers in the brain are closely related and generally reciprocally linked in the brain. When heroin addicts take their drug, for example, they not only feel pleasure or euphoria but also a waning of whatever negative sensations they had been experiencing prior to taking the drug. Tension and depression, pain and self-doubt—all are dissolved in the heroin high. Many abused drugs also have important roles in medicine as painkillers. Medicines used to treat several painful mental illnesses, such as panic attacks, can also, at high doses, produce feelings of euphoria. This is no accident; it is the result of fundamental brain biology.

Both physicians and the public often find the relationship between positive and negative reinforcement confusing, especially when it comes to the use of potentially abused medicines and drug abuse. We saw this earlier when we considered the role of withdrawal in maintaining addiction. Withdrawal symptoms are distressing. Addicted animals, including humans, find relief from acute symptoms of withdrawal to be reinforcing or rewarding. Scientifically, but confusingly, this is called negative reinforcement, because it involves removal of a painful feeling.

One reason cigarette smokers find pleasure by lighting up each hour is that the jolt of nicotine, which hits their brains within eight seconds after the first puff, begins to relieve the nicotine withdrawal discomfort they had been experiencing. That is also why the first cigarette in the morning is uniquely satisfying. Addicted smokers have gone for an unusually long time without a cigarette when they wake up in the morning, so nicotine withdrawal symptoms are relatively severe, and the relief that comes with the first cigarette of the day is particularly reinforcing. This is an example of negative reinforcement. It is seen universally in addiction to alcohol and other drugs.

Making Excuses for Irrational Behavior

As a young resident in psychiatry, I attended a lecture on hypnotism that has stayed with me throughout my career. I was fascinated when a professor hypnotized a patient in front of our class. He told the patient that ten minutes after the patient came out of the hypnotic trance he would go to the window and open it. The doctor gave the patient no reason to do this. It was a cold day, and the classroom was chilly.

The patient came out of the hypnotic trance and, after ten minutes of general discussion with the professor, went to the window and opened it. The professor asked the patient why he had opened the window. The patient said, "I was hot and thought we would be more comfortable with the window open." The professor said, "But this is my room. Are you accustomed to opening other people's windows without asking them?" The patient politely replied, "No I'm not. I am sorry. I didn't even think about asking your permission." Then the professor asked, "But it is cold in here now and it is even colder outside. Are you sure you want that window open?" The patient held his ground: "Yes, I am more comfortable with the window open right now, thank you."

As the professor explained that experiment to our class, he told us that the patient did not have any idea why he had opened the window. He was simply making up the most plausible excuses he could on the spot. Years later I thought of that experience as I saw hundreds of people addicted to alcohol and other drugs who sought to explain why they continued to use alcohol and other drugs despite the terrible things that often happened to them as a result. Like the hypnotized patient, they did not know why they acted as they did. They simply made up excuses for what was irrational and self-destructive behavior.

The brain research on addiction has helped me to understand this mystery. People who are addicted act as if they were hypnotized, as if their pleasure centers, like the professor in the experiment, told them to do things in a voice that was not accessible to their conscious minds. So the addicts made up excuses that seemed as lame as that poor patient's excuses for opening the window on a cold day.

This is the process of denial at work. It is as if the disease of addiction whispered softly in the ear of the addict: "Do it again, right now. Go ahead. It's okay." Without consciously hearing that voice, the addict nonetheless acted as the voice directed. Even more mysteriously, denial can prevent the addict from seeing the addictive behavior at all. It is as if the hypnotic voice of the addictive disease said, "This is not happening. You are not doing it." It would be as if the patient in the experiment said, when challenged by the professor, "What window? I don't see a window. And if I did see a window, I can assure you that not only did I not open it, but I would positively refuse to open it. What do you take me for, a fool? Anyone can see that it is cold in here as well as cold outside today. Why did you even ask me such a ridiculous question?"

When you confront addicts about their addictive behavior, they deny it. Are they consciously lying, or are they deceived by their own disease? After many years of studying this fascinating process, I have concluded that the answer is "both." It is about as rewarding to ask addicts why they behave as they do as it was for that professor to ask that patient fifty years ago why he opened the window. To confirm once more the nature of the disease, I can ask the addicts I see in my practice why they continue to use alcohol and other drugs, but I no longer have hope of finding a useful answer to the question because I have learned that addicts have no idea why they are doing what they are doing when it comes to alcohol and other drug use. Their reason, if they admit use at all, is usually, "I do it because I like to do it." When asked why they lie about their use of addictive drugs, addicts give similarly direct answers that usually come down to, "Because if I told the truth, someone would try to stop me from using my drug."

We saw in the previous chapter how every human culture has developed rules governing common pleasurable behaviors in order to contain the destruction that occurs when people lose control over pleasure-producing behaviors. These rules are seen in social conventions, in religions, in laws, and most especially in the family-based management of behaviors. Addicts not only have lost control of their lives, they not only deny their addiction-caused behaviors and the problems these behaviors cause, but they pursue their addictive behaviors in clear conflict with social norms, laws, and religious values. It is remarkable to see the ability of addiction to overcome even the most moral and sensible person. I have seen many physicians, teachers, ministers, and others of high intelligence and great moral strength turned into destructive, dishonest, and irresponsible people by their addictions. Both they and those who know them well are amazed by this, because they underestimate the power of addiction to control human thought and behavior, regardless of intelligence or character. In this way, addiction is like some psychiatric disorders in that the irrational behavior of someone with severe depression, anxiety, or other neurochemical disorders can alienate and confuse the people around them. It's common to see addiction and psychiatric disorders occurring together, which can raise the questions of how each affect the other and which to treat first.

Self-Medication and Co-occurring Brain Disorders

The drug abuser's behavior has sometimes been explained as an attempt to self-medicate. "Self-medication" means the use of mood-altering drugs to treat unpleasant feelings (such as severe anxiety, depression, or physical pain). Although psychological distress or physical pain are reasons some addicts first use drugs—whether alcohol, street drugs, or prescription drugs—I am skeptical of the self-medication hypothesis as an explanation for persistent addictive behavior. Drug abusers do not abuse any medicine that does not produce brain reward or reinforcement. For example, people do not abuse arthritis medicines or antibiotics, two effective and commonly used classes of medicines that reduce distress. People with panic disorder do not abuse antidepressants, even though they block panic attacks. Drug abusers do, however, abuse stimulants and narcotics. The reasons certain drugs are abused, but most medicines are not, have less to do with self-medication and more to do with feelings produced in the brain's pleasure centers.

Infections and arthritis, both of which can be terribly painful, are treated with powerful medicines. Once people with these diseases understand the importance of specific treatments, they are highly motivated to use the medicines. This is not self-medication, and these medicines have no appeal to drug abusers. Such medical patients, if they are denied access to their pain-relieving medicines, will exhibit "drug-seeking behavior" in the sense that they will take steps to ensure they get the medicines they need. When drug addicts and alcoholics talk of self-medication, they refer only to their use of abused drugs such as alcohol, opioids, and cocaine, never to routine, non-abused medicines such as antibiotics or anti-arthritic medicines.

Because of my own professional involvement with both addiction and anxiety disorders—which, like addiction, as well as depression, post-traumatic stress disorder (PTSD), and other psychiatric disorders, are caused by neurochemical imbalances in conjunction with other biological and environmental factors—I am drawn to the more complex aspects of the self-medication controversy in addiction, using anxiety as an example. Most clinically anxious people fear loss of control, so they do not drink alcohol or, if they do drink, they do so on a very limited basis. On the other hand, some people who suffer from anxiety disorders do use alcohol and find that it reduces their painful panic and anxiety, at least for an hour or so.

A small percentage of all anxious patients get trapped in their use of alcohol, escalating their use over time in an alcoholic pattern.

Some anxious people become addicted to alcohol, using it in repeated doses throughout the day (maintenance drinking) or in great amounts over short periods (binge drinking). Anxious patients who continue to demonstrate either of these patterns of alcoholic drinking once the anxiety disorder has been treated often, but not always, have a predisposition to alcoholism and have a family history of alcoholism. This tells us that these people found not just brief symptomatic relief from their anxiety in the alcohol, but reward, or a high, with which they literally fell in love. It was the reward that produced the addiction, not the antianxiety effects of the alcohol. They probably would have abused alcohol or another drug, such as Valium, Xanax, or another antianxiety medicine, at some point, even if they hadn't experienced anxiety and would have eventually lost control of their drinking.

Addicted anxious patients show the typical alcoholic pattern, which is easily distinguished from the common drinking or other drug-using behavior of the typical person with an anxiety disorder who is not an addict. For these addicted people, their anxiety disorder does not explain their addiction to alcohol or other drugs, but occasionally it does explain how they started using mood-altering drugs in the first place.

The relationship of addiction to anxiety disorders is more complex than this initial picture suggests. Over hours, and even more over days and weeks, alcohol makes panic and anxiety worse. When antianxiety medicines are taken, not as prescribed to reduce anxiety, but nonmedically in higher doses to produce brain rewards and by using them with alcohol and other drugs of abuse, it's common for addicts to eventually experience tolerance and need larger and more frequent doses to achieve the same effect. In fact, many alcoholics and addicts to other drugs, as part of their addiction, become clinically anxious, even sometimes suffering from panic attacks and other anxiety disorders, especially when the drug use is interrupted. For most such addicted and anxious people, simply stopping drinking (which usually requires a program of lifelong recovery in Alcoholics Anonymous) will eliminate the symptoms of their anxiety disorder after they have gone through withdrawal, their bodies are rid of the toxic chemicals, and their brain chemistry has had sufficient time to normalize. In other words, for these alcoholic or other drug addicted people, their anxiety disorder is secondary to their addiction—their anxiety problem followed and was caused by their addiction. Once the primary addiction to alcohol or other drugs is under control, the *co-occurring* anxiety disorder commonly diminishes or even disappears. Even so, it's important that both disorders are treated at the same time with the specific treatment protocols that are required for each.

Anxiety disorders can also be an excuse for addictive drug use as self-medication. Even worse, this connection of alcoholism and anxiety can lead physicians to prescribe addicting medicines to addicts in the mistaken belief that such treatment will improve both their anxiety and their addiction. When anxiety or any other psychiatric disorder coexists with addiction, I suggest treating the addiction at the same time as that disorder, which means generally not prescribing addictive drugs as a part of the treatment protocol.

Addicts regularly speak of using drugs to "feel normal." This is the result of their having so disturbed the normal function of the pleasure centers in their brains that they feel lousy without their alcohol or other drugs. Nevertheless, the drugs that addicts seek for purposes of self-medication are the chemicals that stimulate the brain's pleasure centers. Usually this drug-using behavior is simply addictive behavior hiding behind the rationalization of self-medication.

Whether the bad feeling being "treated" by the addicted person is anxiety, depression, anger, pain, or some other intensely unpleasant state, or whether the bad feelings are the result of prior drug use (as is often the case with hangovers from drinking alcohol or withdrawal from opioid use), the reason the addicted person is using alcohol and other drugs over a prolonged period of time can be traced primarily to the person's love affair with the chemical stimulation of brain rewards, not to the discomfort of a preexisting disease. People who do not use alcohol or drugs addictively, and who experience anxiety, depression, pain, and other uncomfortable feelings, seldom become addicted to alcohol and other abused drugs, even if they are exposed to them in the course of medical practice and even if they find some temporary relief from their discomfort when they use these substances.

Brain Biology and Self-Medication

Although called pleasure, the drug high bears little relationship to the joys of natural activities like painting, dancing, climbing a mountain, or simply talking with a friend. The drug user's high is far more intense and gripping—it is much closer to the experience of sexual orgasm or eating a large meal than it is to visiting an art museum. The drug high is a primitive profound brain stimulation, a sledgehammer blow to the brain's normally subtle pleasure system. Self-medication simply does not explain the experience of persistent use of addicting drugs despite the problems that this use typically causes addicted people.

Brain biology offers a useful way to think about the self-medication hypothesis of addictive drug use. Anxiety and panic are governed by the locus coeruleus in the brain stem. When the ventral tegmental area and the nucleus accumbens in the midbrain—the principal pleasure centers—are stimulated, they send signals to quiet the locus coeruleus. When an addicted person experiences physical withdrawal, the locus coeruleus sends out distressing alarm signals for days, making sleep difficult or impossible and producing profoundly uncomfortable anxiety and even panic attacks.

Drugs that stimulate the ventral tegmental area and the nucleus accumbens, as all addicting drugs do, calm the locus coeruleus. Once addiction has taken hold in the brain, when drug use stops, the locus coeruleus is sent into action, helping to produce the painful withdrawal syndrome. With repeated alcohol and other drug use over time, the pleasure centers of the brain require more and more stimulation to produce pleasure, raising the risks of withdrawal when drug levels fall in the brain. Worse yet, brain reward is reset to a lower level because of this intense, unnatural stimulation. For this reason, drug users when not using drugs, not only miss the drugs but their brain biology has set a trap so that activities that normally produce brain reward are now far less rewarding. What started as a self-controlled search for pleasure, and relief of discomfort from an anxiety or other mental or physical disorder, increasingly becomes a desperate out-of-control search for a feeling of normality and a way to escape the brain's distressing alarm mechanism managed by the locus coeruleus.

For most people who do not have a preexisting vulnerability to addiction, the process of using addictive drugs to suppress uncomfortable feelings is short-lived as they learn that the stimulation of the brain's pleasure centers by the nonmedical use of drugs from alcohol to heroin is a fool's game. At best, they get short-term gains at the price of long-term disasters. One hangover or one episode of uncomfortable intoxication is enough to convince them that large doses of alcohol and other drugs are, in the end, no fun at all. In contrast, people who are biologically vulnerable to addiction are seduced by the experience, despite the problems their use causes. For addiction-prone people, it is often difficult to sort out the positive rewards of addictive drug use (the positive feelings from stimulating the pleasure centers of their brains) from the negative rewards (the relief of discomfort from quieting of the locus coeruleus, whether it is stimulated by withdrawal or an underlying mental disorder).

A Simple Look at Who Is Most Vulnerable to Addiction

What makes some people more vulnerable or at higher risk of addiction than others? Mostly there are two reasons. First there is biology—some people have a genetic family history of addiction that predisposes them to vulnerability to addiction. Second there is the fact that repeated use of drugs addictively—that is, at high doses, with other drugs of abuse, and by powerful routes of administration (like smoking, shooting, and snorting)—can trigger addiction even in the absence of a heightened genetic vulnerability.

The All-Too-Human Disorder of Addiction

Any pleasurable action can be addictive, meaning it can lead to continuing the behavior despite negative consequences of the behavior and dishonesty. There are some simple, and old-fashioned, guidelines that protect people from addictions. The antidote to addiction is honesty with respect to alcohol and other drug use or other addictive behavior. That approach is fairly easy for most non-addicted people to understand and even to practice. It is difficult for addicts to practice because the addiction has taken hold of their brains and has induced distortions in their thinking, including dishonesty. They rationalize their addictive behaviors to protect the forbidden fun of their addictive alcohol and other drug use. When a person gets well from any addiction, the inner experience is similar to a person being released from slavery, the experience of a prisoner being freed from captivity. The slavery of addiction is especially painful, humiliating, and cruel because while it's a brain disease, it appears to be self-imposed; because of the harms caused while drinking and using; and, in the case of illegal drug use, because it was irresponsible (they have no other purpose but to get you high) and against the law. Yet every one of the mysteries of addiction that are briefly recounted here is the direct result of brain biology. The process of hijacked brain reward is complicated by the permanent changes that occur in the brains of addicts with drug use, changes that leave addicted people vulnerable to relapse throughout their lives.

Addiction: A Harsh Teacher

Brain research is in the early, but very exciting, stages of answering many questions about the cunning, baffling, and powerful disease of addiction, including one of the fundamental questions addressed in this book: Why do people use drugs and why do some people abuse drugs and others do not? One the most important discoveries we've discussed in this chapter is that drugs are chemicals that hijack the normal workings of brain reward. "Reward" sounds abstract and superficial, but it is anything but that. Reward is how brain scientists describe the stimulation of the brain's "do it now" and "do it more" mechanisms. Reward is how the brain gets what it, and the rest of the individual, needs. Brain reward is fine tuned to meet the imperatives of biology. As we've seen, it is not unique to humans but characteristic of all animals—even fruit flies respond to brain reward.

We called the brain's reward centers the "pleasure" centers, which may give the erroneous impression that using drugs always makes people happy. The reward center is about much more than the temporary state of happiness: It is driven by compulsion or urgent demand. Stimulation of brain reward is not simply on or off; it is graded from mild to intense. The pleasure of drug use is not like the pleasure received from stamp collecting or looking at a painting in a museum. It is far more driven and urgent.

Drugs of abuse stimulate brain reward many times more, sometimes hundreds of times more, than natural rewards. This explains the puzzling extreme priority given to drug use by addicts as well as why relapse is so common despite often dreadful consequences. Brain reward shapes human behavior and thoughts, including among the smartest people. Addiction swamps intelligence and produces the peculiarities of thinking that are obvious to those around the addicts. The addicted brain pushes aside the negative consequences of the drug use, blaming others for their problems and preserving access to the drugs at virtually all costs, including otherwise unacceptable dishonesty.

To further complicate matters, while the initial drugs of abuse were relatively few in number (such as alcohol, nicotine, marijuana, opium, and cocaine), in recent years chemists have invented thousands of new synthetic chemicals that stimulate brain reward. Meanwhile the older drugs have been made available in new forms, often with ever higher potencies. This is easily seen in smoked marijuana, which has seen a dramatic increase in potency of tetrahydrocannabinol (THC) from the roughly 2 percent in the 1970s to about 20 percent today, with new products like waxes and oils that contain upwards of 90 percent THC.

***

So, to our question "Why do people like to use drugs?" the answer is because they produce intense brain reward—that is, they powerfully hijack the healthy brain. This leads us to a related second question: "Why do some people abuse drugs and become addicted while others do not?" This is more complex because brain biology is complicated by multiple factors. Brain biology is affected strongly by age and a person's stage of brain development, the presence of psychiatric disorders (such as depression, anxiety, or PTSD), genetic factors, and the social environment in which the user exists, including family life. All of these factors can also shape a person's personality. For example, traits like impulsiveness and risk-taking can become contributing factors to whether a person abuses drugs or not. High on the list of contributing factors is availability and acceptability of drugs of abuse. Having friends use alcohol and drugs addictively also increases a person's vulnerability to addiction.

The bottom line is that addiction is a harsh and demanding teacher. This education not uncommonly is lethal. Recovery is brain healing but the addicted brain never forgets and remains capable of re-ignition at any time, even years into recovery. Triggers to use can spring up at any time, often unexpectedly—getting an innocent pain pill, spending time with drug-using friends, attending a wedding where there's pressure to drink and "have a good time." Relapse often starts before actual drug use has begun, before any real thoughts about resuming alcohol and drug use even formulate. It can start with no intention to drink or use drugs. But suddenly, the situation to use presents itself and the dormant addicted brain switches to automatic pilot. This perpetual risk of relapse can be the driving force in an addict's life, which we'll explore in the next chapter.

4. AN ADDICT'S LIFE

Addicts never use alcohol and drugs to become addicted—that is never the intent. Addiction is an unwanted and unexpected side effect of the substance use. When an addict begins using, it's not always clear that addiction will develop, but in retrospect we can see that becoming hooked was a natural progression of the disease of addiction.

This chapter outlines the full spectrum of an addict's life. To put it simply, we can say that addicts who are successful at beating addiction go through four stages in their relationship with drugs: fooling around, getting hooked, hitting bottom, and entering recovery. Not everyone who starts out reaches the fourth or even the third stage. Many die in the first or second stage. Many addicts, however, do go through all four stages. The stages are the same for addicts of all drugs, but each drug produces characteristic effects that distinguish it from the other drugs.

Stages of Addiction

- **Fooling around**: This is the honeymoon stage, typically marked with few problems.
- **Being hooked**: Loss of control, denial, and accumulating negative consequences of drug use are features of this stage.
- **Hitting bottom**: Now the addict pays the price for living out of control and is forced to recognize that a drug-using life cannot continue.
- **Recovery**: This stage offers freedom from the pain and chaos of addiction and a better more meaningful drug-free life.

Fooling Around

Fooling around often is the honeymoon stage of addiction. It usually starts between the ages of twelve and twenty, often with alcohol and/or marijuana use, but occasionally with other drugs such as inhalants and hallucinogens—and more frequently of late, with opiates. Like a marital honeymoon, this stage of the experience usually includes few problems, but it may also be marked by many problems.

At the age of twelve, the daughter of a medical colleague of mine set two national swimming records in four-person medley relays. My colleague's daughter was dead at sixteen because of her drug use. After smoking marijuana at the home of one of her neighbors, she walked into the path of a speeding car on her way home. She became a victim of marijuana, what I call the "careless drug." She was not an addict—she never progressed past the initial stage of fooling around—but she and her family paid for her drug use with her life.

Generally speaking, however, there is a continuum in drug use from a single use of a drug to a pattern of occasional use. Some people use a drug once and stop, while others use it for a while and stop. But some others use the drug more often and show a progression to increasing use and problems resulting from that use. This continuum is commonly seen with alcohol. It is less often seen with cigarettes where the common pattern of use is to smoke a few cigarettes for a while and then stop or to use progressively to full-blown nicotine addiction. After the teen years, when there are many people who smoke a little now and then, this pattern virtually disappears. Adults either smoke many cigarettes a day every single day or they do not smoke at all. This contrasts sharply with the common pattern of adult alcohol use where there are many people who use a little alcohol from time to time—often for their entire adult lives—and a smaller number of people who drink heavily whenever they drink, often frequently, and even daily. There are similar patterns in the use of other drugs with no sharp dividing lines between relatively mild and extreme patterns of use. Often, the use of drugs varies every day except when the addiction is severe, in which case it is every single day and the amount used is similar day after day, influenced only by the availability of the drugs.

In the early stages of addiction, the addict seeks a good feeling, ideally a kind of euphoria. As the drug use continues over months and years, the low point in the feeling cycle drops so that in time the addict is no longer seeking "good" feelings as much as "less bad" feelings. Experienced addicts sometimes say, "I use now just to feel okay for a little while." As the disease of addiction progresses, addicts are "treating" their own drug-caused bad feelings, known as dysphoria. The selfish brain remembers those early highs, and it experiences the continued immediate reinforcement of the better feelings that come after each use of the drug. Fooling around is the stage in which the addict learns to ride the drug swing, the mood changes, the highs and lows caused by repeated drug use.

How long does the fooling around stage of addiction last? This is determined by many factors. The stronger the person's genetic predisposition for addiction, the faster he or she passes through this stage and moves on toward getting hooked. This is because the drug user with a stronger biological predisposition for addiction likes the drug high more than do drug users who lack this heightened risk. People who have had a malignant course of addiction—meaning that they progress rapidly from fooling around to being hooked—often say that they fell in love the first time they tried the drug or after only a few uses of the drug. Right away, they say, they liked the feeling that the drug produced.

In contrast, many people who fool around with drugs and then drop them, without ever progressing to having a love affair with drug use, say that the drugs did little or nothing for them. A number of people will become social drinkers, enjoying a glass of wine with a meal or a cocktail or two and will generally avoid drinking to intoxication or using illegal drugs—with occasional marijuana use, especially where recreational use is now legal, being an exception for some. Alcoholics who drink alcohol for many years without loss of control but then lose control later in their lives often say that alcohol was of some interest, but not much, until they had some change in their lives that led to their turning increasingly to alcohol for pleasure. The same is true for other substances of abuse. In such cases, there commonly has been an environmental change that shifted the use from benign to malignant. There was no change in the drug and no change in the brain of the user. What changed was the life of the future addict, and this led to different feelings from using alcohol or other drugs and triggered the previously latent progression of the disease of addiction. A job loss or a divorce can trigger a more active phase of the illness, as can a new job, a promotion, or a new group of friends.

The first pattern—rapid and severe addiction—is most often seen in people with parents and siblings who are also addicted to alcohol or other drugs. The second two patterns—those who use a drug but drift away from it, and those who fool around with a drug for a long time without loss of control only to develop an addiction after a life event change—are more often seen in people who do not have close relatives with addiction problems.

Although it is not possible at this time to test for the genetic traits associated with addiction, it is possible to determine just how much the addictive substance means to the person using it by simply asking the person. The more important the use of alcohol and other drugs are to anyone, the more rewarding the experience of using the substance, the greater the risk of addiction. The single best way to avoid the risks of addiction, no matter what one's genetic makeup, is not to use the substance at all. Figuring out this genetic risk by actually trying a drug is a hazardous gamble with the potential for a hefty price tag. Sometimes people who lose this gamble pay with their own lives or with the lives of other people.

As we've discussed in earlier chapters, genetic vulnerability is not the only important influence on the relative risk of addiction among those who try drugs. The younger the person is when drug use starts, the more rapid and the more likely the progression to loss of control over drug use. Individuals who begin nonmedical drug use at a young age also tend to have more character disorders than people who begin using when they are older. Youth who are impulsive, prone to lying, and interested mostly in the present, not the future, are especially vulnerable to rapidly progressing addiction. The brains of younger users are more vulnerable to the seduction of the drug highs, just the way youth are especially vulnerable to brain-based pleasure disorders involving eating and sex. Adolescence turns up the heat in the brain's pleasure centers.

Environments that permit and even encourage drug use at a young age tend to promote addiction. When people use drugs in settings and with people who encourage alcohol and other drug use, they are more likely to progress to full-blown addiction. Especially risky are peer groups of heavy users of alcohol and other drugs. One of the top predictors of addiction is having a best friend who is an addict. Having personal values favorable to drug use and spending time with others who have the same values increase the risk of trying drugs and, once having tried them, of progressing to loss of control over drug use.

It is said that individuals who are destined to become addicts will find alcohol and other drugs no matter how restrictive the environments in which they live. It is also said that some people will never become addicted to alcohol and other drugs no matter how permissive their environments are toward the use of alcohol and other drugs. Both statements have some truth, but both are dangerously misleading.

Surely there are some people who hone in on addictive drugs the way air-to-air missiles seek out their targets. The more important reality, however, is that whereas a small percentage of people seem either utterly destined for addiction or completely immune to it, the large majority of people lie at neither extreme. This large middle group is composed of the people who are influenced by their environments when it comes to addictive substances. Thus, the size of the vulnerable population for addiction to alcohol and other drugs rises in permissive environments, and the size of the invulnerable population rises in relatively restrictive environments. This is an important perspective not only for prevention but also for the treatment of addiction.

Fast and Slow on the Road of Addiction

The route of administration and the choice of a particular drug also play big roles in the speed of progression beyond the stage of fooling around with drugs. Smoking, vaping and shooting, which get drugs to one's brain rapidly at high doses, are more likely to produce rapid progression from fooling around or being hooked than is oral use of a drug. Heroin and cocaine are more likely to produce rapid progression than are alcohol and marijuana. People who use a drug more often are more likely to progress rapidly than those who use the same drug less often.

All these factors interact in powerful and sometimes mysterious ways. A rapid, malignant development of addiction usually signals a combination of many risk factors, including a high genetic risk, character disorder, early use, frequent heavy use, and an environment that is permissive for nonmedical substance use. Slow development of addiction usually means the opposite cluster: lack of genetic factors, relatively little character disorder, relatively late and infrequent drug use, and an interpersonal environment that is less tolerant of drug use.

This experimental use of addicting drugs is like playing Russian roulette, putting a gun to your head when there is a shell in one of the six chambers, spinning the chambers, and then pulling the trigger with a smile on your face. People who use drugs later in their lives and in lower amounts pull the trigger only once. Five out of six of those people survive without succumbing to addiction. People who use addicting drugs earlier and more heavily pull the trigger two or three times, so more of them are victims of their selfish brains. When young people with close relatives who are addicted smoke or inject drugs, they are pulling the trigger six times. Few survive that gamble without serious addiction.

In the fooling around stage, the addict is likely to become interested in using the substance because a close friend is using it and tells the neophyte user that the particular drug can be used safely and with pleasure. Again, alcohol and other drug use usually begins between the ages of twelve and twenty. As noted earlier, experimenting with opiates, especially opioid painkillers taken from a parent's medicine cabinets or purchased from friends or on the street, has become more common in recent years. Youth are unlikely to pick up drug-using habits from end-stage addicts. Their lives make unappealing role models. On the other hand, novice or early users who are having fun using drugs and who have experienced few if any problems as a result of their drug use are often enticing role models.

Character plays an important role in addiction. In this book, I use the term "character disorder" to describe a specific constellation of thoughts and behaviors. This term is often used by psychiatrists and others in the fields of mental health and education. More technically, the syndrome is classified as a personality disorder, an unhealthy pattern of behavior that appears in childhood and usually persists throughout a person's life. The specific personality disorder that most closely fits what I call character disorder is antisocial personality disorder. However, in the Diagnostic and Statistical Manual of Mental Disorders (DSM), the official diagnostic manual for mental disorders, this diagnostic term is restricted to the most severe cases. When I use the term character disorder, I am referring to a group of enduring characteristics that vary in severity from mild to extremely severe. The severe cases are labeled as antisocial personality disorder.

The most prominent features of character disorder are thinking about the present rather than the future when making decisions and frequent dishonesty. Other features include being insensitive to the feelings of others, rebelling against authority, and being relatively unbothered by punishment. Character disorder is more common in males than in females, and it is at its peak from the ages of about fifteen to twenty-five years, tending to diminish at older ages. It is seen in all ethnic and economic groups. (See chapter 5 for a discussion of preventing addiction among high-risk youth as well as a checklist for youth at high risk of addiction to alcohol and other drugs.) In this book, high-risk generally refers to character disorder, because character disorder creates a uniquely high risk of addiction to alcohol and other drugs.

The more the future addict suffers from character disorder—meaning the more the new drug user is focused on current pleasure instead of on future consequences—and the more the person lies and is reckless, the more likely the person is to use any particular substance and to subsequently progress in that use to addiction. Also, the more a person suffers from character disorder, the lower the "bottom" of the addict's career is likely to be. This means that with more character disorder, the negative consequences of drug use must be severe before addicts conclude that they can no longer continue their love affairs with alcohol and other drugs.

This sounds more complex than it is. People, especially youth who focus on the present rather than the future, are relatively immune to the painful consequences from using alcohol and other drugs because painful consequences are usually delayed and uncertain for each person. That is why ever-optimistic character-disordered youth repeatedly engage in pleasure-producing behaviors without learning from their many negative experiences. They learn only in the present tense. If the negative consequence of a behavior is delayed and uncertain, they are unfazed and undeterred. When a bad outcome occurs as a result of drug use, it is brushed aside as an accident because it did not happen every time and so it produces no useful learning. In the right-now world of the selfish brain, drugs work right now, every time they are used. Ask such people why they continue such apparently senseless behavior that produces such painful long-term consequences and they will explain that each and every time they use the drug, they think they can get away with it. They truly believe they can have their drug fun without a painful result this time. Every time they do experience a painful result from their use, they are surprised anew. Painful results typically do not occur every time the addict uses the drug, and, when they do occur, are usually delayed after the drug use and subject to excuses and explanations that hide the connection of the distressing outcome to the drug use.

Think of training a dog and rewarding or punishing the dog on an irregular basis hours or days after the behavior about which you are concerned. For example, the dog jumps up on people who come to your home, and you punish the dog for this behavior two days or even several minutes later. Would the dog ever learn? No, never. Only by pairing the reward or the punishment immediately with the behavior does the most basic form of learning take place. The human brain acts like the dog's brain when it comes to addiction, unless the human has a highly developed sense of future consequences. People with character disorder, and most youth, do not learn well under such circumstances. In truth, most of us have trouble learning from delayed and personally uncertain consequences. This is precisely the reason that laws had to be passed to make wearing seat belts mandatory in airplanes and automobiles, and to make the use of drugs such as cocaine and heroin illegal for everyone.

For addicts, the painful consequences not only have to come often and soon after alcohol and other drug use, but they have to be painful enough to produce meaningful learning about the dangers of drug use. This is true both because many addicts are relatively unfazed by punishments and because the rewards of drug use are so powerful. That said, high-risk people can also learn from others who are addicted because they can more easily identify with kindred souls. They discover not only that other people learn the first time something bad happens to them as a result of alcohol or other drug use, but also that they often do not have to engage in such risky behaviors by using in the first place.

Low-risk people learn quickly and easily when they are warned against such risky behaviors by others, such as their teachers, parents, and the police. High-risk or character-disordered youth seldom learn this way, which is unfortunate for them and for everyone who cares about them. They mainly learn the hard way, through their own personal pain, and this comes after they are already hooked.

Being Hooked

The most remarkable of the four stages of the journey of addiction is being hooked. In an earlier chapter, I likened the experience to falling in love, another common and near-magical process. Who can explain what it's like to lose control to the intense infatuation that can be true love? I recently talked with the parents of a college freshman, a youth with a low risk of addiction. He was an honest, open young man who had suffered from moderately severe phobias as a preteen. He had been slow to get involved with his peer group, whom he considered generally to be frighteningly out of control in their lives. He fell in love for the first time when he went to college. This was his first real girlfriend. He assumed she would be his lifelong soul mate, but she dropped him without warning and without a second thought a few weeks into his marvelous state of rapture.

He was devastated and utterly confused: "If I love her so much, how could she love me so little?" This despondent young man found it suddenly difficult to stay in school, let alone study. Hard as it was, he had found it much easier to study when the brief, intense romance had been hot and heavy. Life had meaning then, even though he was preoccupied with his girlfriend to the point of distraction much of the time. Most of us have been through times like this. After a few such painful experiences, we gain a finely developed sense of both the delight and the despair that go with this natural "disease" of falling in love.

Although the feeling of being hopelessly, intensely in love can happen at any age, it is more likely to hit a person hard during the ages of roughly fifteen to twenty-five, precisely when alcohol and drug addictions are likely to start up. This is when people who have been fooling around with alcohol other drug use, confident that they can handle their substance use, are most likely to get hooked. Like falling in love, being hooked on a substance can happen with lightning speed and intensity, or it can happen slowly, almost without noticing it. The person in love looks outwardly normal. The "disease" can be seen only in the lover's behavior. People in love can lose objectivity and rational control of their lives when it comes to the object of their love. They often hide their out-of-control behavior from others so as not to appear as bizarre as they feel on the inside.

There are built-in feedback loops that, to a greater or lesser degree, help people lost to love in human relationships regain their equilibrium over the course of months or years. This does not happen with alcohol and other drugs, which have, unlike a relationship with a person, direct access to the brain's pleasure centers. Also, unlike a person in love, addicts can buy and control their supply of alcohol and other drugs. It is possible to have your own supply and to use the substances whenever you want to, night or day. There is no natural feedback loop in the brain turning off the drug addiction, even though the search for the drug high will typically result in an increase in negative consequences with each use.

Each time the person uses drugs, regardless of the sinking baseline of the feeling of well-being, there is a prompt and certain reward that is powerfully reinforcing. The brain's hardware says, "Yes, more" to the drug after every single use. The drug is a chemical lover that takes over the brain's natural control mechanisms. As we saw in the previous chapter, addiction is a perversion of brain biology and of the behavior that the brain controls, because, unlike eating, aggression, and sex, there is no biological purpose to the use of addicting drugs. Addiction is brain stimulation devoid of biological meaning.

One of the consequences of falling in love with alcohol or other drug highs is that a subtle but profound distortion of thinking sets in that leads addicted people to deny the negative consequences of their use, both to themselves and to anyone who might try to come between them and their chemical lovers. These distortions of thinking are partly conscious, leading to outright lying, and partly unconscious, leading addicts to trick themselves into thinking that their alcohol and other drug use really is perfectly fine. This characteristic distortion of thinking produces one of the most distinctive features of the addictive disease: dishonesty and deceit when it comes to the use of rewarding chemicals.

Addicts are often outgoing and gregarious before their disease, but once the addiction has taken hold, other people matter less, except as they relate to drug use. Once an addict is hooked, all that really matters is the use of the drug. Of course, that does not mean that the addict does not socialize with others, but the socialization is progressively more limited to experiences that permit, and even encourage, drug use. Absent that, there is a progressively more limited basis for human relationships and a diminishing pleasure in being around anyone. Drug-using friends are not friends; they are allies and accomplices in drug use. They help provide the drugs, and they sustain the environment in which drug use takes place. They help the addict rationalize the drug use with the view that "everyone is doing it, not just me."

The stage of being in love with the drug is of variable length, depending on many of the same factors that determine the speed of progression in the first stage of addiction, fooling around. When people use alcohol and other drugs relatively infrequently, when they do not have a character disorder, and when their substance use is oral (as opposed to smoked or injected), the progression tends to be relatively slow. Some users can stay in this stage of being hooked for months, years, or even decades.

Addicts commonly make strenuous efforts to control or limit their substance use, especially once they experience negative consequences or if they encounter resistance to their use. To the extent that they succeed in limiting their use, this stage is prolonged. Hooked addicts in every case are disasters waiting to happen, because sooner or later they will lose control over their substance use, and painful, negative consequences of their use will flood over them.

Let's again talk about how social use and addiction are different. Social drinkers are not hooked on alcohol. They are people who have not fallen in love with alcohol despite recurrent alcohol use, often over many years. Usually they do not progress to become alcoholics. Social drinkers stay in the stage of fooling around with alcohol, and for them alcohol continues to be not very important. They drink moderately and seldom or never to intoxication. Social drinkers generally do not like the feeling of being out of control when they are intoxicated. For them, intoxication is an unwanted alcohol overdose. Once an alcohol drinker learns to drink heavily and to enjoy the experience of intoxication, then the disease of addiction progresses. The love affair takes off. An alcoholic who starts out as a social drinker will typically progress to drinking to intoxication more and more often until the person eventually loses control of the amount and frequency of use.

The stage of falling in love, of being hooked, like all stages of addiction, is progressive. Over time, addicted people give up more and more of their lives that do not involve satisfying their addiction. Addicts first ignore and then abuse their friends, then their families, and then often, only at the final stages of the disease, their employers. This typical progression relates to the environment in which the addict lives. Friends are often tolerant of whatever the addict does. Families often hide behind denial, not wanting to see the alcohol and other drug use or its negative consequences. It is usually only late in the disease that family members confront their loved one's addiction and then only with great reluctance and hesitancy.

The fact that work is spared as much as possible by most addicts does not mean that serious problems cannot develop at work, even in the early stages of addiction. Addicts are not in control of their lives, so they often cause harm accidentally. Impaired workers show up at work, think they are not impaired, and cause serious accidents that may cost their own or someone else's life. Characteristically, addicts do show up at work, despite intoxication and terrible hangovers, as well as other drug-caused problems, because they do not want to be penalized for missing work or expose their addiction and lose the income that supports it. They are far less likely to meet with a friend or to honor a family obligation when they are feeling bad from their alcohol or other drug use and they will lie to hide the reason.

What turns addicts into liars is not just the pharmacology of drugs, or even the psychology of their love affair with drugs, but the societal reaction to that love. Their social environment makes them liars. Cigarette smokers who are permitted by their employers and families to smoke are reasonably honest about their behavior. But prohibit cigarette smoking and watch what happens. I recall a husband-and-wife team who were leaders in the drug abuse field. The wife was a cigarette smoker for many years but gave up the habit, encouraged by her health-conscious husband. She often talked about how she continued to dream about cigarettes, even years after she had quit smoking, as a way of dramatizing and personalizing the grip of physical dependence.

As I got to know these two brilliant people, I learned that the wife had not stopped smoking at all; she just hid it from her husband. She lied to him, she told me, to protect her self-respect and to please her husband. She later died of a heart attack, no doubt hastened by her continued smoking. After her death, I learned that her husband, unbeknownst to her, had known all along that she continued to smoke. He wanted to let her believe he did not know the truth to protect her.

The more an addictive behavior is prohibited, the more it is lied about. Addiction to alcohol and other drugs always leads to lying because the negative consequences and the abnormality of the behavior caused by the addiction are inescapable. It is not possible for those who really care about or who have to regularly relate to an addict to make peace with an active addiction to alcohol or other drugs. Those who have to be around the addict, either out of love or necessity, always object to their behavior sooner or later for their own sakes and for the addict's sake. Although most addicts primarily use one or another of the most commonly used drugs, they are likely to use multiple drugs simultaneously in the pattern of polydrug use. Addicts who use more than one drug are said to be cross-addicted to the drugs they use. For example, an alcoholic may be cross-addicted to a tranquilizer such as Valium, a cocaine addict cross-addicted to meth, and both of them cross-addicted to nicotine. The more intense the addiction, the more likely the addict is to be cross-addicted to multiple substances.

This polydrug pattern is less common in alcoholics who grew up before there was widespread use of drugs other than alcohol. Addicts older than forty, and especially those older than sixty, are seldom cross-addicted to illegal drugs. In contrast to the pattern with illegal drugs, both older and younger addicts can become cross-addicted to prescribed controlled substances (addicting medicines prescribed by physicians), especially the opiates, stimulants, and antianxiety medicines.

Hitting Bottom

The stage of being hooked is open-ended in the sense that addicts do not outgrow addiction. Addiction is not a self-curing disease. Addicts cannot learn or think their way out of it. Addiction just gets worse over time, slowly or rapidly. The next stage in the journey of addiction is hitting bottom. Addiction persists until there are painful and inescapable consequences to the alcohol or other drug use that lead addicts to finally seek help or until they die. These consequences can be either negative physical (such as medical issues) or behavioral problems or both. Often the painful consequences from addiction come from problems in the workplace or from the law, including arrest. Today in the US, addiction arrests are usually for driving while impaired (DWI), as more than one million Americans are arrested each year for drunk driving.

The highest prices for addiction usually are paid in the family, but because of the workings of "codependence"—where family members protect and enable the addicts in their use (more about this in in chapter 8)—the family is seldom the place where the addict hits bottom until later in the disease. Families are, like the addict, caught up in denial, and they usually need outside help if they are to create bottoms for the addict. Families create bottoms for addicted people when they conduct interventions and confront the addicts with the impact of their drug use on their family. (See chapter 6.) They can create bottoms for addicts that do not have the danger often seen in lower bottoms such as loss of career, accidents, health events, and arrests. This requires tough love and real determination. Simply saying, "We think you should stop using alcohol (or other drugs)" will not do the job.

Drug Courts

One of the biggest advances in the legal response to repeat DWI offenders is the growth of drug courts where offenders are sentenced to get an assessment for alcoholism and given the opportunity to get treatment instead of doing time. Offenders still face the appropriate punishment for any crimes committed while driving drunk, which for alcoholics in recovery becomes a part of their healing through making amends for the harms they've caused.

The less the addict suffers from character disorder, the higher the addict's bottom—meaning that less suffering is required before the addict reaches the conclusion that further alcohol or drug use is incompatible with living a reasonable life. The more there is character disorder, the lower the bottom—meaning that more painful episodes are required to convince the addict that the use cannot continue.

A high bottom is deciding to get help after waking up one morning and not remembering what happened last night, or having a frightening paranoid episode as a result of smoking pot or snorting cocaine. Some alcoholics hit a high bottom when their physicians tell them their liver function tests are slightly abnormal. Addicts with no character disorder, especially those without relatives who are also addicted, sometimes conclude as a result of such relatively mild experiences that they should not use alcohol or other drugs anymore. For people with character disorder and/or a strong family history of addiction, these mild bottoms may be barely noticed. They are shrugged off as minor but inescapable costs of the intensely valued pleasures of getting high.

For these and other dedicated addicts, bottoms are often far lower. The negative consequences have to be truly terrible to get some addicted people to recognize that their lives cannot continue if they keep using alcohol and other drugs. For many addicts, severe automobile crashes, arrests, imprisonment, life-threatening health problems, family disruption, and disastrous financial losses are still not enough to convince them that they need to stop their alcohol and other drug use. For some addicts, the use stops only at their death. This is the ultimate bottom

Seldom do addicts have one bottom. The negative consequences from using alcohol and other drugs keep coming at addicts over the course of their addictive careers. An addict may have several times where one or more of these consequences is enough for them to realize they have a problem and decide to get help, but either denial kicks in again or they make a failed attempt at Alcoholics Anonymous (AA) or treatment and go back to using. Over time, bottoms tend to get more severe, or lower, as the disease worsens. The process of hitting bottoms and then making strenuous efforts to regain control of their lives—without giving up the use of alcohol and other drugs—is part of the disease of addiction. Addicts desperately try anything and everything that will let them have control of both their lives and the alcohol and other drugs they crave. They may even stop using for periods of time, like obese people go on calorie-restricted diets. But they continue to harbor the dream of returning to controlled, moderate, and safe use. They experience the period of abstinence the way dieters experience a strict diet, as a temporary deprivation.

Addicts "white knuckle" through the experience of willful abstinence, meaning they mentally grit their teeth and cling desperately to their short-term resolve not to use alcohol and other drugs. Just stopping drug use without doing the work of recovery is more likely to cause addicts to be resentful and angry than to give them the relief they seek. They often ask, "Other people can drink and use drugs. Why can't I?" These episodes of white-knuckle sobriety are not part of recovery, but are part of the active disease of addiction. Sometimes these episodes of abstinence are imposed by family, employers, or the courts. As such, they are always temporary unless the process of recovery takes hold, and that comes only from the heart of the addicted person. Recovery is a healing of the whole self—body, mind, and spirit. Unlike white-knuckle abstinence, the sobriety that comes with real recovery is a sustainable state dependent on the addict's daily effort.

When families begin to face the addiction of one of their members, they often resist drawing clear lines and imposing tough consequences because they fear that without family support, the addict will die. "How can I turn him out of the house when I know it is only my love and my nagging that keep him from using even more drugs than he does already?" Employers, judges, friends, and physicians face the same difficult dilemma and often avoid confronting the addiction, using similar rationalizations. The sad truth is that such an understandable attitude feeds and prolongs addiction. Just as addicts have bottoms, so do their codependent family members, friends, and colleagues at work. The people around an addict are destined by the nature of the disease to continue the enabling behavior until they get sick enough of being hurt that they disengage out of self-preservation, or they become convinced beyond a shadow of a doubt that to continue such behavior only prolongs and worsens the addiction, leading eventually to death, and decide to confront the addict and get help themselves.

Some codependents reach their bottoms only when the addict is dead, reminding us that not only do many addicts have tragically low bottoms but so do many codependent people. One of the major objectives of this book is to help addicts and their families recognize the bottoms they experience and to know what to do when they hit bottoms in their own lives. Another goal, the environmental approach to prevention and treatment of addiction (see chapters 5 and 6), is to create more and earlier bottoms for addicts and their families, to begin to pull back the disaster-producing veils of denial and enabling.

Recovery: Getting Well

Getting well, unlike hitting bottom, is not a natural or inevitable part of the progression of the disease of addiction. Fooling around, being hooked, and hitting bottom are inescapable parts of the addictive disease itself. Recovery does not just happen; it requires a plan and hard work over the course of many years. Getting well does not mean the disease of addiction is gone or cured. While the person's brain chemistry can stabilize and the addictive thought processes retrained through a rigorous recovery program, the addict's brain remains predisposed to addiction and so the person is at risk of relapse, which is lifelong. Instead of a cure, recovery is a strategy that manages the addicted brain to stay sober through abstinence from all addictive drugs and to work a recovery program that prepares addicts to live full and successful lives. Usually recovery begins with the painful educational experience of hitting bottom, of realizing that continuing to use alcohol and other drugs will necessarily mean repeating the intolerable pain of hitting bottom after bottom after bottom. Getting well usually means learning about the disease concept of addiction. In most cases, it also means that the addict and the addict's family go to a treatment program for initial education and that they attend Twelve Step fellowship meetings for many years to support recovery.

The first three phases of addiction—fooling around, being hooked, and hitting bottom—usually take their own natural and virtually irresistible course. The selfish brain experiences the drug high and wants more of it, blocking out contrary forces with the iron curtain of denial. To some extent, addicts can cover up their secret chemical love affairs, but over time they all hit one bottom after another. Addicts and their families simply do what comes naturally throughout these first three stages of addiction. It's like a plane flying on automatic pilot; no thought from the pilot is necessary.

The heart of the addict's job and the family's job is the getting well stage of the process. This stage requires a true dedication from both the addicted person and everyone in the addict's family. It requires stripping away the denial and fully accepting the role each member of the family has played in the addiction. Often the addict's denial is no more intense or resistant to change than that of the codependent family member. They both are frighteningly difficult to break through. The stage of recovery, if it occurs at all, requires taking responsibility for one's life and flying with skill and courage. The Twelve Step recovery movement is an expression of the plan needed to get well from addiction.

Almost all addicts and families of addicts need to stay in a program of recovery, since it's so easy to be seduced back into denial and active addiction and codependence. The payoff for recovery is nothing short of miraculous for both addicts and their family members. But the gains, important as they are, have to be earned one person at a time by sustained hard work. Indeed, the gains of recovery are elusive. The process of getting well sometimes includes false starts, slips (relatively short reversions to alcohol and drug use), and relapses (more prolonged reversions to alcohol and other drug use). Getting well is hard because it requires overcoming the powerful direction of the addicted brain. Getting well means saying to one's own brain, "I know where that road leads and I will not go down it" and seeking help outside of one's selfish brain's control. Getting well is almost never successfully done alone; it requires help, a plan, and a lot of hard work.

We talked in chapter 1 about how a substance use disorder as defined in the DSM-V—like a character disorder, diabetes, and asthma—is not all-or-nothing. It exists along a spectrum from relatively mild to serious. In milder cases, it is more accurate to call it substance abuse than a disease or addiction. Some people in the fooling around stage use alcohol and other drugs to reckless excess, especially in permissive environments, only to conclude that they are better off without alcohol or other drugs. They simply stop or limit their use to occasional episodes without intoxication, as is typical of social drinkers. In my practice, I do not see people seeking help for use like this, but I have met such people in many settings, including when they seek professional help for problems other than addiction. Such people are not rare.

They do not need addiction treatment, regular drug tests (unless they get a DWI), or Twelve Step meetings to limit or stop their use of alcohol and other drugs. For them, the ability to stop using or to use only occasionally is possible with little or no effort.

These people never met the criteria for loss of control of their use that characterizes a severe substance use disorder, what we know as addiction. Their addiction switches never got turned on—they never fell in love with the alcohol or drug high—even though they may have used a lot of alcohol and other drugs, and even though they may have even had serious problems as a result of that use. That they are able to stop or limit their use with such ease gives hope to many who are truly addicted—leading them to believe that they, too, can return to controlled use of alcohol and other drugs. That hope, in my experience, is invariably both false and dangerous. People who have problems as a result of their use of alcohol and other drugs and then simply stop using the drugs and stay stopped all their lives don't need treatment or Twelve Step fellowships. These are for the people who cannot stay stopped, even if they can stop for a while. The true test is not whether the person with an alcohol or drug use disorder can stop use, because almost all of them can stop and do stop both voluntarily and involuntarily (such as when in the hospital, in prison or when they don't have the money to buy drugs). What they cannot do is to stay stopped. It is this group that finds it necessary to use treatment for their substance use disorders and who needs to commit themselves to the Twelve Step fellowships or similar community support networks.

Would anyone ever suggest that a heavy smoker could return to the use of cigarettes, perhaps smoking only three cigarettes a week? I have never seen that happen. If heavy smokers are to get over their dependence on nicotine, they must stop smoking—completely. Zero is the only stable number for addicted smokers. On the other hand, there are a few people who do smoke only three cigarettes a week over many years. These people have never been addicted smokers. They are people who did not get out of the fooling around stage with cigarettes, and their addiction switches were never turned on.

Almost every alcoholic and drug addict I see in my practice wants to go back to the long-ago time when they believed they could use alcohol and other drugs relatively under control. That simply cannot work. That futile hope, sometimes fostered by well-meaning but ill-informed physicians and critics of the disease concept of addiction, is a major reason people relapse into the depths of addiction.

Getting well requires addicted people to make a range of efforts. Some can do it fairly easily after a single episode of treatment and a year or so of Twelve Step meetings, whereas others repeatedly relapse and must attend

Twelve Step meetings virtually every day throughout their lives. I do not see many people like those in the first group. The people I see are those who are deeply caught in the denial of their disease and who are struggling to hold on to their secret chemical lovers by any means they can, including doing their best to deceive themselves, their families, and me. When I hear someone who bargains to use alcohol and other drugs socially, or to limit their involvement with treatment and Twelve Step programs, I am sure I am seeing the full-blown, hard-core disease of addiction yet one more time.

Relapse: Remedial Work on Addiction

Recovery from addiction often includes one or more returns to the active use of alcohol and other drugs as the grip of the disease tightens. Typically, relapses occur when the addicted person begins to think, "Maybe I was not really addicted at all," or "I was not as bad as many of the people I met in treatment and at meetings." Once the addict's life has stabilized in the beginning phases of recovery, the pain of addiction fades from the addict's thinking. Denial reappears. Usually, the person stops attending meetings long before returning to the active use of alcohol and other drugs.

Relapse has nothing to do with withdrawal symptoms and everything to do with the selfish brain's selective memory of the good times associated with alcohol and other drug use, and its selective forgetting of the bad times that came with the same drug use. A return to the use of alcohol and other drugs may be prolonged, lasting many years, or so brief that it is called a "slip" rather than a "relapse."

Relapses are learning opportunities for everyone involved. The saddest part of a relapse is to see the disease come back in full force as it reclaims its victim. Dishonesty reappears, as do the character traits associated with active use. In those cases, it is especially hard to get out of a relapse. The addict may face a new bottom that is even lower than the one that preceded the previous episode of sobriety. Looked at rationally, a relapse is not so bad; it is just further research into the process of addiction. But addiction is not rational. Observers of the addict in a relapse often cannot believe how rapid and deep the person's fall as the disease once again takes over the addict's thinking.

Sooner or later, if the addict does not die first, the relapse ends with a new bottom and a new period of sobriety, often initiated by going through another round of addiction treatment or heading back to Twelve Step meetings. At that point, it is important for everyone involved to take advantage of the new opportunity for recovery, including fixing in everyone's memory, as best they can, the pain and humiliation that came with the renewed period of addictive behavior. Most of all, however, it is important to understand that relapse prevention is not a logical process and recovery does not mean being forever deprived of pleasure. Recovery is rooted in continuous participation in one or more of the Twelve Step fellowships and the determination to keep coming back to work the program, including daily involvement with a personal sponsor. When this leads to a new life of stability, serenity, and the ability to enjoy the natural pleasures that the healthy brain experiences in life, then lifelong sobriety is possible.

People in recovery often tell their stories of addiction at Twelve Step meetings and elsewhere in their lives. These stories typically have a distinctive structure: (1) What my life was like when I was using, (2) What happened to get me on the path to recovery, and (3) What my life in recovery is like. I have never heard one of these stories without being spellbound. They are all similar yet different. These real-life unique stories are also all powerful and all inspiring. The life of active using as told by the addict in recovery is often filled with self-deprecating humor despite the grim nature of that existence. The second part of this narrative is equally fascinating. The crisis that finally led them to surrender and recognize that by themselves they could not overcome their addictions was seldom the first serious negative consequence they experienced as a result of their addictive substance use. The turning point, or bottom, was often a serious illness or accident, an arrest, the loss of a job, or the breakup of a family. The third part of this narrative is also dramatic as the recovering addict describes the joy and relief of no longer having to be dishonest and of experiencing far more success in life. The life in recovery is not a life of strawberries and cream. It is a life after chemical slavery that is filled with all of the normal successes and failures—joys and pains—of life. But it is free of the special hell that was the addiction.

More on Addiction versus Substance Abuse

A friend told me about his experiences with drinking and overeating. He habitually drank two or three martinis at night, almost every night. His family did not like this behavior and labeled it alcoholic drinking. They tried to get him to stop drinking. He liked alcohol and saw no reason to stop, reasoning that, other than the fact that his family did not like it, he had no problems of any sort because of his drinking. He had struggled with his weight for decades, having an especially intense and enduring relationship with ice cream. In his family, obesity was common, but none of this man's blood relatives had been an alcoholic or a drug addict.

Late in his life he was diagnosed with type 2 diabetes. His physician advised him to stop using both alcohol and ice cream for his health. My friend told me that he effortlessly stopped drinking the day the doctor asked him to do so. He had not had a drop of alcohol in the following four years. On the other hand, he continued to struggle with his ice-cream habit, alternating periods of white-knuckle abstinence with periods of relapse to eating ice cream despite his knowledge that both alcohol and ice cream were harmful to his health and despite his resolve to stop both behaviors.

Voluntary stopping is a common pattern in workplaces that introduce drug testing programs—many illicit drug users simply stop using to protect their jobs. The same sort of positive change is taking place in the US today as the DWI programs linked to alcohol tests curb drinking and driving. People who routinely drank, sometimes heavily, and then drove now have a reason not to drink and drive, so they stop the behavior. Dietary advice to limit fat consumption and to maintain a healthy weight has a similar effect, as the people who have not lost control of their eating have a relatively easy time changing their behaviors once they are convinced it is in their interest to do so. However, other people, who are equally motivated to be healthy, simply cannot change their diets or, if they do change them, are unable to sustain the new, healthier eating pattern.

True addiction does not end with a simple decision to quit a particular behavior. The grip of addiction on the addict's brain is too firm for that to happen. Addicts and chronic abusers look alike until they are confronted with a reason to quit, until they face serious consequences as a result of their using behavior, or until they try to stop. Then the two groups separate: the chronic abusers simply quit, and the addicts either are not able to stop or they do for a time but then relapse, often to a level of use that is even more intense than before they attempted to stop these pleasure-producing behaviors. It is the behavior of the addicts that is both irrational and puzzling. Such addictive behavior is the behavior from which this book seeks to learn.

Many addicts claim they can stop their behaviors any time they want to. They say they continue because they do not want to stop. Sometimes chronic abusers, confronted by social disapproval, perceive themselves to be addicted even though they have never tried to stop using. Addiction is a disorder of the entire self and both loss of control and denial are central features of this disorder. Only when the environment sends a strong message to quit is the person who is engaged in pleasure-producing, potentially addicting behavior likely to quit. And only when the person tries to stop and stay stopped can the distinction be clearly made between addiction and mild to moderate substance misuse.

In the example I gave of my friend who stopped drinking alcohol easily but could not stop eating ice cream, we see the distinction between addiction and abuse, a distinction that even this smart and self-aware man would have had a hard time making until he had a good reason to try to stop those two pleasure-producing behaviors. It is important to understand that potentially addictive behaviors, including the use of alcohol and other drugs, can have serious consequences for the person engaging in the behaviors and for others, even in the absence of addiction. Furthermore, people cannot get addicted unless they engage in potentially addictive behaviors. The powerful role of the environment in both promoting and curbing addicting behaviors is hard to overemphasize.

Why was it that my friend found his doctor's advice so convincing and his family's concerns so unpersuasive? There are many mysteries in addiction that are close to the human heart. Could it be that this man was genuinely afraid of dying, especially as he was aging and the inevitability of his death became more palpable? In contrast, why was the unhappiness of his family less important to him? Perhaps he retained a streak of rebelliousness from his own childhood that prevented him from accepting the good advice of his family, whereas his physician escaped this link with his childhood. Which bottoms lead to behavior change and which do not is hard to predict. One thing is clear, however. In real addictive behaviors the bottoms keep coming, ever deeper, until the addicted person dies or figures out that life cannot go on without real change. This includes committing to abstinence from addictive drugs, not engaging in the behaviors associated with their use, and, in most cases, getting help in a treatment program and ongoing group support, usually a Twelve Step fellowship, to make that change permanent.

The difference between addiction and substance abuse where loss of control is not a factor, especially for chronic abusers, helps explain a disturbing problem. Some critics of addiction treatment and of the Twelve Step recovery programs point out correctly that many people stop drinking and stop using drugs with little effort and no expense at all. They label addictive behaviors as "simple bad habits." Complaining about people like me who encourage the wider use of both addiction treatment and the Twelve Step programs, they have a point. All of the follow-up studies of potentially addicting behavior do show that many people who engage in these behaviors, even some who have serious problems as a result of these behaviors, do stop—and stay stopped—once they have good reasons to do so.

My answer to these critics of the disease concept of addiction is that they have mistaken non-addicted substance abusers for addicts. It is true that many substance abusers do not need addiction treatment or Twelve Step programs because they do suffer from simple bad habits. However, it is also true that virtually all addicts need real and sustained help if they are to stop and stay stopped. Addicts have fallen in love. They are hooked on their addictive behaviors. Chronic abusers are still fooling around. They have not lost control of their potentially addicting behavior.

People in Alcoholics Anonymous and Narcotics Anonymous are amazed at the claim that alcoholics and other addicts can simply stop using on their own. They have never seen such an occurrence. They are right. They are describing the experience of true addicts, people who, despite having plenty of good reasons to stop, nevertheless continue to use alcohol and other drugs, doing no end of harm to themselves and to those around them.

When it comes to treatment and the use of the Twelve Step fellowships, the right course of action is to do whatever is necessary to help the particular person stop using alcohol and other drugs. Less is more. This means that it is both unnecessary and wasteful of scarce resources to do more than is necessary to achieve sobriety, just as it is wasteful to do less than is necessary to achieve that goal. For true addiction, less is not likely to do the job. For addicts, recovery is an inside job, a matter of changing thinking as well as changing behavior. For most addicts, getting well and staying well means regular attendance at Twelve Step meetings, probably for a lifetime. For many substance abusers, all it takes to get well is a reason to stop.

When I visit cancer patients and their families in a hospital, I think about what a joy it would be if I could tell them that all they had to do to get well and stay well was to go to meetings once a day for an hour or so and do a few things differently in their lives. With that approach, they could be free of the ill effects of their disease. When I visit an alcohol or drug unit in the same hospital and see someone equally close to death's door, I can actually deliver that message. The cancer patient and the patient's family would leap at the opportunity. They are desperate for any help.

On the other hand, the polite addicted person responds to my offer by saying, "No thanks, Doc. I can handle this myself." Addicted patients who are less polite simply say, "Get lost. I've heard that before, and I don't need it." The difference between the cancer patients and the addicts, who are both suffering from potentially fatal chronic diseases, is that the disease of addiction tells the addicts they are okay. The cancer patients know they are seriously ill. When I see a person in stable recovery from addiction, I see a person who is as grateful for recovery, and the means for recovery, as I would see if I could offer that opportunity to a cancer patient. That is what it means to get well: the disease is held at bay, and the addicted person can get on with his or her life with sobriety and gratitude. Denial has also been held at bay, but it remains lurking—ready to return and cause a relapse at any time.

Although understanding the nature of the disease of addiction cannot cure addiction, it can set the stage for recovery. Having words to describe the intensely personal experiences of addiction that are otherwise confusing and overwhelming can help both understanding and communication.

Recovery is contagious, like addiction, at least in its early stages. But unlike addiction, recovery is also inspiring to others around the person in recovery. Whether treatment is long or short it is important for addicted people to actively participate in community-based recovery support which often but not always means one of the Twelve Step programs both during and after treatment. Many addicted people find their ways into recovery communities without going to treatment. One of the most remarkable new developments is organized recovery support which often involves a professional recovery coach or a mental health or addiction specialist supporting the recovery process. This is a hugely important development as it links health care with recovery to the benefit of addicted people, outside of addiction treatment itself.

One of the most inspiring examples of recovery support is the Oxford House movement which began in 1975 and was founded by Paul Molloy, an alcoholic now in long-term recovery. When Paul's government-funded halfway house closed for lack of funding for the coming year he organized the other residents to rent the house themselves. It worked. In the following four decades Paul has built on this simple concept of self-help to create a remarkable program that has created over 2,200 Oxford Houses with over 18,000 recovery beds, in 44 states and Washington, DC and four other countries. Addicts, when leaving residential treatment, or for any other reason, who need a supportive living environment dedicated to recovery apply to a specific Oxford House. They are voted in or out by the residents who run the house using the experience-based principles of the organization. Everyone in the house must actively and routinely attend recovery support meetings and be abstinent from any alcohol or other drug use. The houses are all rented and the rent is paid by the residents themselves. Participants can stay for as long or short a time as they need for their individual recovery. I think of Oxford Houses as recovery houses. They are an excellent example of addicted people themselves organizing to support recovery. I'll end this chapter with a case history that demonstrates, more than theory ever could, the life of an addict.

A Case History of the Life of an Addict

Sam, age twenty-five, was eager to go back to a highly competitive college that he left during his sophomore year because of his drug use and gambling. He had been in addiction treatment twice and had an on-again/off-again relationship with Alcoholics Anonymous and Narcotics Anonymous. He needed my approval for him to go back to college. He tried to return two years ago but dropped out again during his first semester. Since starting college seven years ago, he actively used marijuana, cocaine, and alcohol with the complication that he was a dedicated, and often successful, gambler.

I saw him for about six months during which time he moved back home with his parents while he reapplied to college. I urged him to re-enter treatment and to become steadily active with the Twelve Step fellowships. He told me he started high school as an indifferent student partly because of his marijuana use but in his junior and senior years he devoted himself to his studies and did exceedingly well in math and science. Based on this academic record, he was accepted into a very competitive college where he started with a bang. But he got derailed by his return to drinking and using marijuana. His grades suffered and he was asked to leave the college.

He had some big drug debts that scared him because his drug dealer threatened his life. His father gave him $15,000 to pay the debt. Sam decided to leverage that and headed to a casino, where he got drunk and gambled the entire amount away. His father stepped in again and paid his debt. Later, Sam had a remarkable series of gambling wins and losses culminating in his winning $30,000 at a local casino. He was set for college financially—until he got into day-trading in the stock market. Once more he lost most of his money. He convinced his college to give him another chance. In my work with Sam, I was clear that he must stop all alcohol and drug use and all gambling if he was to have any hope of making it in college. I also made clear that I did not think this would be possible unless he became a dedicated participant in both Gamblers Anonymous and Narcotics Anonymous or Alcoholics Anonymous. He was sure this time he would make it. That was the last time I saw Sam, so I don't know how this worked out. I tell this story to emphasize the power of addiction to cloud a smart person's judgment so that the addict keeps using drugs despite repeated defeats. When I see patients like Sam I tell them that, through their behavior, they are doing personal "research" on addiction and clearly they are not yet finished with their self-destructive study. Based on my study of addiction, I am confident that the path ahead of Sam is more lessons and more suffering until he surrenders until he accepts that he must stop using alcohol and other drugs permanently to reclaim his life.

PART 2: HOW TO STOP THE DRUG EPIDEMIC

There is no quick fix for either the global modern drug epidemic or the individual's plight with addiction. Recovery from both will require change in multiple areas and sustained efforts over the long term.

Support will be needed for most addicts, many of whom will find hope and healing through participation in a mutual aid group such as Alcoholics Anonymous or Narcotics Anonymous. Likewise, the recovery of our population at large and the required efforts to prevent future generations from being engulfed in the ravages of addiction will demand the support that comes with collaboration—we need the criminal justice system, treatment, and prevention programs to work together for shared goals; we need the medical community, educators, and many others on board. Experience tells us that bandage fixes don't heal. We need to do the real work to get at the roots of addiction in order to stop this epidemic and find lasting recovery.

Here are ten steps rooted in widely shared values that can reverse this epidemic:

1. **Prevention**: Establish the prevention goal for youth as One Choice: no use of alcohol, tobacco (nicotine), marijuana, and other drugs before the age of 21 for reasons of health. Educate adults caring for youth, starting with parents, but including pediatricians, educators, and other youth workers to reinforce this message. We must especially give voice to the growing number of youth who have made the decision to grow up drug-free; they can lead this campaign.

2. **Treatment**: Establish long-term recovery as the goal of all addiction treatment. Pay attention to what happens after treatment: Often it is relapse, the continuation of active addiction. All substance abuse treatments, those that use medicines and those

that do not, need to be assessed on the basis of their ability to produce long-term recovery which includes no use of alcohol and other drugs as well as character improvement. Look to the individuals in the large and rapidly growing recovery community to see what they did to get into lasting recovery. They are the teachers and the inspiration for a dramatic improvement in treatment outcomes.

3. **Health care**: Persuade all of elements of health care to treat addiction as a serious chronic disease. Focus on prevention – not only prevention of addiction but prevention of drug use. Make health care responsible for the full range of services: prevention, intervention, treatment, and long-term monitoring—just the way heath care manages other serious chronic disorders like diabetes, heart disease, and cancer.

4. **Prescribed controlled substances**: Educate physicians and patients about the significant risks of these often valuable medicines when they are used along with alcohol and other drugs of abuse and when they are used in ways and in doses not intended by the prescribing physicians. Identify patients with substance use disorders by their history and by drug tests. Ensure that they are carefully monitored when using controlled substances and given effective treatment for their substance use disorders when that is needed.

5. **Criminal justice system: supply reduction**: A balanced, successful drug prevention and treatment effort depends on an effective law enforcement effort to prosecute sellers of illegal drugs, including physicians who run pill mills, drug lords in this country and abroad, and the new chemists around the world who are selling an expanding range of clandestinely manufactured synthetic drugs. Availability of drugs is one essential driver of the drug epidemic. Reducing drug availability is crucial to turning back the epidemic.

6. **Criminal justice system: demand reduction**: Many of the five million offenders in the US on parole and probation have substance use disorders. These diseases must be identified, monitored, and treated to help these offenders become and remain drug-free. There are promising models, including Drug Courts, HOPE Probation, and 24/7 Sobriety, to make the criminal justice system a common pathway to long-term recovery. The essential collaboration of the criminal justice system and health care is not

being sufficiently coordinated at present to deal more effectively with the drug epidemic. Effective criminal justice programs in both supply reduction and demand reduction are essential to a successful public health response to the drug epidemic. It is now commonly said that we cannot arrest our way out of the drug epidemic. That is true. But it is equally true that we cannot treat our way out of the epidemic. We need both law enforcement and health to work better together.

7. **Focus on the family**: The family lives the addiction with the addict. Educate and empower families to prevent substance use and to intervene to stop substance abuse when it occurs. Addiction is a family disease; recovery is a hard-won family miracle.

8. **Redirect harm reduction from short-term goals to the goal of sustained recovery**: Providing clean needles, naloxone treatment for overdoses and safe injection sites must focus not just on the immediate drug crisis but the long-term outcomes of these interventions. The goal of all harm reduction must be recovery— successful drug-free living. We need to assess all harm reduction efforts on the basis of their success, or lack of success, in achieving this goal.

9. **Healthy living**: Drugs hijack the brain. Healthy living requires living drug-free. Put the message of no use of drugs of abuse into the context of other healthy living initiatives, like healthy diet, exercise, and wearing seat belts.

10. **Research**: Defining the drug epidemic as a modern plaque prioritizes the need for a massive new effort to create and evaluate effective strategies to control, contain and eventually eradicate it as much as possible. This research should build on the success of the existing fine biological research into brain biology in a manner similar to the response to the HIV/AIDS epidemic that created a massive, research-driven global public health response involving both prevention and treatment. Drug overdose deaths now exceed the number of HIV/AIDS deaths in the US at the peak of that epidemic. The recent engagement of the US Surgeon General and the US Centers for Disease Control and Prevention in drug abuse policy is an encouraging step in this new effort.

The chapters in the second half of the book dig deeper into these areas.

5. PREVENTING SUBSTANCE ABUSE

"Prevention is much more about strengthening resilience in children and young people to cope with difficulties and instead choose healthy lifestyles. Prevention initiatives must involve caring adults, schools and the whole of society. Successful prevention should be built on sound structure, long-term visions and committed adults. Effective prevention also includes the promotion of health and social well-being. It is especially important to prevent young people from using drugs. The adolescent brain is more vulnerable than the adult brain to damage caused by drugs. We also know that an early introduction to drugs raises the likelihood of dropout from school.

Substance abuse is preventable. Today, we have better knowledge of what is effective prevention and what should be implemented. We know that prevention is highly cost efficient for the society and that it saves individuals and families from enormous suffering. Policy makers, scientific communities and non-governmental organizations (NGOs), as well as representatives from the social services, health-care and schools, must continue to invest in preventive efforts and to learn what works and what does not. The work must be evidence based, evaluated thoroughly and benefit from the guidance provided by the international standards on prevention. Prevention work must also be culturally sensitive and be adapted to specific context.

It is my strong belief, and that of the Swedish government, that drug policy should focus on prevention, treatment and control, with the aim of reducing both supply of and demand for illegal drugs."

— Her Majesty Queen Silvia, UNGASS special side event on drug prevention, April 19, 2016

Drug abuse prevention is the great hope for reducing substance abuse and addiction and over the long-term putting an end to the modern drug epidemic. Setting prevention policy in this country is not simple, either in defining clear and achievable goals or in determining how to make prevention work. To put this in perspective, I see drug abuse prevention existing in three broad layers:

1. The prevention of any drug use by youth (which I define as under

the age of twenty-one) and the prevention of illegal drug use by everyone;

2.   The prevention of the problems associated with drug use; for example, preventing DWIs or opioid painkiller misuse that might lead to addiction or overdose; and,

3.   The prevention of complications of drug abuse and addiction; for example, prevention of HIV infection in addicted intravenous drug users or lung cancer from smoking tobacco.

These three levels are called primary, secondary, and tertiary prevention, respectively. While all three levels of prevention are important, the major focus in this chapter is on primary prevention, because if more young people do not use drugs, there is less need for secondary or tertiary prevention—which I address in the next chapters on intervention and treatment and in chapter 8 on the role of the family.

While primary drug prevention involves all ages, here we focus on adolescence because the overwhelming majority of adult drug abusers, including those who become addicts and alcoholics (90 percent or more), began their drug and alcohol use before adulthood. This focus on primary prevention does not mean that secondary and tertiary prevention are not also important, but these later prevention stages are enhanced by being built on a solid primary prevention strategy.

Defining the Goal of Primary Drug Prevention

Drug abuse prevention comes in many forms. Some prevention efforts target particular drugs, most often cigarettes and alcohol. These substance-specific prevention goals often consider some youth drug use as inevitable and so they have focused on reducing youth binge drinking or drunk driving rather than youth drinking itself. In an earlier book, *The Selfish Brain*, my explicit prevention objective was to prevent addiction or other serious problems resulting from drug abuse, especially among teenagers where the road to addiction begins. I have come to realize, much to my chagrin, that once an adolescent has begun using drugs, it can be hard to stop, even if the use is occasional and mostly social, and it can be easy to escalate. For that reason I have switched to a clear message targeting young people at an earlier age, even before they reach their teenage years. Primary prevention is One Choice: no use of any alcohol, tobacco (nicotine), marijuana, and other drugs by young people under the age of twenty-one for reasons of health. This does not mean, of course, that every child who uses alcohol, marijuana, nicotine or other drugs becomes a drug addict or even has problems resulting from the drug use. But the safer and healthier choice for youth is not to use any substance at all.

Those who espouse alternative prevention strategies believe that most adolescents drink, smoke, or "try" other drugs, especially alcohol, nicotine, and marijuana, and the prevention goal of no use is unrealistic or even counterproductive. In this alternative point of view, kids will simply turn off any parent, educator, or physician who advises them not to use any drugs at all, seeing this advice and the adult delivering it as hopelessly out of touch with reality today.

Why Primary Prevention Is So Important

- Primary drug prevention: The prevention of any use of alcohol, tobacco, marijuana, and other drugs by young people under the age of twenty-one as well as the prevention of illicit drug use by anyone regardless of age.
- Benefits of no use for youth: Young people who reach the age twenty-one without using drugs are far less likely ever to use drugs. If they do use any drug after that age, they are less likely to have problems with their drug use than are youth who begin using drugs in adolescence.
- Risks of drug use for youth: Youth are uniquely vulnerable to addiction because the adolescent brain is especially susceptible to drug effects and because the frontal lobes of the brain, which put the brakes on risky behaviors, are not fully developed until the mid or late twenties.
- See also appendix C "Reducing Future Rates of Adult Addiction Must Begin with Youth Prevention."

Let us consider some reasons to refute the objection to the message of One Choice: no-use of alcohol, tobacco, marijuana or other drugs for reasons of health. Think about cigarettes. Most youth today do not smoke cigarettes and few would dispute that the top prevention goal for cigarettes is for youth never to start smoking them; however, an increasing number of young people are vaping nicotine and become just as addicted to it that way. Many youth who vape then transition to smoking cigarettes. Further, if youth do start smoking cigarettes or vaping, the health goal for them is to stop—not to cut down or to smoke only outdoors or not to smoke more than five cigarettes a day.

When it comes to youth use of alcohol and marijuana, the prevention goal is not so clear for many people, adults and children alike. An argument is often made that many youth do use one or even both of these two most commonly used drugs and that most of them either stop using them after a few years or continue to use them without obvious problems in their adolescence and even later in their lives. Given these facts, how can the case be made that no use of alcohol and marijuana is the right health decision for all youth? The reason is that no young person and no family can know whether any particular young user of alcohol, marijuana, or other drugs will be among those who encounter serious problems as a result of that drug use.

With the possible exception of new marijuana industry executives – who rely on heavy use to make money – no pro-marijuana groups openly argue that youth use of marijuana is a good or healthy behavior. Even NORML, the major marijuana lobby, advises young people not to use marijuana even as the group supports adults being able to use marijuana legally. In its Principles of Responsible Use NORML states, "Cannabis consumption is for adults only. It is irresponsible to provide cannabis to children. Many things and activities are suitable for young people, but others absolutely are not. Children do not drive cars, enter into contracts, or marry, and they must not use drugs."

A useful analogy for youth drug prevention is the use of seat belts. The universal safety message, and supporting laws throughout most of the country, is that everyone should wear a seat belt every time they are in a car. This is true even though many people can drive their entire lives without being saved from injury in a car crash by wearing a seat belt. Although no one in a car can know on any trip whether or not his or her life will be saved by wearing a seat belt, the prevention message is clear. This same is true for youth drug use.

Put simply, the decision to use any drug opens an endless series of subsequent decisions for youth, ranging from which drugs to use to when and how much to use. On the other hand, the single decision not to use any drugs—including the three most frequently abused drugs, alcohol, tobacco (nicotine) and marijuana—is associated with many positive health and other important outcomes in youth and beyond. Strikingly, over the past four decades, more and more youth have made the decision not to use any drug: in 2014, 26 percent of all high school seniors had never used any drug—including alcohol, cigarettes, marijuana, or other drugs—in their lifetimes, and 52 percent had not used any drug in the past thirty days.[1] These numbers are up from about 3 percent of high school seniors who reported no use in their lifetimes and 16 percent who reported no past month use three decades earlier. This is a strong, still growing trend toward more and more American youth deciding not to use any drug. I call these youth who choose not to use any drugs "abstainers." Compared to youth who do use drugs, young abstainers were more likely to report higher grades, lower

---

[1] Levy, S., Campbell, M., Shea, C. L., & DuPont, R. L. (2018). Trends in abstaining from substance use in adolescents: 1975-2014. *Pediatrics*. doi: 10.1542/peds.2017-3498

truancy, spent fewer evenings out, and worked fewer hours during the school year.

Binge drinking (defined as drinking five or more drinks in a setting) is a major focus of youth prevention efforts. The problems resulting from binge drinking are not limited to potentially developing an addiction but also include the health *and* safety problems of intoxication from even a single episode of binge drinking—car crashes, increased violence, including date rape and other sexual abuse. There have also been cases of alcohol poisoning when enough alcohol is consumed, resulting in brain damage and death. The dangers of binge drinking also go up when combined with the use of other drugs, such as benzodiazepines like Xanax, marijuana, and opiates.

Marijuana specifically has become more problematical recently because as more states legalize recreational use (nine and the District of Columbia to date) and medical use (twenty-nine states and the District of Columbia to date), the message becomes that marijuana use isn't dangerous and is the safe drug. That is a dangerous myth. Besides the fact that marijuana can cause developmental problems and contributes to lower grades and social isolation, there are clear links to other drug use. For example, youth who decide not to use marijuana are far less likely to use tobacco, alcohol, or other drugs.

Take a look at figure 5–1 from a study analyzing data from the National Survey on Drug Use and Health.[2] Notice that young people who report having used marijuana are more likely to have used alcohol, tobacco, and other drugs than youth who made the decision not to use marijuana. Notice that the difference between the twelve- to seventeen-year-olds in the left-hand group is that they have never used marijuana in their lives. The twelve- to seventeen-year-olds in the right side of figure 5–1 have used marijuana at least once in their lives. What's significant is how consequential that single factor is in terms of their use of cigarettes, alcohol, and other drugs.

Of the youth ages twelve to seventeen who have never used marijuana, 20.8 percent had used alcohol, 5.9 percent had used cigarettes and 8.2 percent had used any other drug. By contrast, of the youth who had used marijuana, 73.0 percent had used alcohol, 49.6 percent had used cigarettes, and 39.0 percent had used other illicit drugs. Those are huge differences related to the single decision not to use marijuana. It is important to recognize, however, that similar huge differences are shown for youth who decided not to use cigarettes and alcohol: Youth who have not used

---

[2] DuPont, R. L., Han, B., Shea, C. L., & Madras, B. K. (2018). Drug use among youth: National survey data support a common liability of all drug use. *Preventive Medicine, 113*: 68-73.

cigarettes are far less likely to have used alcohol, marijuana, and other illicit drugs than are youth who have used cigarettes.[3] In this regard, marijuana is similar to both cigarettes and alcohol. In fact, those three drugs travel together for youth.

Figure 5–1

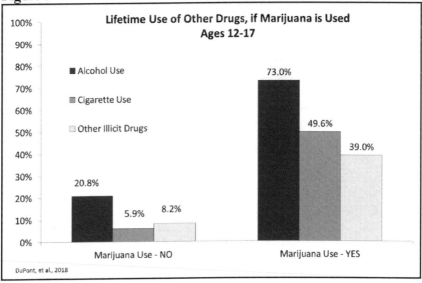

Now look at figure 5–2 for the levels of use of these drugs in American youth age twelve to seventeen and the jump in usage between that age and youth in the eighteen- to twenty-five-year-old age group. Again, my point is not to single out marijuana; it is to emphasize that these three drugs—alcohol, tobacco (nicotine), and marijuana—are commonly linked to all other drug use and that they dominate the youth drug scene. Looking over the entire lifecycle, drug use rates peak in the eighteen- to twenty-five-year-old age group.

For these reasons, and without ambiguity, the first principle of drug prevention is to encourage all youth to make the One Choice to grow up drug-free. After the age of twenty-one, there is time to make new decisions about drug use. The available evidence is that when young people reach age twenty-one (or even later) without using drugs, they are far less likely ever to use drugs. If they do use any drug after reaching the age of twenty-one, they are less likely to have problems with their drug use than are youth who

---

[3] DuPont, R. L., Han, B., Shea, C. L., & Madras, B. K. (2018). Drug use among youth: National survey data support a common liability of all drug use. *Preventive Medicine, 113*: 68-73.

begin using drugs in adolescence. Among youth who do initiate drug use in adolescence, the earlier they begin using drugs and the heavier that use, the more likely they are to have problems with their drug use later in life.

Figure 5–2

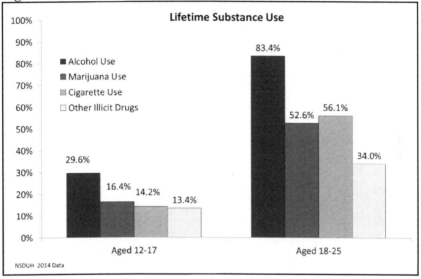

What is the prevention goal for the large number of youth who do use alcohol, tobacco (nicotine), marijuana, and other drugs? The health goal remains the same: to encourage and support them to stop using all drugs for their health, now and in the future. Getting young people who have initiated drug use to stop their use is seldom easy. Nevertheless, it is important to make this no-use goal explicit when working with drug-using youth. Youth drug prevention is needed in all areas of the lives of young people, including home, school, health care, athletics, and religion. Of these, the most important is in the home where parents and caregivers hold the keys to success in drug prevention. Success is most likely when parents and other adults in a child's life start the no-use-for-health message when that child is age ten or even earlier. When the no-use message is first articulated to an adolescent who is seventeen or eighteen, especially when that young person has already been using drugs for several years and most of his or her friends use drugs, it is far more difficult to get the youth's buy-in to not use. Nevertheless, even then, it is important for parents and others dealing with older drug-using adolescents to promote the goal of no use for their physical, emotional, and social health.

For many parents and other adults, to say nothing of most youth, the central goal of primary youth drug prevention as no use of alcohol and other drugs for reasons of health seems not just radical but utopian. It is neither of those things. It is eminently practical and achievable. The challenge facing the nation—and every family—is to support and extend the powerful, healthy trend of drug abstinence.

In the remainder of this chapter, we explore how to implement this central prevention goal in three interrelated settings: the family, health care, and education.

Making Prevention Work in the Family

I am under no illusions about what family means today in America. It is often not two parents and two kids but can include many configurations, from divorced or single moms and dads with kids from previous marriages to grandparents as primary caregivers for kids whose parents are unable or unwilling to care for them.

What I mean by family is the adults who are managing the lives and the environments for youth under the age of twenty-one. Often that is two parents but not always. The adults raising youth sometimes are not related to them at all. When I use the words parent and parents I am referring to whomever these caring adults are. I assume the best—that the responsible adults do care for the children and not only do they wish them well but they are committed to working hard in the best interests of the children. I realize this isn't always the case. Without this commitment to responsible parenting, a consistent no-use message is less likely. Furthermore, I know that drug use is not the only thing that parents have to worry about, with just putting food on the table and paying rent often a more pressing challenge.

When children reach the teenage years, parent-child relationships typically undergo dramatic shifts as the bodies and minds of the children go through major developmental changes, changes that often are tumultuous and challenging for both parents and children. Parents are not all the same and neither are teenagers. Teens tend to fall somewhere on a broad spectrum from compliant to rebellious. I am not ignorant of how resistant many young people are to the idea of their growing up without using any drugs, especially alcohol, nicotine and marijuana.

Compliant teens are focused on their futures and usually are happy to work collaboratively with adults including parents, teachers, physicians, religious leaders, and others. Most of the time these youth are willing to work hard for uncertain future rewards. They see doing their homework as an important part of reaching their goals. They also tend to be honest, are often self-critical, and are prone to worry more about what people think about them and about the prospects of being successful.

On the other end of the spectrum, rebellious teens are more resistant to adult guidance and eager to chart their own course, often in opposition to the adults in their lives. They tend to be less willing to delay gratification so that homework, with its delayed and uncertain rewards, is seldom of much interest. Some of these youth eagerly take risks and tend to worry less about what people think about them or whether they will be successful in school or socially. They are less receptive to adult guidance than compliant teens and may lie to adults to get what they want and to avoid punishment. Few youth are all one or the other of these two extremes, and many youth don't fit into these extreme categories. Generally speaking, compliant, low-risk youth are more receptive to prevention messages while the rebellious, high-risk youth are less so.

The earlier that parents start with the drug prevention message, the better. Most ten- to twelve-year-olds are receptive to the One Choice no-use message unless they have drug-using—or not drug using—older siblings who can be attractive role models—one way or the other. Many times, I have seen younger siblings of drug-using youth who see the trouble caused by their older siblings' drug use behaviors and who respond by being eagerly receptive to the no-use message. This message needs to be expressed over and over again, linked to negative family-imposed consequences for use and positive re-enforcement for no use. Life is full of teaching opportunities for this message because the problems of youth drug use are so common. It is the rare youth today who does not have friends or family who have spectacularly bad outcomes from substance use, from school or legal sanctions to overdose deaths and fatal car crashes. The kids who fail at or drop out of school or who are arrested because of their drug use are far more numerous but less visible in the media because these more common tragedies are less spectacular than overdoses and fatal crashes.

The One Choice no-use prevention message is not negative. It is a positive goal, protecting youth and their futures. The drug-free message needs to be linked with praise for not using drugs and linked to the achievement of positive outcomes in school and in later life and for better long-term health.

A clear no-use message should also be given to youth who are already using alcohol and other drugs. When alcohol or other drug use has caused serious problems such as school failure, arrests, car crashes, or overdoses or have led to addiction and substance abuse treatment, it is critical for parents to stress the no-use message and to set clear negative consequences for further substance use. These can include loss of privileges, closer monitoring of school work, and restrictions on spending time with drug-using friends. At the same time, praise should be given for successfully abstaining from drug use and sanctions should be lifted as trust is restored and the young person demonstrates compliance with a no-use family policy.

The identification of those two large groups—those young people who don't use drugs at all, and those whose use of drugs caused clear-cut and serious negative consequences—leaves an even larger group of youth: those who are using one or more drugs but who have not yet experienced negative consequences from this use. For this large group, I recommend maintaining a persistent no-use goal and being watchful for clear evidence of any problems resulting from drug use, which should be met with immediate and consistent consequences by the family.

Drug Policy: The Legal Drinking Age and Prohibition

When I speak to sophisticated American high school and college students, I focus on binge drinking and on the fact that no use of alcohol, tobacco, marijuana, and other drugs is the healthy choice for youth under the age of twenty-one. Usually some of the students oppose the age restrictions for legal drinking, and I can count on at least one of them to bring up the fact that there is no (or often very low) minimum legal drinking age in Europe. According to these skeptical students, the youth of Europe have far fewer problems with alcohol than do their American peers. This argument appears to go easily to the next step: It is the prohibition of youthful drinking in the US—and the "mistrust" that underlies it—that causes teenage drinking problems. How could the solution to this problem be simpler? Eliminate the drinking age and, presto, there will be fewer youthful drinking problems in the US! The logic here is as breathtaking as I have found it to be commonplace. This is a central argument used by advocates of fully legal drugs. In this misguided view, it is the prohibition of drugs that causes drug problems. Therefore, get rid of the prohibition and we can solve our alcohol and drug problems.

Before responding to this critique of current US alcohol and drug policies, we need to review a few facts. Prohibition in the US came about because of the problems created by the use of addicting substances, not the other way around. The biggest cause of problems with alcohol and other drugs is not prohibition.

It is the effects of drug use. In every situation, in every nation, prohibition reduces drug use, and legalization of every drug results in an increase in the use of that drug.

Problems such as teenage drunk driving deaths would go up if the legal drinking age were lowered. The national experience during a decade in which the US drinking age for alcohol was reduced to eighteen (roughly 1974 to 1984) was a clear lesson on this point. Drunk driving deaths for teenagers rose. When the legal drinking age was returned to twenty-one, where it had been in the US since 1933, teenage drunk driving deaths fell.

When societies have tight controls over adolescent behavior, based on widely observed family and community values, it is less important to place legal controls over drinking and drug use by teenagers. To the extent that any community moves toward the modern high-risk approach to the teenage years—with looser adult supervision and greater socializing among adolescent peers—then there is a greater need for legal and other formal limitations on adolescent behaviors that are clearly destructive both to the youths themselves and to their communities.

Adult drug use is also a crucial prevention challenge in the family when it comes to the messages we give youth. Adults who drink socially—that is, they enjoy an occasional glass of wine, a beer, or a cocktail as a beverage and don't drink to intoxication—can be role models to young people for responsible drinking when they become adults. The message should still be no alcohol use until you're an adult and to avoid abusing alcohol, including not driving after drinking when an adult. The US Centers for Disease Control and Prevention recommends these guidelines for moderate drinking:[4]

"According to the Dietary Guidelines for Americans, (1) moderate alcohol consumption is defined as having up to 1 drink per day for women and up to 2 drinks per day for men. This definition is referring to the amount consumed on any single day and is not intended as an average over several days. However, the Dietary Guidelines do not recommend that individuals who do not drink alcohol start drinking for any reason." [5]

As for illegal drugs, a no-use policy for adults as well as youth is the best course. The only reason adults in a family can have for using illegal drugs is to get high. This contradicts any no-use message they are giving to their kids.

Addictive prescription medications must be kept out of the reach of children and only used as prescribed. Adults should explore all alternatives to addictive medications such as opioid painkillers and, if legal in their state, medical marijuana and use them only if other measures haven't worked. Adults should never use drugs to get high. It is especially important that adults use caution when potentially addictive medications are prescribed for their children and that they monitor the use of these drugs closely.

Drinking, smoking, and other drug use are often romanticized and even glorified on TV, in movies, and in social media. News reports of drug busts, celebrity drug use, and overdoses occur regularly. When youth hear about drug abuse in the media, this is a good opportunity for family discussions about your no-use policy and why you have it. Parents' responsible social

---

[4] Centers for Disease Control and Prevention. *Alcohol and Public Health – Frequently Asked Questions.* Available at www.cdc.gov
[5] US Department of Health and Human Services and US Department of Agriculture. (2015). *2015 – 2020 Dietary Guidelines for Americans.* 8th Edition, Washington, DC: Author.

drinking and appropriate use of prescription drugs also present opportunities for them to talk to their children openly and honestly about their own and other adults' alcohol and drug use. It's when kids don't know the facts about drug use or hear only exaggerated horror stories about the dangers of drugs that they are more likely to want to experiment or will be tempted by peer pressure to try drugs.

Children can also learn from adults' personal struggles with their alcohol and drug abuse. As we'll see in chapter 8, when addiction isn't confronted, families can learn the hard way that this is indeed a family disease with everyone, especially vulnerable children, suffering the consequences. However, families who confront the addiction of adult family members, and support their treatment and recovery, become stronger, including raising stronger children.

Making Prevention Work in Health Care

Young people see family physicians, pediatricians, or adolescent medicine specialists, usually with their parents. It is essential that parents check to be sure that their children's physicians embrace the prevention of youth substance use, that they are aware of adolescent vulnerability to addiction, and that they understand that adolescence is when drug use often begins. There is a strong movement in today's health care to focus on highly prevalent, serious, and chronic disorders. Youth substance abuse fits that description to a T. Health care reform, and the response to the current drug abuse epidemic, have led to two landmark laws that guide these dramatic changes in health care: the Mental Health Parity and Addiction Equity Act and the Patient Protection and Affordable Care Act. These laws drive the recent effort led by the American Academy of Pediatrics (AAP). In 2016, the AAP published an important clinical report calling on health care providers, including all pediatricians, to focus on youth substance abuse beginning with the prevention message that for the health of youth, the best option is to use no drugs, including drugs that are legal for adults— alcohol, nicotine, and, in some states, marijuana.[6] The AAP report goes beyond previous prevention messages for youth, to encourage all providers of health care to adolescents to ask all of their patients about their substance use and to encourage any youth who are using alcohol or other drugs to stop using these drugs, including alcohol, nicotine, and marijuana, for their health. For adolescent patients who have serious problems because of their substance use, the APP recommends referral to treatment as needed and follow-up monitoring for signs of relapse to drug use after

---

[6] Levy, S. J. L., Williams, J. F., American Academy of Pediatrics Committee on Substance Use and Prevention. (2016). Substance use screening, brief intervention, and referral to treatment. *Pediatrics, 138*(1), e11-e15.
http://pediatrics.aappublications.org/content/138/1/e20161211.long

treatment. This wraparound engagement of all adolescent health care in the substance abuse problem is new and promising. When this becomes the norm in all youth health care, family physicians, pediatricians, and adolescent medicine specialists will become a major factor in both the prevention and treatment of substance abuse.

The goal of these new efforts to put substance abuse prevention and treatment solidly in routine health care of adolescents has several elements. First, every youth on every visit should be asked by their health care providers if they use alcohol, nicotine, marijuana, or other drugs, including the nonmedical use of prescription drugs. Those youth who answer "no" should be praised for this healthy decision and encouraged to maintain their no-use status. Those who say "yes" should be asked which drugs they use, how much they use, and what the consequences of that drug use have been. They should then be encouraged to stop all drug use for their health. On all future visits, these youth who have reported using should be questioned about their current use and encouraged to stop any use of alcohol and other drugs. It is generally wise to bring the young person's parents into this discussion with the consent of the patient. When children have serious and repeated problems as a result of their drug use, it is critical to include their parents in the discussion and to consider substance abuse treatment for the child and the entire family. When youth enter substance abuse treatment, the health care provider should actively monitor the aftercare requirements and recommendations following treatment, including drug testing, and to be sure to intervene quickly and decisively if a relapse to alcohol or other drug use occurs, as would be the case with any other serious chronic illness.

Physicians now routinely counsel young patients about wearing seat belts in cars, using helmets when riding bicycles, and avoiding sugary beverages. They do this repeatedly for all of their young patients as an essential element of health promotion. It is important that they also address substance use as another part of every wellness visit routine.

There are several reasons why many pediatricians and other physicians do not address youth substance use at all. Some think it is "preachy" and would alienate their young patients. Others believe that adolescent experimentation with drugs is common and normal. Others think substance abuse prevention is best handled in schools and at home rather than by them and that the more serious substance abuse problems in their patients are best handled by addiction specialists. Concern about confidentially is also a factor in the decision by some physicians to avoid this topic of drugs, since they don't want their young patients to censor what they tell them out of fear that their doctors will tell their parents. Adolescent patients are generally difficult to keep engaged in health care, so anything that discourages continuity in health care is worrisome for providers.

In its 2016 report, the AAP took on these resistances and clearly stated that substance abuse is a major adolescent disorder and that pediatricians owe their patients the best care possible, which includes supporting the no-use policy. This no-use view is not moralistic or political; youth drug use is a serious health matter, with adolescent health being a medical imperative.

Families with children whose drug use is out of control should get a professional assessment for possible addiction and for referral to an adolescent substance abuse treatment program. As we'll learn in chapter 8 on the family's role, it's important for the entire family, including parents and siblings, to embrace the treatment opportunity and work to improve their function as a family in order to support the addicted child's recovery. Families with youth who have serious drug problems are commonly caught in a struggle that is prolonged and painful. They often experience repeated failures. It is important that these families get professional help and connect with other families facing similar problems with drug abuse. When young people get into recovery—and that means no use of alcohol or other drugs and regular attendance at Twelve Step or other mutual support meeting—families need to recognize that recovery is fragile even years after abstinence has been achieved. They and their recovering youth must stick together and do the work necessary to support family recovery on an ongoing basis.

For families faced with failure, with youth who relapse and continue to use alcohol and other drugs, and who sink deeper and deeper into the slavery of addiction and possibly leave home, I have a message based on my five decades as a physician dealing with addiction: There is always hope no matter the depths of the losses and no matter the length of the suffering. Some of my most dramatic stories of recovery have taken place after years, even decades, of losses to addiction. These late recoveries are truly wonderful for the recovering people and for their families—and for their grateful physicians like me. Successes like this confirm my belief that we should never give up and never quit caring.

It is worth noting that even people who condone or encourage adult use of alcohol, nicotine, and marijuana are unanimous that it is unwise and unhealthy for youth to use any drugs, including those that are legal for adults. These three most commonly used drugs—alcohol, tobacco (nicotine), and marijuana—are usually not condoned for use by youth because they are illegal. This illegal status is reinforced by new brain research that shows that the adolescent brain is uniquely vulnerable to addiction, as described in chapter 3.

When it comes to the prevention of drug problems, the role of health care generally extends far beyond the treatment of adolescents. As is often the case with pediatricians talking to their young patients about drugs, for a long time physicians saw drug use by their adult patients as outside their scope of concern—perhaps as a legal or a moral problem but not as a medical issue. Neither prevention nor treatment of substance use disorders has historically been seen as an integral part of routine health care. It has been relegated to parents, teachers, and substance abuse specialists. As the stigma around addiction has lifted and more is learned about addiction as a disorder—a brain disease brought on by drug use—and not a matter of bad morals or lack of discipline, more health care professionals have become comfortable talking about substance use with their patients.

The overdose death crisis, largely driven by opioids, has contributed recently to physicians seeing substance use as an increasingly common and often serious health threat. Effectively addressing this issue with patients of all ages means asking both adolescent and adult patients about their use of alcohol and other drugs and educating them on the health consequences of substance abuse, including addiction. But the national opioid problem is not limited to the nonmedical use of prescription opioids. Almost all opioid deaths involve multiple drugs and many overdose deaths do not include opioids at all. Prescription opioids remain a serious health threat but are increasingly dwarfed by the use of purely illegal opioids, especially synthetic opioids like fentanyl. At the same time the over prescription of opioids remains a serious public health problem must be addressed not only to reduce overdose deaths but also to improve the care of patients with chronic pain. This means better education and behavioral changes for both physicians and patients. Specifically for physicians it means counseling patients of all ages about the dangers of the nonmedical use of prescription drugs and monitoring patients' use of opioid painkillers and other addictive drugs. Further, it means following up with patients returning from addiction treatment to support their aftercare plans and to identify and quickly to intervene if relapses occur.

Prevention in Schools

Adolescents see their physicians typically once a year for well-patient visits and more often when specific health problems arise. Contrast that health care exposure with the adolescents' exposure to school. It is obvious that prevention of the use of alcohol and other drugs, including nicotine, in the school is essential. But, as in health care, there is a deep-seated resistance to taking this on in education today because many educators do not view drug use prevention as their responsibility. Some teachers and administrators also view youth drug use as a legal or moral problem that is more properly managed in the family, by law enforcement, or by substance abuse professionals. This denial of responsibility by educators occurs in middle and high schools but it is most pronounced in post-secondary education – colleges and universities – where rampant drinking and other drug use, especially marijuana use, is all-too-often ignored and seen as an inevitable rite of passage.

It is not that educators don't recognize or care about drug problems among youth. Instead, this widespread failure to act reflects confusion about education's role and the message that should be delivered to youth about drug use. There is confusion about the law, what is legal for adults and what is legal for young people, and there are value conflicts about whether the health objective is no use, or if some use is normal and a rite of passage. And finally, there is uncertainty about the relationship between drug use and the students' problems: has the drug caused the problems or is it the result of the problems? Because so many young people use drugs, especially alcohol and marijuana, without negative consequences, many educators see the problem as not drug or alcohol use per se, but a problem only if there is excessive or pathological drinking and other drug use. With marijuana, many educators have permissive attitudes toward use, especially as marijuana legalization becomes more widespread. They don't think it is as harmful to use marijuana as other drugs, including alcohol. Generally, while binge alcohol drinking, nicotine vaping and smoking, and regular marijuana use are frowned upon, youth drug use is still not recognized as the health problem it is, especially for students with addiction in their families.

Prevention programs in schools, such as D.A.R.E., and evidence-based programs, such as Raising Healthy Children, Mentor Foundation USA, Building Assets, Reducing Risks (BARR), and Project Northland, have been effective in reducing substance use and abuse but because of lack of funding, both for research and implementation, they do not meet their full potential nationwide. A 2014 report from the US Centers for Disease Control and Prevention, *Best Practices for Comprehensive Tobacco Control Programs*, concluded:

"When research-based substance use prevention programs are properly implemented by schools and communities, use of alcohol, tobacco, and illegal drugs is reduced. Such programs help teachers, parents, and health care professionals shape youths' perceptions about the risks of substance use. While many social and cultural factors affect drug use trends, when young people perceive drug use as harmful, they reduce their level of use. Parents, community and government leaders need to make supporting these programs a priority if prevention efforts are to be successful."[7]

One additional reason that some well-meaning educators, government

---

[7] Centers for Disease Control and Prevention. (2014). *Best Practices for Comprehensive Tobacco Control Programs—2014*. Atlanta, GA: US Department of Health and Human Services, Centers for Disease Control and Prevention, National Center for Chronic Disease Prevention and Health Promotion, Office on Smoking and Health. https://www.cdc.gov/tobacco/stateandcommunity/best_practices/index.htm

officials, and community leaders have given for ignoring drug use among youth is that they are focused on education and do not see youth alcohol and other drug use prevention as a core educational objective. Many of them know that drug-using youth have more educational problems than youth who do not use drugs, but they also see a lot of drug-using students who do fine academically and socially. They see the connection of drug use with academic failure as being just one of many contributing factors, which may also include mental illness, economic or social disadvantage, or family dysfunction.

There are two sources of evidence that show clearly youth drug use adversely impacts core educational goals. First, the academic failure seen in many drug-using youth only began when they started using alcohol and other drugs, even though the other problems in their lives preceded their drug use. Even more compelling is the evidence presented by drug-using youth who enter recovery. Their grades and social engagement improve dramatically when they stop using drugs. This is most clearly seen on college campuses all over the country where drug-free recovery dorms are popping up. Go to any of them and ask the students who are in recovery about their academic performances when they were using alcohol and other drugs compared with their performances now that they are living drug-free Ask them why that change is so dramatic. They will tell you, as they have told me, that when they were using drugs, they didn't care about their grades or their futures and they didn't study. In recovery, they do care about how well they do in school and about their future careers and they are motivated to study. They are typically proud of their remarkable transformations and are eager to share their inspiring recovery stories.

There is, however, still a problem: A lot of youth who are using alcohol, marijuana, and other drugs appear to be doing fine while using these substances. Like the thousands of people who drive without incident while intoxicated, not all are harmed by their drug use—but eventually many are. Who is harmed and who is unharmed is not predictable, but it is clear that there are many injuries and deaths caused by drunk driving and drug use. Similarly, many drug-using youth eventually have serious negative effects. For a significant percentage of young people, casual use turns to abuse and their brains are primed for drug-induced brain reward, increasing the risk of addiction and all the negative consequences of this insidious chronic disease, not just in adolescence but throughout their lives.

If educators get it—if they recognize that youth drug use is a widespread and serious health and education threat both in adolescence and beyond—and if they recognize the unique vulnerability to addiction of the adolescent brain; and further, if they recognize that they should work to reduce youth drug use, what exactly can they do?

Educators need to give clear repeated health messages to all youth: *Do not use alcohol, tobacco (nicotine), marijuana, or other drugs for your health and for your academic success.* And for youth who do use drugs, advise them to stop. Caution them on the risks they face from their decision to use alcohol and other drugs. Care for them, be interested in them, and respect them, but hold to this view, which in their interest. Not driving while intoxicated is the law. The law concerning drug use by youth is similarly clear: Even alcohol and nicotine use (and marijuana use, in some states) that is legal for adults, is illegal for youth. All drug use that is illegal for adults is also illegal for youth.

***

Prevention has as its first priority increasing the percentage of youth who grow up drug-free and a second priority of encouraging those who do use drugs to stop. This also means responsible use of legal drugs and no use of nicotine or illegal drugs by adults, young and old. A third prevention priority is to reduce the harm created by young adults' alcohol use to the extent possible by discouraging those who drink to not drink to intoxication and especially to not binge drink. The simple motto is "Don't drink and drive," not "Don't drive drunk." This admonition applies to all drug use: "Don't use drugs, including marijuana, and drive."

This straightforward and clear prevention message—One Choice: no use of any drugs for youth up to the age of twenty-one for health—needs to be given consistently and repeatedly by families, health care professionals, community and government leaders, law enforcement, and educators including administrators, teachers, and counselors. The 2016 report *Facing Addiction in America: The Surgeon General's Report on Alcohol, Drugs, and Health* confirms the importance of an integrated approach to prevention, specifically related to alcohol use:

> "Well-supported scientific evidence shows that federal, state, and community-level policies designed to reduce alcohol availability and increase the costs of alcohol have immediate, positive benefits in reducing drinking and binge drinking, as well as the resulting harms from alcohol misuse, such as motor vehicle crashes and fatalities. There is also well-supported scientific evidence that laws targeting alcohol-impaired driving, such as administrative license revocation and lower per se legal blood alcohol limits for adults and persons under the legal drinking age, have helped cut alcohol-related traffic deaths per 100,000 in half since the early 1980s."[8]

---

[8] US Department of Health and Human Services (HHS), Office of the Surgeon General. (2016). *Facing Addiction in America: The Surgeon General's Report on Alcohol, Drugs, and Health.*

The same proved true for the concerted efforts by government, health care, schools, and communities to crack down on tobacco (nicotine) use since the landmark 1964 Surgeon General's report *Smoking and Health* by labeling tobacco products with warnings about cancer, using TV and other media to educate the public about the dangers of tobacco use, instituting rigorous no-smoking policies, raising the tobacco tax to make tobacco products less affordable, and making free cessation programs readily available. I have confidence that, like the Surgeon General's landmark 1964 report on tobacco, the 2016 report on alcohol, drugs, and health will mark a turning point on preventing drug abuse in our country with its key goal of no use of alcohol, nicotine, or marijuana by youth.

There is more to prevention than helping youth grow up drug-free. Prevention also has major roles for adults, specifically in helping people who have problem-generating drug use, including addiction, to become drug-free. When we see friends or family members endangering themselves and others by using addictive drugs, we should express our concern and refuse to support that behavior rather than condoning or ignoring it. If it's clear someone has lost control of their use and is addicted, we must offer support to the person and their family in finding professional help to achieve abstinence. In addition, there are prevention priorities for adults in many other settings besides their family, including the workplace, in the community, and in social settings. In all of these places, the prevention goal for adults is no use of nicotine, no nonmedical use of prescription drugs, and no illegal recreational drug use. For alcohol, the prevention goal is no use to intoxication and no use in settings where alcohol use is dangerous, including before or while driving.

Washington, DC: HHS. https://addiction.surgeongeneral.gov

6. INTERVENTION AND TREATMENT

Addiction to alcohol and other drugs is the malignant disease of the entire self. It has two central features: first, the continued use of alcohol and other drugs despite repeated serious negative consequences, one of the key criteria indicating loss of control; and second, dishonesty about that use and the problems caused by that use. This disease is progressive and often fatal. It is not self-curing. The disease of addiction involves the entire family, not just the addict. As we'll see in the next chapter, getting well—recovery—involves more than not drinking or using other drugs. Recovery from addiction means a new and far better way of living for the addicted person and for the codependent people in the addict's life.

Addiction treatment is often the start of a long-term, difficult, and uncertain process. It is not a magic bullet for addictive disease. Treatment does not fix or cure the addict. It is the beginning, and only the beginning, of the work of recovery. Formal addiction treatment, whether inpatient or outpatient, explains the disorder of addiction and it identifies the path to lasting recovery. It starts addicted people and their families on the road to recovery. When people come out of treatment programs, they are just beginning that journey as they discover the challenges of lifelong abstinence from addictive drugs and the freedom from the chemical slavery of addiction. The deeper aspects of addiction—aspects that involve the character of addicted people and of their families—require years of hard work to achieve the full promise of recovery. Not only is tough love needed, but so are patience, persistence, and a sense of humor. Most of all, hope. Hope for the addict and hope for the addict's family that a better life awaits as a reward for the work of recovery. Relapses are common, but not universal, in recovery. Relapses must be met by immediate and definitive interventions by the family and others. Failures on this path are growth opportunities that can enrich and deepen recovery. Recovery is possible for everyone facing addiction. The reward of recovery is worth the sustained effort of the addict and the addict's family.

There are three stages in the process of getting well from the disease of addiction:

1. Intervention, which includes identifying the disease of addiction, often involves a formal assessment and precipitating the addict's painful and humiliating experience of hitting bottom where serious consequences of addictive behavior lead the addict to surrender to the unequivocal recognition that life using alcohol and other drugs cannot go on. This stage culminates in the addict agreeing to treatment.

2. Treatment, which may start with detoxification, involves a formal inpatient or outpatient care program, with or without medication, and with structured and intensive aftercare upon discharge.

3. Recovery, which is a lifelong stage, almost always includes attending mutual support groups, usually Twelve Step programs such as AA or NA, many times a week, even daily, at first and one or more times a week after a person's recovery is more stable. This community support in a recovery community is essential to ensure ongoing abstinence and the fundamental changes in mental, emotional, and social/spiritual outlook that define sobriety.

We will cover the first two stages of this near miraculous process in this chapter and then devote the entire following chapter to recovery.

Intervention

Intervention has three phases: Identification of addiction by the addict and the family and other loved ones; the actual intervention, which may involve a professional interventionist along with the addict's family members, partners, friends, and even co-workers; and finally, getting the addict into treatment.

Identification

The first, and usually the hardest, part of intervention is identification, which may include a professional assessment. This is the step in which the family, and sometimes the addicted person or a social institution such as the school, workplace, or the courts, recognizes that they are dealing with a serious disease and that someone's life is out of control or, in the language of recovery, "unmanageable." The individual, ideally with the involvement of the family, must identify and name the problem. Identification grows out of a painful and usually long process in which the person's alcohol and drug use grows progressively worse and the negative consequences of that use become more frequent and more serious. The family and community interactions with the person become increasingly dysfunctional because of addiction. Denial is a powerful and crippling feature of the disease for everyone involved. In the addict's view, the problem is about everything but the alcohol or drug use. The family avoids facing the addict's use and refuses to accept their own self-defeating roles in the process of addiction.

A simple and useful way for an individual to identify alcoholism or other drug addiction is to use the CAGE alcoholism screening tool, which was developed in 1968 at the North Carolina Memorial Hospital. CAGE is the acronym for the key terms Cut down, Annoyed, Guilty, and Eye-opener in the following questions, which have been adapted to include other drug use in addition to alcohol.

1. Have you ever felt you ought to cut down on your drinking or drug use?
2. Have people annoyed you by criticizing your drinking or drug use?
3. Have you felt bad or guilty about your drinking or drug use?
4. Have you ever had a drink or used drugs first thing in the morning to steady your nerves or to get rid of a hangover (used an "eye-opener")?

An answer of yes to two or more of these questions indicates the strong potential for alcoholism or other drug addiction.

The assessment criteria for addiction most widely used by professionals comes from the fifth edition of the American Psychiatric Association's *Diagnostic and Statistical Manual of Psychiatric Disorders*, or DSM-V, which we described in chapter 1. To recap, the manual includes a list of specific criteria commonly seen in substance use disorders (SUDs), such as continued drug or alcohol use despite persistent or recurring problems (health, social, interpersonal, work, school, and so on), tolerance (that is, over time more of the drug is required to get the same effect), craving, inability to quit or cut down on use, withdrawal, and using more of a drug than intended. The diagnosis of an SUD only applies if at least two of the eleven standard criteria listed in the DSM are met over the past year. With two to three criteria met, the SUD is judged to be mild; four to five criteria indicate a moderate disorder; and six or more is considered severe.

While the DSM-V can be a helpful guide for laypeople, it is written to be used by health care professionals since the boundary between substance abuse that hasn't progressed to addiction (usually mild to moderate) and full addiction (severe), where a person has lost control of use, can be hard to define. Untrained people using these criteria run the risk of "over-labeling" someone as an addict.

What is the danger today of over-labeling someone as addicted? The worst possibility of such an error, in my experience, is that the person would be advised to stop nonmedical drug use, including the use of alcohol, and possibly to go to meetings of a Twelve Step fellowship. Because I do not consider either of these two outcomes to be negative for anyone, I am not concerned that a small percentage of people who are labeled (by themselves and other nonprofessional people, including their families) as addicted would not have been so labeled some years ago, or that such people might unnecessarily stop drinking or using addictive drugs and go to a few Twelve Step meetings. The basic solution for the disease of addiction is downright healthy living in its own right, so one need not be worried about families over-diagnosing addiction. The major danger is not over-labeling by families but "under-labeling," as most people suffering from addiction continue to use denial to perpetuate their diseases. Under-labeling is usually a manifestation of denial by both addicts and their loved ones and it only leads to an escalation of the disease and even more destruction.

Denial can prevent addicts from getting a formal assessment and referral to treatment, even when everyone but the addict recognizes that the person's drinking and/or other drug use is out of control and is wreaking havoc on the lives of everyone involved. This is when a formal intervention may be needed to bring addicts to face-to-face with their addiction and precipitate their hitting the bottom necessary to accept help.

Formal Intervention

Before a formal intervention is held with the addict, the process typically begins with the entire family coming together, often with other concerned people, and focusing on what they have each observed that leads them individually to the conclusion that this person is facing addiction. Sometimes the family predicts that the addict will accept this judgment quickly and without resistance. More often, however, the group concludes that addicted person will likely continue to be in denial and resist facing this conclusion. In these cases, it is useful to find a trained intervention specialist to help the family plan and conduct a formal intervention. An interventionist can be found by calling local substance abuse treatment programs and asking for recommendations or by searching for addiction specialists online where you'll also find ratings and reviews by people who have worked with the specialists. Libraries and bookstores also carry books devoted to intervention and addiction treatment.

Successful formal interventions are planned and structured meetings with the addict that usually involve family members and possibly friends, co-workers, or bosses—anyone who has witnessed the negative effects of the addict's alcohol and other drug use—and that are led by a trained professional. During the intervention, family members should remain calm and focus on what they have personally observed and not on hearsay. Emphasis should be put on love and concern, not on anger or punishment. Before the intervention, family members need to figure out what they want as a result of the intervention. In most cases, the goal is for the addicted person to be admitted to a specific inpatient or outpatient addiction treatment program. When confronted by an organized intervention or even by a family concerned about their addictive behavior (an informal intervention), it is common for addicts to be angry and resentful. It is important for the family and others involved to remain calm and to stick to the facts. Most of all, it is important for the addict to see that those conducting the intervention, formal or informal, are united. The addict needs to realize, however dimly at this time of crisis, that the family and often others are dealing with facts and that they are united in their care and respect for the addict as a person. Not only that but the addict needs to see that there is a clear path to recovery, to a better life.

For many addicts, a traditional formal intervention won't break through their denial and convince them to enter treatment. In some of these cases, a less confrontational approach called Brief Intervention proves successful. In this type of intervention, an addiction professional trained in this technique works with addicts to identify their readiness to change using the Stages of Change model developed by James Prochaska and Carlo DiClemente and to motivate them to move through five stages to get the help they need:

- Pre-contemplation—still denies there's a problem;
- Contemplation—agrees there's a problem and help may be needed;
- Preparation—takes the necessary steps to find a solution to the problem;
- Action—does what's required to address the problem; and
- Maintenance—continues to find and apply solutions to the problem long-term.

Many people find their way to addiction treatment as a result of a confrontation with a judge or an employer rather than through a family intervention. Often the legal system gets a hold of addicts and alcoholics through driving while impaired (DWI) programs, which funnel more than a million Americans each year into educational programs involving once-a-week films and discussions, plus for some, especially repeat offenders, Twelve Step meetings once or twice a week for a period of time. In some states, repeat offenders may also be sent to a drug court where the judge takes the role of an interventionist and may sentence the offender to enter a treatment program in lieu of going to prison.

In the workplace, the initial confrontation with addiction can involve a supervisor's intervention or a routine drug test that indicates the person violated the company's drug-free standard. This may trigger the employee being sent to an Employee Assistance Program (EAP) for evaluation, and then, if indicated based on the evaluation, going on to formal addiction treatment. What's important is that all addicted people find their own unique springboards into a new life of recovery.

Addiction is a pernicious disorder, accurately called "cunning, baffling, and powerful" in AA. Unfortunately, there are addicts whose denial is so entrenched that no intervention approach works. Almost all eventually endure enough serious consequences from their alcohol and other drug use that they hit their bottoms and agree to get help. For too many, however, this is a fatal disease. They succumb to addiction's power despite everyone's best efforts. As tragic as this is, family members and other loved ones need to find healing for themselves and move on, hopefully using their new, hard-won knowledge to help others avoid this terrible fate.

Getting the Addict into Treatment

The admission to addiction treatment is best worked out in detail before the intervention, including the costs of treatment, so the addicted person can go directly from the intervention into a treatment program chosen by the family. Family members and other loved ones do not enter treatment but will benefit from regular attendance at Al-Anon meetings to help them deal with their own roles in this family disease. Sometimes the family members are handicapped by denial of their self-defeating roles in the addicted person's life. Family members may be more than willing for the addicted person to enter treatment but quite resistant to the idea that they need help to overcome their part of the disease of addiction. We'll discuss this more in depth in chapter 8 on the family's role in recovery.

Ninety Meetings, Ninety Days

For some people with less severe addiction and especially those without significant co-occurring psychiatric disorders, Twelve Step or other recovery support meetings can provide an alternative to treatment as a starting point on the road to recovery. The simple standard, developed over many decades by the AA program, is "ninety meetings, ninety days": Go to at least one Twelve Step meeting a day for ninety days. For many newly recovering addicts, the beginning stages of recovery involve two or three meetings a day. You simply need to take your body there and stay for the entire meeting: Take the body, and the mind (as well as the heart) follows. You can also go to meetings before you or your family member enters professional addiction treatment, especially if there is a waiting list. Most treatment programs require patients to attend Twelve Step meetings during treatment and strongly encourage them to regularly attend Twelve Step meetings after treatment as a necessary part of ongoing recovery.

Having said that, however, a major door into recovery has for decades been the residential addiction treatment program or one of the alternative intensive outpatient addiction treatment programs. Recognizing that, how can you find the best treatment program for you and your family? Below is a checklist to help you make wise choices.

Treatment Selection Checklist

1. Talk with local physicians and others specializing in the treatment of addiction to identify the best treatment programs available.
2. Visit the addiction treatment programs you are considering.
3. Find out the nature of the treatment offered.
4. Even if you are sure which program you would like to select, consider alternatives.
5. Determine if there is adequate initial evaluation of the addicted person and the family.
6. Find out the costs of the treatment program.
7. Ask about aftercare.
8. Determine the extent of family involvement.
9. Ask whether the program integrates Twelve Step programs into the treatment.
10. Ask how long patients stay in treatment and what percentage of patients complete the program.
11. Go to open meetings of Al-Anon, Alcoholics Anonymous, and Narcotics Anonymous to learn what these veterans of addiction treatment have to say about specific programs and about the role of treatment in their recoveries.

Checklist for Addiction Treatment

If you do an online search for "Alcoholism Information and Treatment" or "Drug Abuse and Addiction—Information and Treatment," you will find a list of addiction treatment programs in your community. You can also contact your local medical or psychiatric society and ask for addiction treatment recommendations. Likewise, you can call your state, county, or city alcohol or drug abuse treatment agency to get their suggestions. If you live near a medical school, call them and ask about their addiction program. You own physician may also have useful suggestions. Sometimes your best referral source is a trusted friend or relative who has already faced addiction and has had a successful experience in a particular facility. Once you have compiled a list of the two or three programs you are most interested in, use the following checklist to help you make your decision:

1. Talk with local physicians or other health care professionals specializing in the treatment of addiction. You can obtain a list of specialists in your area from the American Society of Addiction Medicine. Find out what addiction specialists in your area think of the treatment programs you are considering, especially specialists who do not work for those particular

programs. Here you will find out what the competition thinks about the programs you have selected. If the doctors with whom you are speaking do work for the particular treatment program in which you are interested, ask them which other programs in your area they would pick if they, or a member of their family, needed treatment for an alcohol or drug problem and they could not use their own treatment program.

2. Visit the addiction treatment programs you are considering. Talk to the staff. Do staff and patients appear to be glad to be there and busy at all times of the day? You may not be able to go into the unit because of concerns about confidentiality, but get as close as the staff will let you. You can often feel the difference between a good and a poor addiction treatment program simply on the basis of the atmosphere of the place. Good programs are happy, active places. Poor programs are often morbid places where not much is happening, where patients and staff mostly just let time pass.

3. Find out the nature of the treatment offered for addiction. For example, is it inpatient or outpatient, residential or hospital; what are the treatment modalities used; and how long does the treatment usually last?

4. Even if you are sure which program you would like to select, consider alternatives. Get details about two or three programs before you choose one. This is too important a decision to be made without careful consideration of all of the facts. Consider at least one intensive outpatient program.

5. Determine if there is an adequate initial evaluation of the addicted person and the family. Does the program have a pre-treatment evaluation process in place to identify particular problems, including medical and psychiatric problems, that may complicate the treatment of the addicted person and to confirm that the person needs formal addiction treatment?

6. Find out if you can afford the costs of the treatment program. How much does the treatment cost? How much of that cost will be paid for by your insurance, and how much will you have to pay out of your own pocket? The treatment program staff can help you figure out these costs. Often the best addiction treatment costs less than the not-so-good treatment. Do not let a high price tag convince you that a particular addiction treatment program is the best.

7. Ask about aftercare. In particular, ask what type of aftercare is available for the treatment program besides Twelve Step programs. Is it built into the treatment? Is aftercare both intensive and prolonged? Six weeks or longer is typical.

Recovery support is often a key part of successful aftercare plans following treatment, but a note of warning for families to scrutinize so-called "sober houses" that are often unregulated, may permit ongoing substance use, and have high costs. As discussed in the chapter 4, Oxford

House is one of the most inspiring (and well-researched) examples of exemplary recovery support.

8. Determine the extent of family involvement. If the family is not actively involved in all stages of the treatment, then the treatment program is not likely to work because addiction is a family disease and recovery is a family affair. Good residential addiction treatment programs include one week of intensive treatment for family members during the three to six weeks the addicted person is in treatment.

9. Ask whether the program integrates Twelve Step and other recovery support programs into the treatment. In both the intensive treatment and aftercare phases, does the program include the Twelve Step program and their principles, including the disease concept, into all aspects of the treatment? Is the program an abstinence model treatment?

10. Ask how long patients stay in the treatment and what percentage of patients complete the program.

11. Go to open meetings of Al-Anon, Alcoholics Anonymous, or Narcotics Anonymous to learn what these veterans of addiction treatment have to say about specific programs and about the role of treatment in their recoveries. At these free meetings, you will find a community of consumers of addiction treatment. This consumers' eye view of addiction treatment in your own community is priceless. Use it.

This checklist can be used for individuals and families searching for treatment for any age, including addicted teens. I encourage parents and their teens to discuss treatment options and programs with their children's primary care physicians. Although these physicians may have limited experience in addiction medicine, the act of linking primary care to treatment and subsequent aftercare can help physicians follow-up and monitor teens in their recovery.

I also encourage parents to find a support network of other parents who have faced their own children's addictions and learn from their experiences and recommendations for treatment. Many community support meetings are geared toward adults and may not be suitable for teens. Increasingly many community support meetings are geared to the needs to teenagers. Parents can help their teens navigate and manage the network of community support often with the help of therapists who routinely work with youth. In addition Al-Anon meetings can help parents help their teenagers get into and stay in recovery.

Be an informed consumer. Ask questions. Use all the resources available to you in making a decision about which addiction treatment program your family will use. This is one of the most important decisions you will ever make.

Treatment

Formal addiction treatment is a central step on the road to recovery for both the addicted person and for codependent family members. But, surprisingly, it is not the hardest part of the process for most families. Usually the toughest steps are identification of addiction in their loved one and acting on it with some form of intervention to get their loved one into treatment. By the time the family has made it to addiction treatment, the healing process from addiction is under way. The treatment phase is almost a relief compared with the uncertain outcome of an intervention and compared with the uncertainties of aftercare. Treatment is often an island of calm between the turbulence and uncertainty both before and, all too commonly, after treatment.

For addicted teens, parents are typically the most significant force that motivates them to enter treatment because of the leverage parents have. Parents of addicted adults can feel particularly hopeless because of the powerful grip addiction has on their children. After her son died from addiction, a Kentucky mother helped pass Casey's Law which allows families to seek court-ordered involuntary treatment for their addicted loved ones.[1]

Two basic settings of treatment for addiction are available in the US today: inpatient and outpatient. Inpatient addiction treatment involves a more or less prolonged stay in an addiction treatment program, often in a hospital or in a residential treatment center. The typical private sector addiction treatment program has been the twenty-eight-day residential program pioneered in Minnesota in the 1950s and 1960s, known as the Minnesota Model, an abstinence-based, multidisciplinary approach based on the Twelve Steps of AA. Increasingly, residential treatment for addictive disease has evolved into diverse structures, from relatively brief (a few days) to quite long (a year or longer), reflecting a program or a continuum of care appropriate to individual needs and financial limitations.

Because addiction is a lifelong disease, regardless of how long or short is the residential phase of care, addiction treatment almost always includes prolonged and intensive outpatient aftercare. Recovery is possible, but it is never a quick fix. Relapse to addiction remains a possibility long after even the most successful treatment.

The forms of addiction treatment that grew out of the Minnesota Model are sometimes called recovery-based because of their commitment to abstinence from all alcohol and other drug use and to the Twelve Step model of addiction and recovery. This approach is the opposite of treatment models that focus on a single substance and those that encourage controlled or moderate use of the substance as part of the process of

---

[1] http://www.CaseysLaw.org/

getting well. For example, some earlier addiction treatment programs dealt with only one drug, such as alcohol, cocaine, or heroin, and attempted to help patients stop the use of that substance while permitting or even encouraging continued use of other addictive substances. Many early programs designed to combat heroin addiction permitted the continued use of marijuana or alcohol as long as that use was not deemed excessive. Similarly, some alcohol treatment programs attempted to teach alcoholics to drink moderately, as social drinkers do. Although these earlier approaches to addiction recovery can still be found today, they are becoming less common as they are more widely seen as ineffective. I am skeptical of addiction treatment approaches that define only one substance as the patient's problem, permitting other alcohol and/or drug use, and approaches that encourage alcoholics to learn to become social drinkers.

A Note for Addicts upon Entering Treatment

Once you and your family have chosen an addiction treatment program, put aside whatever misgivings you had before starting treatment and put your whole heart and soul into the recovery process. Make full use of your addiction treatment program and your counselors. Addicts and their families became sick and stayed sick by trying to run their own lives in their own ways. Do not do that with your addiction treatment. Work the program and do what the program staff tells you to do. The people in your Twelve Step fellowship and in your addiction treatment program are the experts you have chosen to help you and your family.

Detoxification

Detoxification, or detox—structured treatment to overcome the withdrawal symptoms of physical dependence to become drug free—was once the heart of inpatient treatment. Today detoxification, if needed at all, is usually a brief part of the first few days of either inpatient or outpatient treatment for most alcoholics and other drug addicts. Many addicts have no withdrawal symptoms when they stop use or, if they do, their withdrawal symptoms are handled with routine medical treatment, depending on the specific drug they had been using.

Some people who are physically dependent on alcohol, barbiturates, benzodiazepines, and opioids such as heroin and prescription painkillers face more difficulty when they detoxify from drugs. Their detoxification requires medical skill because there are potentially serious risks if the detoxification is not managed well. A variety of medicines are commonly used in detoxification, including naltrexone and Suboxone for detoxing from opioids.

Generally speaking, the period of detoxification is usually brief—lasting for a few days to a week or so—and it is relatively easily handled in an appropriate setting. With good medical care, detoxification is usually neither painful nor dangerous, although it is sometimes distressing. The biggest danger during the detoxification period is not that the addicted person will flee from treatment due to distressing withdrawal symptoms, because when addicted patients are medically managed, the withdrawal symptoms are not that severe. Rather, the biggest danger during this period is that the addicted person will terminate the treatment prematurely to resume the abusive chemical love affair with alcohol and other drugs. Because of the powerful grip that physical dependence and the fear of withdrawal have on the public, the detoxification period of addiction is exaggerated in most discussions about treatment.

Treatment that involves the use of medications, called medication-assisted treatment (MAT) now often continues throughout and beyond the treatment stay as a key part of the aftercare protocols.

Medication-Assisted Treatment
For Alcoholism

In recent years two medicines have been marketed to treat alcohol use disorders. By decreasing cravings for alcohol, they reduce relapses in people with alcohol use disorders. Their effectiveness is measured by reductions in alcohol use after taking the medicines.

In 1994 the Food and Drug Administration (FDA) approved the use of naltrexone (ReVia) as a part of a comprehensive treatment of alcohol use disorders. Naltrexone, which is often also used in the treatment of opioid use disorders, reduces cravings by blocking the opioid receptor system that may play a role in the reinforcement of alcohol use. Naltrexone is used as a once-a-day tablet or as a once-a-month implant under the skin.

Acamprosate, approved by the FDA for the treatment of alcohol use disorders in 2004, is another medicine that reduces alcohol use. A delayed-release capsule that is taken three times a day, the medicine is thought to reduce drinking by reducing the imbalance of the glutamate and the GABAminergic brain system that is produced by chronic alcohol use.

Naltrexone and acamprosate have joined the long-established medication Antabuse (disulfiram), introduced into medical practice in 1951, for the treatment of alcohol use disorders. Antabuse works by temporarily poisoning the liver enzyme needed to metabolize alcohol in the body. Antabuse allows acetaldehyde, a toxic intermediary metabolic product, to build up in the drinker's body. Acetaldehyde causes flushing of the skin, headaches, stomachaches, and elevated blood pressure. Drinking a lot of alcohol while using Antabuse can even cause death. The alcoholic seeking motivation to avoid drinking needs to take Antabuse only once a day, usually in the morning when the determination not to drink is relatively high. Then, if the alcoholic is tempted to drink later in the day, the fear of illness or death from drinking alcohol after using Antabuse serves to protect the person. Because Antabuse poisons enzymes in the body for quite a while, the person must stop Antabuse use for one to two weeks before drinking alcohol; otherwise, disturbing and potentially dangerous symptoms are likely to result.

There are two serious problems with the use of Antabuse to treat alcoholism. The first is that it is specific for alcohol, which makes it possible for alcoholics to use other drugs and get high while taking the medication. For example, they can use closely related medicines such as Xanax and Valium, or they can use quite different substances such as opiates or marijuana. The second problem is that alcoholics can simply stop taking Antabuse. The people most familiar with alcoholism—those in Alcoholics Anonymous—generally take a dim view of treating the disorder with Antabuse because this type of treatment does not deal with the alcoholic as a whole person.

Antabuse treatment alone does not lead to long-term recovery. At best, Antabuse or any of the other anti-craving medications provides an opportunity for the person to get alcohol out of the brain and make some long-term decisions about getting—and staying—well. I have found that Antabuse treatment usually does not lead to recovery unless the alcoholic also attends meetings of AA or NA. This is especially true for those using other drugs of abuse. If Antabuse is used only with psychotherapy, I have rarely seen it lead to long-term, stable recovery. In fact, like using psychotherapy in the place of working a Twelve Step program for addicted people, it can become a "cover" for continued addiction as alcoholics delude those around them into a false sense that their problem with alcohol is under control.

These three medicines, now underused, are helpful for many people with alcohol use disorders, although not all people who use them find them helpful. Those who have trouble stopping their use of alcohol with standard treatment methods and AA are wise to try one or more of these medicines.

For Opioid Addiction

Vincent Dole, MD, who had worked for many years on the serious chronic diseases of obesity and diabetes, teamed up with his psychiatrist wife, Marie Nyswander, to develop methadone maintenance treatment for heroin addiction in 1964. (The synthetic opioid methadone was developed in Germany in the late 1930s by Gustav Ehrhart and Max Bockmühl and was introduced into the US in 1947 by the drug company Eli Lilly to treat pain and withdrawal in opioid addicts, especially heroin addicts.) In these programs, methadone is usually taken orally once a day in dosage forms that are non-injectable. Taken that way, it does not produce a high but has three dramatically useful effects: It blocks the high of injecting heroin and other opioids, it prevents overdose deaths, and it prevents withdrawal symptoms and therefore permits the methadone patient to live a stable, productive life. Methadone has been approved by the US Food and Drug Administration (FDA) to treat heroin addiction since 1974. There are nearly a million Americans now using methadone treatment in regulated and comprehensive treatment programs.

Methadone maintenance does not cause intoxication or obvious impairment because of the virtually complete extent of tolerance to opioid effects on the brain (sedation and euphoria) with once-a-day oral methadone administration. It is not possible for people to function normally when taking continuous doses of alcohol, marijuana, cocaine, or heroin, but it is possible for users of methadone to function normally — that is, not to be intoxicated.

Agonists and Antagonists

Let's take a closer look at how different medications can help in the treatment of addiction. First, recall what we learned in chapter 3 about how the transmission of messages throughout the brain requires specific "locks and keys" to fit together—an axon's neurotransmitter needs to fit into the receptor site on the dendrite for the message to go through. Neurotransmitters are agonists—the keys—that work to communicate messages across synapses in the brain. But sometimes the message-receiving nerve cells—the locks—are blocked by chemicals called antagonists. When this happens, the message can't go through.

Opioids—including heroin, prescription painkillers, and methadone—are all agonists, the keys that exactly fit the receptor locks. Many other drugs of abuse, such as cocaine work primarily by blocking the reuptake of naturally occurring neurotransmitters. Several synthetic chemicals block the receptor sites for the opioids. They are called narcotic antagonists. When addicts take an opioid antagonist, such as naltrexone, they cannot get high from an opioid. Narcotic antagonist drugs including naloxone are used to reverse overdoses on opioids. The antagonists cover the receptor sites and block the effects of the opioid. Even if the opioids get to the receptors first, the antagonist knocks the opioid key out of the lock and closes the lock to the key. As a result, the overdose victim not only survives, but rapidly wakes from a deep coma when given a narcotic antagonist.

The effects of antagonists, like all medicines, last as long as they are present in the synapse at adequate levels. Five decades ago, when methadone was introduced as a treatment for heroin addiction, methadone overdoses were relatively common when a patient's methadone was taken accidentally, or for purposes of abuse, by people who lacked opioid tolerance. Methadone overdose victims, sometimes young children, were rushed to hospitals and treated with naloxone. Both heroin and naloxone, the first opioid antagonist to be widely used in medicine, have short durations of action, meaning they stay in the synapses at effective levels for a few hours. Methadone, by contrast, is slowly eliminated from the body, staying in the synapse at effective levels for twenty-four hours or longer.

When methadone overdose patients were treated with the short-acting medication naloxone, which had worked well for heroin overdoses, comatose patients at death's door woke up just as heroin overdose victims did soon after receiving the naloxone. Because medical personnel then assumed these patients were well, they sometimes sent the patients to their hospital rooms or put them aside in busy emergency rooms. In a few hours the rescued overdose patient lapsed into a coma and, in some cases, died when the naloxone was eliminated from their synapses but the longer-acting methadone persisted. Only later did physicians realize that methadone overdoses, in contrast to heroin overdoses, need to be treated with long-acting antagonists or with repeated doses of short-acting antagonists. This same mismatch occurs with the opioid fentanyl, which has a long half-life like methadone. The increasing use of fentanyl raises the same concerns as methadone overdoses—the fentanyl overdose victim wakes up from the overdose only to lapse back to a potentially fatal outcome. This was apparently the case with the popular musician Prince who died of an overdose in April 2016.

Naloxone, the medication used to treat opioid overdoses, is not effective orally, so it must be injected or taken as a nasal spray. The opioid antagonist naltrexone, a more recent addition to the therapeutic armory, can be taken orally and it is effective for twenty-four hours or more. An oral dose of naltrexone once a day, or even every other day, is sufficient to block the effects of opioids, including heroin, opioid painkillers, and methadone. The challenge today for drug abuse treatment is getting opioid addicts to take naltrexone. Because addicts want to get high, they are seldom motivated on their own to take the antagonist because the medicine makes it impossible to get high. Recently a depot injection has been developed for naltrexone lasting for six months. Also, naltrexone has recently been approved to treat alcohol abuse.

Suboxone is another medicated-assisted treatment (MAT) that combines naloxone with buprenorphine, an opioid partial agonist. Buprenorphine can produce euphoria when injected but with effects weaker than heroin, methadone, or other opioids. Buprenorphine was the first drug approved by the FDA for use by physicians to manage opioid addiction, unlike methadone treatment, which can only be used in an approved, structured treatment program. The euphoric effect of injected buprenorphine is dulled when combined with naloxone, lowering the risk of abuse.

Naltrexone and rarely Suboxone are used by physician opioid addicts who are required to remain drug-free as a condition of their medical practice. Although physicians make up a tiny percentage of opioid addicts in the US, they underscore the point that all forms of drug treatment—including the use of opioid antagonists—are highly dependent on the incentives established to promote recovery by raising the cost of continued drug use. Physicians who have been identified as opioid addicts typically have strict supervision, including frequent random drug tests, and strong incentives not to use drugs nonmedically. If physician addicts relapse to drug use, they may lose their licenses to practice medicine, a major cost. Treating physicians with strict testing for drug use is a good example of the environmental approach to addiction treatment.

The discovery of opioid antagonists opened the possibility of finding antagonists for many other abused drugs, especially cocaine. One problem with using medicines to block the effects of abused drugs is that drug users can get high on many different drugs, each acting on the pleasure centers of their brains through entirely different mechanisms. Antagonists that block one mechanism to get high do not block others. This means that while addicts treated with opioid antagonists cannot get high on heroin (or any other opioids),they can—and all too frequently do—get high on alcohol, cocaine, and other drugs not blocked by the opioid antagonists.

The three medicines used to treat opioid use disorders—methadone, buprenorphine and naltrexone—are all specific to opioid use. They have no effect whatsoever on the use of other drugs of abuse. It is rare to find a person suffering from opioid use disorder who does not also abuse other drugs, usually many other drugs, including alcohol.

There is an intense interest in the development of new and more effective medicines for the treatment of severe alcohol use disorders because of the serious consequences of these disorders, their high prevalence (15 million people in the US had an alcohol use disorder in 2016[2])

---

[2] Substance Abuse and Mental Health Services Administration. (2017). *Key substance use and*

and the lack of successful treatments. For these reasons, it is easy to predict that there will be many new medicines to treat alcohol use disorders (as well as other substance use disorders) marketed in the years ahead.

For all addicts, the key word in medicated-assisted treatment is "assisted." The medicine is not the treatment for the disorders but instead the medicine assists in the treatment. These medicines are all prescribed by physicians. Before using any of these medicines, it is essential to have a medical evaluation and to have medical supervision over their use.

Addiction is a disease of the body, mind, and spirit. Reducing cravings with medication only works as long as the medicine is used. Experience shows that few addicts are willing to take these medicines for their entire lifetimes. A combination of talk therapy, co-occurring disorder assessment and treatment, and ongoing attendance at a support group like AA or NA usually is necessary to treat the complex, chronic disease of addiction and to ensure lifelong abstinence from all drugs of abuse. The drug-free treatment programs that are evolved from the Minnesota Model need to use medicines appropriately in support of their goals of long-term recovery. At the same time MAT programs need to integrate the Twelve Step and other recovery support into their programs. Perhaps most importantly, as discussed in the following section, treatments that use and do not use medicines both need to be evaluated on their ability to reduce the all-too common problem of relapse and instead to produce long-term recovery.

Recovery is about a whole lot more than the craving for drugs. It is a major change in the person away from the self-centered, dishonest, and resentful lifestyle of the active addict into a life of caring about others, honesty, and gratitude. No pill or injection can do that. Only the hard work of recovery can.

The Multidisciplinary Approach to Treatment

For many years, the core of modern addiction treatment has included education about the disease concept of addiction and long-term participation in the Twelve Step fellowships based on Alcoholics Anonymous (AA). More recently, the multidisciplinary approach based on the Minnesota Model has evolved to incorporate other research-based therapeutic methods, such as Cognitive Behavioral Therapy (CBT) and Motivational Enhancement Therapy (MET) along with Twelve Step Facilitation (as well as medication-assisted treatment). CBT helps patients gain insight into how their thoughts affect their behaviors and gives them

---

mental health indicators in the United States: Results from the 2016 National Survey on Drug Use and Health (HHS Publication No. SMA 17-5044, NSDUH Series H-52). Rockville, MD: Center for Behavioral Health Statistics and Quality, Substance Abuse and Mental Health Services Administration. Available: https://www.samhsa.gov/data/

techniques for replacing dysfunctional addiction-driven thinking with more rational thinking that promotes healthy behavior. MET, as used with the Stages of Change described earlier, helps patients move from resisting the hard changes they have to make to recover, to embracing these changes based on their own desire for health rather than just complying with their counselors' and family members' wishes. Many treatment programs use Twelve Step Facilitation to take patients through the first three of AA's Twelve Steps, where they admit they have an unmanageable disease, agree they need help, and make the decision to accept that help. Some will add the fourth and fifth Steps where patients do a personal inventory of the harms they've committed while drinking and using other drugs and then tell a trusted person—such as a clergy member, a counselor, or their AA or NA sponsor—what they've written in that inventory

For each patient, all of these therapies are delivered in individual and group sessions according to an individualized treatment plan determined after a thorough addiction and psychological assessment. These are often complemented by lectures on recovery topics, such as the Steps, denial, spirituality, and emotional health. More and more, not only is physical health being emphasized, including exercise and diet, but also non-sectarian spiritual health as well, with mediation techniques taught as a part of the treatment regimen. This holistic approach has evolved to treat addiction as a disease of the whole person—mind, body, and spirit—or as some would have it, as a bio-psycho-social disorder.

Another big change taking place in addiction treatment is a new emphasis on diagnosing and treating co-occurring psychiatric disorders at the same time as the addiction is treated. Previously, it was thought that the addiction needed to be treated before these other disorders were addressed, but high relapse rates among people with depression, anxiety disorders, PTSD, and other mental health disorders sparked research that showed it was more efficient and effective to treat all these conditions in the same space and time, if possible. This has included recognition of the high rates of trauma from sexual and physical abuse, especially among women, and the need to specifically address this issue to ensure long-term recovery. Add to this the unique challenges faced by special populations—such as LGBTQ, racial and cultural minorities, and the disabled—and it becomes clear why the requirements for designing a responsive and effective addiction treatment program have grown exponentially. This has put a burden on treatment programs to retrain their staff and include more social workers, psychologists, and psychiatrists in their programs. Where in the past most addiction counselors had their own recovery in AA and a two-year degree as their credentials, it's more common now for counselors to have a master's degree and even a PhD in addiction counseling.

Modern addiction treatment also involves the family. The disease concept holds that not only is the addict sick but so is the addict's family. Typically, abstinence-based residential treatments have five to seven days for "Family Week," when family members are brought into the treatment process and helped to understand their role in both the disease and the recovery, including the importance of the family attending Al-Anon meetings frequently and for a long time.

Different Treatment Modalities

Although addiction treatment used to mean a twenty-eight-day inpatient stay for people with health insurance or the ability to pay for their treatment, this was seldom the model in publicly funded addiction treatment. Many public sector programs used other methods, such as methadone treatment (described above), therapeutic community programs (yearlong intensive residential programs, now used mostly for criminal offenders), or outpatient drug-free counseling programs.

The widespread use of MAT for opioid use is now dominant in addiction treatment especially but not only in public-sector treatment. The use of MAT for opioid use disorders has also spread to many residential and outpatient treatment settings that previously did not use medicines. To recap, buprenorphine has similar effects to methadone but is much less likely to produce overdose death when abused and it can be prescribed by physicians outside of formal addiction treatment programs. Well over a million heroin and other opioid addicts are being treated with buprenorphine. Naltrexone, which is available in oral daily doses and in once-a-month implants under the skin, is an opioid antagonist so it has none of the opioid effects from pain relief to overdose death potential. It cannot be abused because it does not stimulate brain reward, produce a high. Suboxone combines buprenorphine and naloxone, a drug that prevents the intravenous misuse of buprenorphine. While buprenorphine has been widely prescribed by physicians to treat opioid dependence for more than a decade now, what is entirely new is the recent use of both buprenorphine and naltrexone in recovery-oriented residential and intensive outpatient treatment programs, programs that previously had refused to use medication in the treatment of addiction.

As the multidisciplinary abstinence-based model revolutionized drug abuse treatment in the private sector, similar changes began to take place in publicly funded addiction treatment. The therapeutic communities became the first publicly funded treatment programs to grasp the Twelve Step philosophy and to integrate Twelve Step Facilitation along with other evidence-based modalities into every aspect of their programs. The Twelve Step approach to lifelong recovery also made increasing inroads, being incorporated with both methadone and other MAT treatment modalities as well as in outpatient drug-free treatment programs in the public sector.

I have seen that MAT is fully compatible with attendance at Twelve Step meetings. It takes some skill at times, because some more traditional Twelve Step groups define any use of potentially addictive medicine, especially methadone and buprenorphine, as "active addiction" and therefore consider such medicines incompatible with abstinence-based recovery. However, just as eventually happened with psychiatric drugs—such as antidepressants and antianxiety medications—Twelve Step groups are becoming more accepting of members' use of anti-addiction medications as long as they are taken as prescribed and not to get high. In the methadone program I studied, for example, two-thirds of the methadone patients went to Twelve Step meetings and 90 percent of them considered the meetings to be helpful.

Meanwhile, cost consciousness in health care in the 1970s and 1980s promoted a new generation of addiction treatment programs that use shorter and more flexible inpatient stays as well as intensive outpatient treatment (IOP), which may involve participation in treatment several hours in the evening three to five days a week. This intensive outpatient addiction treatment approach permits addicted patients to continue to live at home and to work while in treatment. Intensive outpatient programs lower the cost of addiction treatment, which is especially important for low-income families or other people with inadequate insurance. As the quality of such services has improved over time and included the same basic elements of inpatient multidisciplinary programs, people who complete intensive outpatient addiction treatment tend to do as well as those who complete inpatient treatment.

There is an urgent need for new and better research on both prevention and treatment, research that is focused on the clear drug-free public health goals. For prevention that means the One Choice of no use by youth under twenty-one of any alcohol, tobacco (nicotine), marijuana and other drugs for reasons of health. For treatment it means achieving long-term or five-year recovery which includes abstinence from the use of alcohol and other drugs. Further, more research is needed on many areas where drug use plays a major role, for example, in education and the workplace. What are the most cost-effective ways to reduce the negative impacts of alcohol and other drug use in schools and workplaces? The roads and highways are now suffering not only from alcohol-impaired driving but also drug-impaired driving. There is little research today on improved strategies to reduce drug-impaired driving, an urgent national safety priority. Over a million Americans are arrested each year for alcohol-impaired driving. Many find their ways to recovery through these arrests. We need to match this with new strategies to deter and detect drug-impaired driving and to channel similar numbers of these drives into education and treatment. We need new research on why drug users so commonly use multiple drugs at the same time and why over 90 percent of drug overdose deaths involve multiple drugs. There are solid biological reasons that drug users spend their money on multiple drugs and don't focus on any one specific drug. Impairment, including the ultimate impairment—death—is often heightened by polydrug use. This too is an urgent research priority.

The central goal of addiction treatment—whether inpatient or outpatient, and whether medications are used or not—is not only to get addicted individuals off drugs, including alcohol and marijuana, but to break through denial and help them and their families accept the reality that they have a brain disorder that requires a lifelong program of recovery based on abstinence from alcohol and other drugs and, usually, long-term use of Twelve Step and other recovery-support programs.

It is important that all substance abuse treatment be evaluated on a single goal, the program's ability to produce sustained recovery. I use the five-year recovery standard. I predict that when this standard is used widely, treatment programs will work to achieve the goal to validate their existence. They will compete with all other treatment programs on a level playing field. For too long substance abuse treatment has been unaccountable for long-term outcomes. Instead addiction treatment programs have mostly been evaluated on their success only while patients are in treatment rather than on what happens to the patients when they leave the treatment programs.

More research on addiction treatment is needed. The most important new research must focus on the tragically common problem of relapse after all forms of treatment, whither using medications or not. The MAT programs see themselves as lifelong but their patients mostly leave in less than a year. The programs that do not use medicines commonly assume their patients will attend recovery support after treatment completion and continue to be drug-free. However, most of their patients stop recovery support and return to drug use. Treatment needs to be improved so that the outcome of treatment is lasting recovery, not relapse as it is today. Integration of the care of addiction into all of health care including long-term, even life-long monitoring for relapse is one good way to extend the benefits of addiction treatment.

The Elements of Good Addiction Counseling

There are three central elements in good addiction counseling in any addiction treatment program. The first element is listening to the unique story of each user of alcohol and other drugs. This is a great gift that the counselor gives the patient and the patient's family. Taking a careful history of one's life and a clear description of one's history of alcohol and other drug use, of the problems resulting from that use, as well as a history of that person's unique life and ambitions separate from addiction, constitutes the vital first step in the process of addiction treatment. The counselor needs help the patient have hope for a better life in recovery.

The second element of good counseling is helping the drug user understand the disease concept of addiction and how it played out in the patient's own life. This is the addict's life story from the initial flirtation with alcohol or other drug use to falling in love with that substance—when the addiction switch is turned on—to hitting bottom and finally to start getting well. Alcohol and other drug users need to understand the disease concept and relate it to their own lives. Initially, most users entering treatment think they are different from other patients. If they are to get well, I have learned that they usually need to see the similarities of their stories to the standard story of the typical addict's life.

The third element of good counseling is to help the drug user find his or her way to one of the Twelve Step programs or to some other community support program. This is the path to lasting recovery. Going to meetings and working the Twelve Steps is the best relapse prevention strategy. This third stage involves identifying barriers to joining a recovery community and helping the addict overcome those barriers in order to achieve a stable relationship with one or more Twelve Step fellowships.

When I see treatment programs built on these ideas of listening, teaching, and guiding to recovery, I have optimism that most of their clients will not only get well, but stay well. The landmark 2016 Surgeon General's report *Facing Addiction in America* on alcohol, drugs, and health confirms this:

> "Well-supported scientific evidence shows that substance use disorders can be effectively treated, with recurrence rates no higher than those for other chronic illnesses such as diabetes, asthma, and hypertension. With comprehensive continuing care, recovery is now an achievable outcome."[3]

Aftercare

Following intensive inpatient or outpatient addiction treatment, some form of systematic aftercare is necessary. This can be a structured outpatient or halfway house treatment, often involving drug urine testing to ensure that drug and alcohol use does not resume, plus regular attendance at Twelve Step meetings and psychotherapy group sessions, with or without individual or family counseling. The formal aftercare period can lasts six weeks or far longer. Aftercare is a continuation of the professional care that

---

[3] US Department of Health and Human Services (HHS), Office of the Surgeon General. (2016). *Facing Addiction in America: The Surgeon General's Report on Alcohol, Drugs, and Health.* Washington, DC: HHS. https://addiction.surgeongeneral.gov

is found in formal addiction treatment and, ideally, a bridge to lifelong Twelve Step fellowship attendance. At the start of aftercare, the therapy sessions may be daily or several times a week. Later in the aftercare process, therapy sessions may be once a week or even once a month. Throughout the aftercare period, Twelve Step meetings may be attended three to seven times a week, or more often. In a very real sense aftercare is all of life after treatment. Like the disease of addiction, aftercare is for life, just like maintenance programs for other serious chronic diseases, such as diabetes, heart disease, and cancer.

Relapse Prevention

One of the main challenges for people in aftercare and in ongoing recovery is to learn ways to prevent the common, and sometimes deadly, problem of relapse. No matter how good a treatment program is, it can't "cure" this lifelong disease. Completing treatment does not mean that addicted people no longer have the problem of addiction. Getting well starts with not using any drugs nonmedically and not using alcohol. Being "clean and sober" was usually impossible for addicts to imagine before they got into treatment. Because the idea of life without alcohol and other drugs is overwhelming and even frightening, the Twelve Step fellowships break the goal down into living clean and sober "one day at a time." One of the central goals of both aftercare and life in recovery is not only preventing relapse, but managing a relapse if does occur. This requires finding ways to solve problems, including dealing with painful feelings, without resorting to the old bad habits of alcohol and other drug use.

Key triggers for relapse include feeling Hungry, Angry, Lonely, and Tired. These common and dangerous feelings are captured in the acronym HALT to help addicted people recognize these common danger signs in their own feelings. Recovering addicts learn that feeling hungry, angry, lonely, or tired is a trigger to relapse. They learn what to do to prevent relapse, including how to manage these and other difficult feelings without turning to alcohol and other drugs, as they typically did when actively using. The best way for addicted people to deal with high-risk feelings on the edge of a relapse is to go to Twelve Step meetings then and/or to call their sponsors—people with solid recovery experience who mentor other members with less experience. (We'll talk more about the role of sponsors in the next chapter.)

We mentioned earlier that Cognitive Behavioral Therapy (CBT) has proven to be an effective treatment tool for changing one's thoughts and behavior when it is incorporated into a multidisciplinary treatment model. This approach to self-management is playing an increasingly positive role in relapse prevention.

The goal of CBT is to increase the addicted person's ability to cope with high-risk situations that commonly lead to relapse, including problems in both relationships and in the management of thoughts and feelings. The therapy trains addicted people to identify their personal triggers for drinking and drug use and to learn new techniques to cope with these problems. For example, the addicted person learns to manage anger in ways that are constructive by identifying and changing the thoughts that trigger that anger. An effective anger management technique is to put the angry feelings into words and to seek direct or indirect resolution of the problem that led to the anger. Other anger management techniques are to let time pass before acting on the anger, to step away from the person or setting that causes anger rather than toward that person or setting, and to talk the feeling over with friends or therapists rather than acting on them.

Preventing relapse means, in addition to handling feelings that can trigger relapses, finding new friends who are clean and sober and who live positive, productive lives. Relapse prevention also has an environmental dimension requiring staying away from the places and situations that were connected with drug and alcohol use. Once common recovery saying sums it up: "If you don't want to slip, don't get into slippery places." Again, a slip is a brief return to drug and alcohol use on the road to recovery. In contrast to a slip, a relapse is a more sustained and problem-generating return to substance abuse. For example, a slip may be a single use of alcohol or other drugs by a recovering person, or it may last a day or two. A relapse may last for as little as a few days or for as long as many years.

Addiction treatment is the beginning of a hopeful, long-term project. The road to recovery is sometimes marked by relapses of longer and shorter periods of time when the person who has been in treatment returns to the use of alcohol and other drugs. Sometimes relapses lead to readmission to the original treatment program or admission to a different treatment program; in other cases, a return to working a solid Twelve Step program, including regular attendance at meetings, is all that's required to get back on the road to recovery. Relapse may come soon after release from treatment, or it may come many years into sobriety. Every addicted person needs to feel the reality of the risk of relapse at all times. It can happen anytime, and it can build over time or erupt in an instant. At Twelve Step meetings, the most important person in the room is not the member with twenty-five years of sobriety; it is the person who last used today or yesterday. Often that person had a period of sobriety, sometimes a long period of sobriety, before the relapse. It is important for the entire group to hear the story of that relapse and to use it to deepen their own recoveries.

Because relapses after treatment are both so common and so frustrating for all involved, a great deal of study has gone into identifying the factors that are likely to lead to relapse. These factors range from psychological changes, such as the emergence or re-occurrence of depression or other mental illness, to environmental factors, such as the loss of a job or family distress. Relapse is usually not a simple, singular event. It is often a long process that begins with distancing from aftercare and from participation in Twelve Step fellowships leading to reemergence of denial that the person is an addict at all and that any use of alcohol and other drugs is likely to quickly lead to full-blown active addiction. Addicts who are at high risk of relapse come to believe that they can use alcohol or some other drug in a controlled fashion, or they give up caring about their own well-being, as the sense of loss they feel in giving up their addictive substance comes to outweigh the benefits they feel from being clean and sober.

A relapse can lead to a worsening of the addiction and a heightening of the pain caused by addiction and can end with a new, and often a lower, bottom. The best way to reduce the risk of relapse is to remain active in aftercare treatment and/or to continue to attend meetings of one or more of the Twelve Step fellowships. Families can help to reduce the risk of relapse by actively continuing participation in Al-Anon.

How Good Can We Expect Treatment Outcomes to Be?

Some time ago I reflected on my career in addiction treatment and thought about how common relapses were after treatment. They are so frequent that many experts have defined relapses as one of the principal features of addiction. Most treatment programs had far more relapsed patients entering treatment than first-time patients. It hit me that in my practice, I had worked with many addicted physicians who were participating in a state Physician Health Program (PHP) who went to the same treatment programs as many of my other patients but the physicians seldom relapsed. They completed treatment and they sustained recovery. What can be learned from that experience? I recruited two colleagues to conduct the first national study of a single episode of care in the PHP system of care management, a study that has now produced ten professional studies and been widely quoted when there is a question about long-term outcomes.[4]

When physicians have an addiction to alcohol or other drugs, there is an understandable concern about the safety of their patients, a concern reflected in the state medical boards which license physicians. When a physician is suspected of addiction by patients, colleagues, family, or others, they are referred to their state PHPs for formal evaluation. Needless to say, most physicians do not welcome this scrutiny and do not think they have a drug or alcohol problem. Participation in the PHP programs is entirely

---

[4] DuPont R. L., McLellan A. T., White W. L., Merlo L., and Gold M. S. (2009). Setting the standard for recovery: Physicians Health Programs evaluation review. *Journal for Substance Abuse Treatment, 36*(2), 159-171.

voluntary. The PHPs have no punishment to deliver for physicians who fail due to drug abuse—physicians found to be addicted only lose the safe harbor provided by the PHPs for physicians who participate in their programs, because participation ensures the medical boards that they are drug-free and complying with their recovery programs. All of the physicians can refuse PHP care—but then they face their medical licensing boards where they may lose their licenses.

If physicians are diagnosed with substance use disorders, they are referred to treatment, often thirty days of residential treatment but sometimes as long as ninety days or, less often, to an intensive outpatient program. They are evaluated for other disorders, including anxiety and depression, and when there are co-occurring disorders, those also are treated. When the physicians leave addiction treatment, they are followed by their PHPs with intensive random testing for any use of alcohol or other drugs. That means that every day for about five years, the physicians are required to go online or to call to see if that day they must be tested. Initially the random testing is often once or twice a week, but after a long period of abstinence from any alcohol or other drug use, the testing frequency may be reduced to once a month. But at all times the testing is random, meaning they can be required to be tested the very next day after they were last tested. Any use of alcohol or other drugs or any missed test generally leads to the physician being removed from practice and reevaluated for more intensive treatment.

Overall, about half of the 904 physicians in our study were alcoholics, about a third were opioid addicts, and about a sixth were addicted to other primary drugs of abuse.[5] They were required to attend community support programs at least four times a week, usually more often. Typically, that meant AA and NA but other community support was permitted. The results: During up to five years of random testing, 78 percent of the physicians never had a single missed or a single positive test for alcohol or other drugs. Of those who had at least one positive or missed test, two out of three did not have a second positive test. About 85 percent successfully completed this single episode of care management. Many of those who failed in a single episode of PHP care management returned to the PHP for a second episode of care and later entered recovery.

A question came up about how stable these remarkable outcomes were after the testing was completed. We conducted a preliminary follow-up study of physicians five years after their last mandatory alcohol and drug test. Remarkably, 96 percent of the physicians examined in this anonymous

---

[5] DuPont R. L., McLellan A. T., White W. L., Merlo L., and Gold M. S. (2009). Setting the standard for recovery: Physicians Health Programs evaluation review. *Journal for Substance Abuse Treatment, 36*(2), 159-171.

study reported that they were in recovery and two-thirds were continuing to go to Twelve Step meetings. We asked them what aspect of their PHP experience was most helpful to them. The number one answer was their participation in the Twelve Step fellowships. Number two was their experience in formal treatment, even though this was a small percentage of their time in PHP care management. Many of the physicians we studied in this follow-up study reported that they entered the programs resentful and angry. They mostly left PHP monitoring feeling that their PHP experiences had saved their lives, their families, and their careers.

Why is this study important? It shows that it is possible to make recovery, not relapse, the expected outcome of treatment. Further it shows how this can be done—how the benefits of good treatment can be extended for years after treatment is complete—by intensive monitoring with serious consequences for any relapse and with attention to all the patient's needs, including co-occurring disorders, and, perhaps most important, with long-term immersion in the Twelve Step fellowships.

While physicians are clearly an unusual population, addiction is a biological disease that can affect anyone. There is an important lesson in the PHP experience that needs to be widely applied: the addict on his or her own is often highly ambivalent about stopping drug use and even when stopping is highly vulnerable to relapse. The genius of the PHP model comes from the sustained, serious leverage applied to physician addicts.

There other similar examples of sustained and effective leverage in the management of commercial pilots and attorneys with addiction showing that these remarkably good results are possible in addicted populations other than physicians. Even more importantly this care management system has resonance with the criminal justice system where 5 million Americans are now on parole and probation, about two thirds of which are suffering from substance abuse problems. A growing range of innovative programs in the criminal justice system use strategies similar to the PHPs, including the well-known drug courts and the less well known HOPE Probation and 24/7 Sobriety. These programs, which I have called the "New Paradigm" of care management use leverage in various forms to shape the initial experiences of the addicted individuals and which impose strict monitoring to discourage any use of alcohol or other drugs.[6] The New Paradigm programs typically encourage active engagement with recovery support including the Twelve Step fellowships and other community programs.

It is important to think anew about the role of the criminal justice system in addiction. I have seen in my practice time and again when my patients are engaged by the criminal justice, they are newly interested in

---

[6] DuPont R. L., & Humphreys, K. N. (Humphreys, K. (2011). A new paradigm for long-term recovery. *Substance Abuse, 32*(1), 1-6.

treatment and newly open to entering recovery. There are two vital roles for the criminal justice system. First and foremost is the role of the criminal justice system in reducing the availability of illegal drugs including both the purely illegal drugs and the diverted prescription drugs. Without effective interdiction our communities are flooded with drugs fueling the drug epidemic and overdose deaths. The growing effectiveness of illegal drug suppliers is adding urgency to this role of the criminal justice system. Commonly overlooked, however, is the second crucial role of the criminal justice system as a uniquely effective engine of recovery. It is essential that the drug policy of the future take full advantage of linking the healthcare system with the criminal justice system to achieve goals that neither can achieve alone. Illegal drug sales are serious criminal offenses needing strong responses. Drug use, including the drug use of drug sellers, is best handled by strict consequences for any continued drug use and when necessary, treatment.

The PHPs and the innovative criminal system programs show that the benefits of these programs are long-lasting to the extent that the participants actively engage recovery support communities both while under supervision and after it ends. These innovative programs use external leverage—for the physicians their licenses and for the criminal justice system the force of law—to require active participation in addiction treatment and recovery including abstinence from the use of alcohol and other drugs. These are powerful engines of recovery. In the process the addicted people transition from being required to be abstinent and to participate in recovery support in to voluntary participation and active endorsement of the values of recovery. A follow-up study of physicians who successfully completed PHP monitoring contracts for substance use disorders five or more years ago showed that 96 percent reported they were in recovery and 67 percent reported they were still active participants in AA, NA or other community support.[7] These physicians were grateful for their recoveries despite the fact that virtually all of them had entered into treatment because of external pressure, and most at admission did not think they needed any help.

My conclusion is that this sustained wraparound approach is just what this doctor recommends to promote recovery. I encourage addiction treatment programs and families to adopt the principles of the PHP care management. This advice also applies to health care generally and to the criminal justice system. It also works for employers seeking to promote recovery in their addicted employees at all levels of the organization, from

---

[7] Merlo, L. J., & DuPont, R. L. (2016). Essential components of physician health program participation: perspectives of participants five years post-graduation. *Physician Health News, 1*, 14-15.

top to bottom.

The Benefits of Treatment

Formal addiction treatment takes a short time in anyone's life; if you are in treatment or are about to attend, give it everything you have from the first day to the last. Be open and honest with the staff, and participate in all of the program's activities. When I see people resisting the recommendations of their counselors and pulling out of some portions, or even all, of addiction treatment, I see people who are headed back to the pain and suffering of addiction, people who are continuing to run their own make-believe programs of recovery, right into disaster.

People who successfully complete addiction treatment commonly say treatment was the most important and busiest time of their lives. They report to whoever will listen that they learned more about themselves and their families, and about how life and addiction works, than at any other point of their lives. The time in an addiction treatment program is a happy and productive time for addicted people, as they develop strong relationships with the program staff and with other patients and families going through treatment with them.

In their treatment programs, addicted people and their family members meet people who have suffered from the same illness for many years and who are working toward recovery. They learn to have hope for a better and more honest life because they can observe people who were "worse than I am" who have gotten well. They learn to express their deep, personal doubts and fears. They learn about recovery. They learn the path to recovery and what it takes to sustain recovery. That word "recovery" is beautiful. It is a beacon toward which to work for the family and for the addict.

Family members come to addiction treatment with their own deep hurts and towering anger and frustrations. Most of all, family members come with their fears. They are angry at their addicted family members and frightened that they will be blamed for the addicts' problems and that their addicts will relapse. They think that all will be well in their families if only their addicted family members become clean and sober. They are reluctant to look at their own issues and work their own programs of recovery because they have spent so much time and energy living their lives in the shadow of their addicted family members. They have all but forgotten that they also have their own lives—lives that have nothing to do with the lives of their addicted family members. These attitudes reflect their codependence and are as common and understandable as are the attitudes of addicted people early in treatment.

Many addicted people and many family members grew up in families dominated by the addiction of parents and siblings, so they have their own painful feelings as adult children of alcoholics and drug addicts. These issues also are opened up in addiction treatment, and the healing process begins for old wounds. The entire family in addiction treatment begins to be honest with each other and with themselves for the first time in a long time, and sometimes for the first time ever. Families undergo this process with other families going through similar experiences in their addiction treatment programs. They deal with their hurts, fears, and hopes. They begin to find better ways of talking with each other and directly expressing to each other the love that they share. Family members go to their own meetings and work their own programs as part of addiction treatment. More about this as we look at the role of the family in chapter 8.

Honesty, the one-word antidote for addiction, is the simplest summary of what good addiction treatment is about. Honesty in personal life, in family life, and in community life—that is central to getting well from addictive disease. In treatment, addicted people and their families begin to think about and discover or rediscover the spiritual foundations of their lives. They often keep journals of their feelings and memories. Their lives are shared with more openness and candor. This may sound easy. It is not. Layers upon layers of dishonesty, grievances, hurts, and secrets must be overcome, and personal fears and insecurities must be faced. Not every addiction treatment program has these goals, and not every addicted person or family member in addiction treatment reaches these goals. I describe these characteristics of treatment because, in my experience, this is how good treatment works and how addicted people and their families experience addiction treatment when they are using it effectively to begin their own personal programs of recovery.

My simple advice to addicted people and their family members is to stick with your treatment program and to keep going to Twelve Step meetings—the longer the better. Find people who are in solid, successful recoveries and work with them. Stick with the winners. Do what they have done to get well.

I know that many addicts and their family members refuse to go to Twelve Step meetings, often telling their counselors that they attended meetings before and found them to be unhelpful or even destructive. Some addicts say they do not go because the people at the meetings "are not like me." Others do not go because the meetings are "religious," because they have difficulty in groups and therefore they cannot use these meetings, or because meetings are full of phonies and failures. We'll talk more about Twelve Step recovery in the next chapter, but for now I recommend that you give these meetings a chance. Go to more than one meeting—each meeting is different with major variations on how they're conducted and the chemistry of the people attending.

I have learned that there are many roads to recovery from addiction.

Whatever addiction treatment works is the one that is right for that person. I have come to my support for Twelve Step fellowships as a central part of addiction treatment not from any ideology, accident of exposure, or personal experience as a member of one of these programs. Rather, I have come to this belief from finding so many addicts in my own practice of psychiatry, in my own family, and in my own life who got well and stayed well through Twelve Step programs. In contrast, I have found few alcoholics and addicts who got and stayed well in any other way.

Facing Failure

Most of this book about addiction is optimistic. Addiction often can be prevented, and it often can be overcome successfully. The greatest enemy of both prevention and treatment is denial, a complex, deeply ingrained set of attitudes and behaviors that link up with enabling to foster addiction. Two of the factors that underlie both denial and enabling are fatalism and pessimism. This is commonly seen in the view that addiction is a hopeless problem or that it is someone else's problem. Addiction is a hopeful problem, and it is everyone's problem.

Although this is an important perspective on addiction, I am mindful of the many readers of this book who have confronted addiction in themselves—and even more often in a loved one—and who have made use of all the best available techniques for prevention and treatment. Some of these people have paid enormously high prices in terms of personal suffering, in financial burdens, and in the efforts they have made over many years to overcome the problems of addiction only to fail, over and over again.

I know that such people feel both guilty and angry. They feel guilty because they believe, down deep, that somehow they could have and should have done something different or something more to save the addicted person about whom they care. They feel angry because they have tried so hard for so long and have devoted themselves so thoroughly to the efforts to help, and still they have failed. They are angry because they know that most other people, whether they say so or not, believe that they should have been able to solve this problem of addiction. They hold themselves responsible for their lack of success, and they know that at some level others hold them responsible also. I am concerned that these good people will read this book and think that I, too, am blaming them for failing to achieve their goals. Nothing could be further from the truth.

My heart goes out to the victims of this desperate disease, both those who use addictive substances and those who love them. I share their feelings of pain daily, as I see in my practice addicts and their families who do not get well and who continue to suffer from this disease in its most active and deadly forms. This suffering falls into one of two distinct patterns. The first and most malignant pattern is continuous active addiction or continuing episodes of relapse into awful addiction alternating at times with brief periods of abstinence. This pattern of active addiction may go on until the addicted person dies, often of an overdose, an accident, an infectious disease such as AIDS, or violence related to the addiction. My cousin died this way in a drug-caused automobile crash during one of his many relapses.

The second pattern of long-term addiction is, in my experience, more common. These people learn from their painful experiences, from treatment, and even from attendance at Twelve Step meetings that they suffer from an incurable disease. They either stop their use of alcohol and other drugs by sheer willpower or they moderate and control their alcohol and drug use, more or less successfully. They seem to have a milder form of the addictive disease because the worst alcoholics and addicts cannot even give the appearance of controlling their use of alcohol and other drugs.

This second pattern of long-term addiction is more subtle and more likely to be chronic than the first pattern. The first pattern is so chaotic and destructive that it is likely to lead to some form of definitive bottom, either to an end of the addiction or to death, in fairly short order. This second pattern, on the other hand, can go on for decades—often decades of suffering for all involved.

For those who experience either of these two common patterns of failure, I can only say that I have seen and shared your suffering. I know that it is awful. Remember that today's failure is often the springboard to tomorrow's success. Life is a learning experience and addiction is a tough, persistent teacher.

The most important message that addiction can teach us and that I can give to you is that recovery, the third stage of getting well from addiction, is always possible as long as the addict is alive. Millions of people have reclaimed their alcohol and drug-hijacked brains. They and their families have gone on to live happy, meaningful lives no longer in under the power of addictive drugs. The next chapter is devoted to learning more about life in recovery.

7. RECOVERY FROM ADDICTION*

Addiction recovery programs based on the Twelve Steps of Alcoholics Anonymous (AA) are the bedrock of lifelong sobriety. When I see people addicted to alcohol and other drugs who have truly changed their lives and found new and better ways to live (what I recognize as a robust recovery), I usually see people who have made an enduring commitment to one or more of the Twelve Step programs. I have never seen anyone who has been harmed by participation in a Twelve Step fellowship, although there are some risks that are discussed later in this chapter. These programs are the biggest and most secure road to lasting, comprehensive recovery from addiction.

They are not, however, the only way to get well from addiction. Other abstinence-based forms of mutual aid and addiction treatments of many kinds offer hope as well. These include SMART Recovery (Self-Management and Recovery Training), which uses a cognitive behavioral approach instead of the Twelve Steps; Women for Sobriety, which de-emphasizes powerlessness and focuses on empowering women to stay sober; and Secular Organizations for Sobriety (SOS), which advocates members taking responsibility for their drinking and drug use instead of relying on a higher power. Whatever works for each addicted person and for his or her family is the best treatment for those people. My focus here on the Twelve Step programs is not intended to push aside alternatives. It is intended to ensure that you know that this is the largest, most well-traveled, and most accessible road to recovery from addiction in the US and throughout the world today. Twelve Step meetings are happening just about every day or night in practically every community in the country and

---

*Note: This chapter is based on material from a book written by Robert L. DuPont and John P. McGovern titled A Bridge to Recovery: An Introduction to 12-Step Programs, published by the American Psychiatric Press. This book helps people in major social institutions, such as religion, health care, and education, to make better use of Twelve Step programs to meet the needs of addicted people and their families.

increasingly throughout the world whereas the alternative organizations are mostly available in larger cities and meet with less frequency. Everyone interested in addiction needs to know what this road looks like and how to use it, even if another road to recovery is eventually chosen.

Twelve Step programs grew out of the experience of addicted people. Their experience, strength, and hope, gained at terrible personal cost, support the view that identifying alcoholism or addiction as a disease helps to overcome the guilt, shame, and isolation of the alcoholic and the addict. Understanding addiction as a disease allows the individual, and the family, to concentrate on conquering destructive behaviors by breaking free of self-defeating denial and futile attempts to solve the problem by willpower. For both the addicted person and the family, admitting loss of control over alcohol and other drug use is the essential first step in overcoming the denial that allows an addiction to maintain control over an addicted person's life. The Twelve Step view of the disease of addiction does not mean addicted people are not responsible for the negative consequences of their alcohol and other drug use. Far from it. As noted earlier, this program includes serious efforts to account for those whom the addict has harmed and making direct personal amends for those harms. This is a program of responsibility not irresponsibility.

Twelve Step organizations are often called self-help or mutual aid programs to distinguish them from professionally run drug treatment or mental health programs addressing the problems of addiction. All people who want help are welcomed at Twelve Step meetings, whether they are drug free or not. All that is required to join a Twelve Step fellowship is a desire, however ambivalent at the start, to stop using alcohol and other drugs. Twelve Step programs are not licensed by a government agency or covered by health insurance, nor do they charge fees. Meetings are usually held in public facilities, such as churches and other community locations, as well as in facilities devoted to Twelve Step meetings. Meetings typically last one hour and are held at the same time and place each week.

In most communities, there are several groups and, in larger communities, there can be hundreds of Twelve Step groups that meet each week. The Twelve Step programs are called "fellowships" because they are made up of members who all contribute actively to the programs. Typical Twelve Step fellowship members attend from one to several meetings a week for long periods of time, often for their lifetimes. Meetings may have ten or fewer members or more than a hundred members.

These programs have been classified as mutual aid as well as self-help because one of the great discoveries of AA is that only by banding together and helping others to get well can addicted people get well and stay well themselves. Twelve Step programs are spiritually based—but nonreligious—programs run by recovering people. They are not traditional self-help programs, because trying to get well the way the individual addicts chose to do it is how their addictions deepened. That's why Twelve Step members often reject the designation of their fellowships as self-help because alcoholics and other addicts have gotten into trouble precisely by doing things their own ways. Many do not like "mutual aid" as a description because they see their strength coming ultimately from a Higher Power. A person's Higher Power can be almost anything—the God of one's religion, the Twelve Step program and group itself, nature, a universal Spirit, and so on—just so it's something greater than yourself.

The Twelve Step programs are also not treatment, because that term is reserved for professionally run programs that charge fees for their services or are paid by taxpayers, health insurance, or some other source. Twelve Step programs are not the result of scientific studies of addiction or its treatment. They have evolved in open and practical ways based on the experience of addicted people, with effective techniques continuing and growing, and ineffective ones withering away over time. Members call these programs "fellowships of recovering people," or simply programs of recovery. This chapter is focused on these spiritually based programs modeled on the Twelve Steps and Twelve Traditions of Alcoholics Anonymous.

Twelve Step programs promote a comprehensive lifestyle of recovery. To halt addiction, it is important that addicts live a recovery lifestyle that includes maintaining honest relationships with family, other loved ones, friends, and co-workers. Recovery means living free of the use of alcohol and other drugs, and developing healthy self-worth. Group process plays an important role in the success of all mutual aid programs, including the Twelve Step programs, which depend on cooperation among members. They are coordinated and led, on a rotating basis, by individuals who are themselves in recovery. The Twelve Step fellowships provide not only guidance on working the Steps but also emotional support to counter the isolation, shame, and agony of addiction. Experienced members of Twelve Step programs inspire and mentor newcomers. Newcomers fresh from active addiction are the most important people at Twelve Step meetings. Newcomers remind other fellowship members of their disease, which always remains just one drink, or one drug use, away. Twelve Step programs help people gain the support and tools to control socially unacceptable and self-destructive behaviors that characterize addiction, through interaction with others who can identify with them and who have found successful ways to overcome these specific problems so that they can live satisfying and productive lives.

Twelve Step programs offer a systematic and carefully planned program for recovery, not just a meeting place or an opportunity to talk about one's problems caused by drinking and other drug use. They help disaffected individuals achieve successful, healthy social values as well as realistic self-worth through a set of lifesaving guidelines represented by the Twelve Steps and Twelve Traditions, healthy rituals, and a language to help them understand and overcome their addictions.

Newcomers at Twelve Step meetings are made to feel welcome and are encouraged to return regularly to fellowship meetings, giving a sense of belonging to addicts who have experienced relentless alienation and rejection. Use of positive verbal reinforcement and supportive attention by other members enhances socialization to pro-social values. Confessing a readiness to accept help is an important part of the Twelve Step philosophy.

The oldest and largest Twelve Step program is Alcoholics Anonymous (AA). It helps people overcome problems specifically with alcohol, although most members have also been addicted to other drugs. Narcotics Anonymous (NA) helps people overcome problems specifically with other drugs besides alcohol. Al-Anon is the program for friends and family members of alcoholics and Nar-Anon is the program for friends and family members of drug addicts. Today, there are literally dozens of different Twelve Step programs dealing with many behavioral health problems. These include Cocaine Anonymous, Marijuana Anonymous, Gamblers Anonymous, Sex Addicts Anonymous, Overeaters Anonymous, and groups for people with co-occurring addiction and mental health disorders, such as Double Trouble in Recovery and Dual Diagnosis Anonymous. Al-Anon, Al-Ateen, and Nar-Anon are Twelve Step groups for families of alcoholics and addicts, which we'll cover in the next chapter.

People new to AA, NA, and other Twelve Step fellowships are encouraged to find same-sex members who have been clean and sober for several years or longer, people whose recovery they see and admire, and ask them to be their personal guides, or "sponsors," to the fellowship and to recovery. Sponsors help their "sponsees" learn about the program and to work the Twelve Steps to recovery "one day at a time." Sponsees typically speak in person or on the telephone with their sponsors regularly—as often as every day early in their recovery. Being a sponsor is a major milestone in personal recovery, as the more senior addicts "pass on" their experience, strength, and hope to newcomers. Even newcomers perform this vital role in serving as role models to everyone in the group for the courage and commitment it takes to admit their powerlessness over their addiction and turn their lives over to working a program of recovery.

Acceptance leading to forgiveness is a vital component of the Twelve Step program for getting well. At meetings, discussion of each member's use of alcohol and other drugs takes place in a secure, understanding, and accepting environment. The promise of anonymity makes a trusting relationship possible, even with total strangers. "What is said here stays here" is the promise members make to each other. A feeling of inclusion is enhanced by the sharing of common experiences. The giving of support is balanced by the expectation of reciprocal encouragement for other members of the group. Complaining and self-pity are not encouraged, neither is telling someone else what to do. Stress reduction is another side benefit of being involved in a supportive fellowship. Abstinence from using alcohol and other drugs is stressful for addicts, with a tempting remedy for bad feelings of all sorts being the substances that have produced their addictions.

Characteristics of Recovery

- Abstinence is necessary for recovery from addiction, but abstinence alone is not sufficient for full recovery.
- Getting well with addiction requires working a rigorous and sustained program of recovery.
- The fellowships of the Twelve Step programs, led by Alcoholics Anonymous and Narcotics Anonymous, offer a program that has proven effective in helping millions of people find and sustain recovery.
- Addiction is a family disease—family members commonly suffer from codependence, where they protect the addict, enable addictive behaviors, and contribute to the progression of the disease. They often benefit from participation in the process of recovery, using Al-Anon, Co-Dependents Anonymous, Adult Children of Alcoholics, and other Twelve Step programs.
- Families can use the crisis of addiction to improve family functioning, including dealing with substance use disorders in other family members.

Alcoholics Anonymous

Before there was Alcoholics Anonymous, in 1934 Bill Wilson, a New York stockbroker with a severe history of alcoholism, stopped drinking after having coming close to death from alcoholism and failing to stop after many tries. Aware of the risk of relapse, in his quest to stay sober while on a business trip to Akron, Ohio, he sought out the companionship of another alcoholic and on June 17, 1935 met a surgeon, Dr. Bob Smith, who had himself tried and failed to stop drinking for years. In that meeting between the two alcoholics, Bill W. passed on what he had learned about staying sober by telling his story of finding the solution to his powerlessness over alcohol in turning his life over to a power greater than himself. Dr. Smith—called "Dr. Bob" in AA circles—was then able to stop drinking and he and

Bill W. became recognized as the founders of AA as they continued this tradition of helping other alcoholics by telling their powerful and inspiring stories of recovery to other alcoholics who still suffered. Within a few months there were around a hundred recovering alcoholics who formed the first AA groups, most of them in New York and Ohio. Bill W., with input from these early members, decided to put down what they had learned in writing and the book Alcoholics Anonymous, which came to be known as the "Big Book," was published in 1939 and became AA's textbook. It was in the Big Book that the Twelve Steps, the heart of the AA program, were first published. And it was with the inclusion of an essay titled "The Doctor's Opinion," by Bill's physician, Dr. William Silkworth, at the beginning of the book that alcoholism was first identified as a disease, and not a failure of will and morals.

The fellowship grew slowly at first. It wasn't until publicity from a 1941 magazine article about AA by Jack Alexander in the Saturday Evening Post brought such growth in the number of meetings and further dissemination of the Big Book that AA began to gain national prominence. Since then AA has become a major international movement with an estimated 118,000 groups and over two millions members in 175 countries world-wide as of 2016.[1]

In one of its many early identity-defining exercises, AA articulated the principle of singleness of purpose, committing itself to deal with one and only one problem: alcoholism. Singleness of purpose underlies AA's not being a job program, or a marital therapy program, or a religious or political program. AA recognized early that members had all of these problems, and many more, but that the AA program must limit itself to doing those things that were essential to achieve and maintain sobriety, nothing more and nothing less. Although AA did not deal with primary problems with drugs other than alcohol, from its beginnings AA has included abstinence from the use of other addicting drugs as clearly within the fellowship's definition of sobriety—a concept vital to the organization's singleness of purpose.

The valuable lesson here is "less is more." By focusing clearly on the major problem, and doing what must be done to solve that one problem, lives can be reclaimed, and families and even communities can be changed. If this single focus is lost, then the iron grip of addiction to alcohol and other drugs is reasserted and none of these worthy goals is likely to be achieved. If they do not maintain sobriety, then alcoholics are unable to solve their myriad other problems, most of which are made worse by, if not caused by, drinking. In the language of AA, "There is no problem so bad that it cannot be made worse by drinking."

---

[1] Alcoholics Anonymous. Estimates 2018. Worldwide A.A. Individual and Group Membership. Available www.aa.org

"Singleness of purpose" led AA to ignore the needs of people who were addicted exclusively or primarily to drugs other than alcohol, including marijuana, cocaine, and heroin. This same singleness of purpose—the focus on the drinking of people whose lives were made unmanageable by their use of alcohol—meant that AA also was not meeting the urgent needs of members of the alcoholic's family. Thus, Narcotics Anonymous and Al-Anon, respectively, were founded.

Narcotics Anonymous

Narcotics Anonymous was founded by Jimmy Kinnon and others near Los Angeles in 1953. Growth of the fellowship, modeled on AA, was slow at first but accelerated in the early 1980s with the publication of the book *Narcotics Anonymous*. Like AA's "Big Book," the NA book contained the program guidelines and a series of illustrative personal stories of addiction and recovery. As of May 2016, there were over 67,000 NA meetings in 139 countries.[2]

Narcotics Anonymous was started by individuals addicted to drugs other than alcohol who sought recovery but who found that Alcoholics Anonymous did not fully meet their needs. Of the five founding members of NA, three were members of AA. The NA fellowship redefined the rule of "singleness of purpose" to cover all of the many different drugs to which members were addicted. NA developed a somewhat broader program than AA had done, recognizing other compulsive activities and self-destructive mechanisms as contributing factors to addiction and comfortably accepting multiple addictions. Young addicts sometimes are drawn to NA meetings because of a general sense of more openness, a greater attention to the extended family, and the NA program's attempts to remain current with drug use trends and treatment innovations. NA meetings also can feel more contemporary since they often have fewer older, long-term members than do AA meetings. Nevertheless, NA adheres to Twelve Steps and Twelve Traditions nearly identical to those that are the foundation, and the strength, of AA with "my addiction" replacing the word "alcohol" and "addict" the word "alcoholic" in the Steps.

From the outset, NA defined alcohol as a drug so that members who were abstinent were expected not to use alcohol or other drugs. A cocaine addict cannot continue to use alcohol (or other drugs), claiming that he or she is addicted only to cocaine and uses alcohol "socially." NA sees mood-altering, or what is better called rewarding, drugs as the central problem, not the use of the one or two specific drugs on which the addict may have been especially hooked.

This NA attitude toward all addicting drugs is fundamentally not

---

[2] Narcotics Anonymous World Services, www.na.org.

different from that of AA. In AA there is a strong belief that alcoholics cannot use other addicting drugs and maintain their sobriety. The differences between AA and NA are not differences of kind but of emphasis. In AA, emphasis is singularly on alcohol, but there is a broader definition of sobriety, including all addicting drugs. In NA, the primary commitment is to addiction or substance abuse broadly defined, and not to the abuse of any one substance, such as alcohol or cocaine.

In many meetings of both NA and AA, these distinctions are now thoroughly blurred. However, in more traditional AA meetings, especially those with older members who see their problems with alcohol (a single, legal drug) as fundamentally different from those of young drug addicts (who use many illegal drugs and who often have criminal records), the distinction between NA and AA sometimes remains clear-cut, even though many alcoholics have arrest records for driving while impaired (DWI), a serious criminal offense.

The Twelve Steps and Twelve Traditions

At the core of AA, NA, and several other Twelve Step fellowships are the Twelve Steps and the Twelve Traditions. The Steps, and sometimes the Traditions, are read aloud at most Twelve Step meetings to provide a basic orientation to the meeting and to ensure that all fellowship members understand and discuss the basic Twelve Step program. The repeated reference to the Twelve Steps and the Twelve Traditions helps maintain the universality and consistency of what are otherwise quite diverse meetings. Although the Twelve Steps are discussed at meetings, their practice is personal and involves each member and his or her sponsor.

The first three of the Twelve Steps provide a foundation for abstinence by acknowledging the problem, coming to believe there is a solution to the problem, and deciding to work to achieve that solution. These steps confront the denial that is the driving force of addiction. The remaining nine steps outline the means of resolving the problem.

Steps Four, Five, Six, and Seven call for a personal moral inventory, revealing the results of that inventory to a Higher Power and another human being (usually one's sponsor, clergyperson, or sometimes a treatment counselor), having identified one's character defects or shortcomings, being willing to remove these defects, and then moving to exorcise them by asking the Higher Power to remove them. Steps Eight and Nine involve relationships to other people, making amends and restitution to others. Step Ten is a lifelong maintenance Step, bringing together all of the elements from Steps Four through Nine into a daily process of awareness, self-evaluation, and making amends. Step Eleven expands the spiritual relationship with the person's Higher Power or "God of your understanding" through prayer and meditation, and Step Twelve brings the individual full circle by practicing the principles embodied in the Steps and by helping others with alcoholism or other addictions. The Steps are meant to be worked through in the order in which they were written in order to have their full effect.

The Twelve Steps of Alcoholics Anonymous

1. We admitted we were powerless over alcohol—that our lives had become unmanageable.
2. Came to believe that a Power greater than ourselves could restore us to sanity.
3. Made a decision to turn our will and our lives over to the care of God as we understood Him.
4. Made a searching and fearless moral inventory of ourselves.
5. Admitted to God, to ourselves, and to another human being the exact nature of our wrongs.
6. Were entirely ready to have God remove all these defects of character.
7. Humbly asked Him to remove our shortcomings.
8. Made a list of all persons we had harmed, and became willing to make amends to them all.
9. Made direct amends to such people wherever possible, except when to do so would injure them or others.
10. Continued to take personal inventory and when we were wrong promptly admitted it.
11. Sought through prayer and meditation to improve our conscious contact with God, as we understood Him, praying only for knowledge of His will for us and the power to carry that out.
12. Having had a spiritual awakening as the result of these Steps, we tried to carry this message to alcoholics, and to practice these principles in all our affairs.

The Twelve Traditions (see appendix B) were first published in the April 1946 AA publication *The Grapevine* under the title "Twelve Points to Assure Our Future," and the final version was adopted at AA's first international convention in 1950. They were published in Bill W's book *Twelve Steps and Twelve Traditions* in 1953 and were included in subsequent editions of the Big

Book. They were later adopted by NA and are published in the NA textbook, *Narcotics Anonymous*. The Twelve Traditions are specific, practical guidelines governing the entire fellowship, not a vague accumulation of practices.

As the Twelve Steps represent the blueprint for an individual's ongoing recovery within the fellowships, the Twelve Traditions represent the constitution of the AA and NA fellowships as groups to ensure the smooth functioning of the Fellowship. The traditions stress such core principles as the primacy of members' common welfare and the primary purpose of carrying the message to other alcoholics, anonymity, protection from outside influence of media and other organizations, each group's autonomy and commitment to be self-supporting, and avoiding controversy by not having opinions on outside issues.

In addition to the Steps and Traditions, AA, NA, and the other Twelve Step programs have structured techniques for getting better, including a routine of regular attendance at meetings, the reading of books and pamphlets published by their organizations, and sponsorship by a more experienced member of the fellowship. The written materials on which the AA and NA fellowships are based are authorized and published by their World Service Offices, in New York City for AA and in Van Nuys, California, for NA.

Types and Structures of Twelve Step Meetings

Twelve Step fellowships have no formal membership or application process and no dues or membership fees. The only money collected is a small voluntary donation, usually a dollar or two, made at meetings to cover such expenses as room rental and coffee for the meetings. Most Twelve Step fellowships do not keep membership records. Individuals become affiliated with a particular fellowship by regularly attending meetings. Although there is a core group of individuals who make up a specific meeting, other participants attend to the extent that the meeting time, place, or availability meets their needs. Meetings of Twelve Step fellowships are open to everyone who seeks recovery.

The composition of meetings frequently depends on group identity, location, and population density. Most meetings have a mix of ages, genders, races, cultures, and sexual orientation but there are also population-specific groups as well, including groups for teens, all men, all women, LGBTQ, African American, Latino, and so on. In rural areas, where there is a smaller and less transient population, memberships of meetings are relatively constant. Urban and high-density suburban areas offer a large number of meetings to a comparatively more mobile fellowship population.

Important Features of Twelve Step Fellowships

- Based on Alcoholics Anonymous, which started in 1935
- Run by recovering people, not by health care professionals
- Use the Twelve Steps and the Twelve Traditions developed by AA
- Spiritually based, nonresidential, open to anyone who wants to stay clean and sober
- No charge to join, no dues for membership
- Lifelong participation

The Meeting

A typical Twelve Step fellowship group meets once a week at the same time and place. Each individual group usually has its own identity with a more-or-less consistent format and membership. In some instances, the membership of a meeting and the focus of the discussion vary dramatically from week to week. Meetings usually last one hour, but some are extended to ninety minutes or two hours. Twelve Step meetings are held at all times of the day, from early morning to late at night. Because of the large number of individual Twelve Step fellowship groups, meetings are available for members to attend 365 days a year in many areas. Many new members go to more than one meeting a day, especially when their lives have been disrupted terribly by their addictions. In NA, meetings may have descriptive names such as "Together We Can," "Monday's Miracles," "Talking Heads," or "Out of the Dark."

Twelve Step members usually have what is called a home group that's convenient in time and location and where they feel the most comfortable with the format and the relationships they've built with other members. This is the meeting that a Twelve Step member attends most consistently, usually varying attendance at several other meetings. Newcomers generally find sponsors at their home meetings and, in time, sponsor other newcomers there. Members usually assume volunteer responsibilities in their home meetings, including leading meetings themselves.

Elected or appointed volunteers fill leadership functions at each meeting. A secretary often convenes the meetings and takes care of paperwork and recognition of anniversaries of abstinence. The treasurer "passes the hat" for voluntary donations and is responsible for paying any rent or other bills for the meeting. A representative from the local Twelve Step fellowship committee may attend and report on organizational activities. Another person or persons may be in charge of setting up for the meeting, making coffee, and cleaning up afterward. At larger Twelve Step meetings, a member may assume responsibility for welcoming newcomers. These leadership functions are usually rotated every six months, providing an opportunity for many members to enhance their own recovery by helping others and ensuring that meetings are not dominated over time by particular leaders.

Types and Formats of Meetings

Twelve Step meetings are divided into two general types, open meetings and closed meetings, each having its own function within the overall fellowship. Open meetings welcome any interested member of the community. Twelve Step fellowships recognize that visitors may be motivated to attend an open meeting for a number of reasons. Individuals may feel a need to explore a personal drinking or drug problem without identifying as an alcoholic or addict, may be concerned about the alcohol or drug use of a friend or family member, or simply may be interested in educating themselves about the Twelve Step process. All people are welcome at open meetings. The only obligation placed on attendance at all Twelve Step meetings, including open meetings, is that of honoring the anonymity of others by not disclosing names outside of the meeting. Open meetings often conclude with a social time when refreshments are served.

Closed meetings of AA are limited to people who want to stop drinking whereas closed meetings of NA are limited to people who want to stop using other drugs. Other drug-specific Twelve Step meetings, such as Marijuana Anonymous or Cocaine Anonymous, focus on members stopping using a particular drug of choice, although people with cross addiction to multiple substances are welcome, as they are in AA (as long as alcoholism is the primary drug discussed) or NA. Closed meetings safeguard the anonymity of members and provide a secure and often more stable forum for the discussion of problems best understood by other members of a specific fellowship. The meetings are usually informal and encourage people to share their thoughts and feelings, either on the topic under discussion or around a personal issue related to drinking or using that they need to talk about. Generally, cross-talk—that is, unsolicited feedback or advice—isn't encouraged so that members feel free to say what they think without fear of criticism or attempts at amateur therapy. The point is to have a non-judgmental atmosphere where the only authority is the group conscience and the Steps and Traditions. Newcomers and those who especially may be concerned about their anonymity within the community often find closed meetings particularly helpful. These meetings provide a safe forum for concerns from troubled individuals that may be inappropriate or awkward to share in an open meeting.

Meetings composed of individuals with similar interests or backgrounds, such as health professionals, usually opt for a closed meeting format. By holding a closed meeting, professionals can discuss issues that would not be appropriate in a diverse group and can reduce the likelihood of encountering a problem with doctor-patient or attorney-client relationships that might occur at an open meeting. A number of professional Twelve Step groups have been established in recent years, such as International Doctors in Alcoholics Anonymous.

Within the two basic types of Twelve Step meetings are several formats that meetings can take. The following paragraphs briefly describe some of the common Twelve Step meeting formats.

A typical Twelve Step meeting opens with the secretary introducing himself or herself by first name only as an alcoholic and/or addict, welcoming everyone to the meeting, and inviting visitors and newcomers to introduce themselves by first names only. During the first part of the meeting, members may recite the Serenity Prayer, attributed to the theologian Reinhold Niebuhr: "God, grant me the serenity to accept the things I cannot change, the courage to change the things I can, and the wisdom to know the difference." Individual members may read a brief section from their organization's textbook, such as *Alcoholics Anonymous* or *Narcotics Anonymous*, usually including the Twelve Steps. General announcements of interest to group members typically take place either at a break midway through the meeting or at the conclusion of the meeting.

Meetings usually end with everyone standing in a circle, holding hands, observing a moment of silence, then reciting the Lord's Prayer, the Serenity Prayer, or whatever closing the fellowship has decided on. As the meeting disbands, the reminders "Keep coming back!" and "It works if you work it!" are often called out. Once a meeting is formed, it usually keeps the same format over long periods of time, even though meetings at other times and locations of the same Twelve Step fellowship in the same area may have slightly different formats. New meetings are founded when two or three fellowship members decide to start one at a new time or in a new location. Meetings that successfully meet the needs of members flourish and lead to more new meetings, whereas those that do not have declining memberships and often disband. There are generally four types of meetings, with some variations, depending on the group.

Topic meetings are usually led by a rotating leader who opens with topics involving recovery and fellowship issues. Recurring themes include denial, surrender, relationships, spirituality, and dealing with emotions that threaten sobriety, such as fear, anger, resentment, and grief. AA and NA slogans—including "First things first," "Easy does it," "One day at a time," and "Let go and let God"—are also common topics. Emphasis is placed on describing one's own thoughts and experiences and not on giving advice to others.

At a speaker meeting, one or more members of the fellowship are asked to speak at the meeting. Although the speaker may talk for the entire meeting, more often the speaker's presentation will be limited to a half hour. The secretary usually tries to achieve a balance between regular members and visiting members when scheduling speakers. The speakers' presentations generally consist of them telling their stories: "What it was like," when they were drinking and using, "What happened" to bring them to hit bottom and seek help, and "What it is like now" as they live a life of sobriety. After the presentation, the speaker may act as moderator for the discussion portion of the meeting. The first time a member speaks at a meeting is an important personal occasion marking a passage to a more responsible role within the fellowship. Although new speakers may find the experience difficult, it is nearly always a positive experience and a valuable aid in the process of recovery for the speaker and for the group. Sincerity and honesty are highly valued rather than polished presentations.

Step meetings, incorporating the Twelve Steps, provide a blueprint for developing individual spiritual growth within the Twelve Step fellowship. When a Step meeting is initiated, it usually begins by working on Step 1 at the first session in a discussion format and continues to focus on one Step at a time through Step Twelve; then the group returns to Step 1. Some meetings elect to work their way sequentially through the Twelve Traditions as well, so the cycle of meetings lasts twenty-four weeks rather than twelve weeks.

Big Book meetings are similar to Step meetings but involve readings from the basic text of the Twelve Step organization: AA's "Big Book" *Alcoholics Anonymous*, NA's basic text *Narcotics Anonymous*, or other fellowship publications. Passages are read and discussed by those attending the meeting.

At the opening of most meetings, the group leader will ask if anyone has an anniversary or "birthday" and will present a "chip" or token to acknowledge the length of the member's abstinence since entering the fellowship. The more commonly acknowledged intervals in the first year of recovery correspond with times when a newly recovering individual is most vulnerable to relapse, such as twenty-two hours or thirty, sixty, or ninety days. After that, chips are received annually on a person's anniversary. Fellowship members are on the honor system in these self-reports of abstinence. No drug tests are conducted, and no one falsely claiming a chip is confronted, even for obvious lies. The underlying value of the Twelve Step programs is honesty. Having seen many chip awards, I cannot imagine that more than a few people would want to go to the front of the group and claim a chip dishonestly, simply because of the strong value of honesty that motivates the group. In any event, chips have no force in dealing with employers, courts, or other authorities outside the Twelve Step fellowships, so there is no incentive for dishonesty in false claims within the fellowships.

Most meeting times and locations adopt one particular format, which may be reflected in the meeting name, such as "Stepping Free" or "Walking Thru the Pages." Some meetings vary their format by holding rotations of three weeks of speaker/discussion meetings, then one Step study meeting, or a similar combination. There are no established rules on meeting format, and meetings vary among fellowships, regions, and groups. In larger communities, there are Twelve Step meetings of many different types held at the same time throughout the week, so members have a wide choice of meeting formats throughout every day of the week. Individual members choose the meetings that best meet their needs. Some meetings focus on the needs of newer members of the Twelve Step fellowships, whereas others are more centered on the needs of long-term members.

Finding a Meeting

Typical Twelve Step meeting locations include community centers, church halls, schools, and club rooms. Meetings also may be held in institutions such as health centers, hospitals, social service agencies, drug and alcohol treatment centers, and correctional facilities. In urban areas, there are NA and AA clubs that rent space, including general meeting rooms, and hold meetings virtually around the clock, twenty-four hours a day, 365 days a year. This means that at any time of any day, a person can show up at the club and attend a Twelve Step meeting. At such Twelve Step clubs, meetings are often held for all the larger fellowships and many of the smaller fellowships. For example, there are often simultaneous meetings of AA, NA, and Al-Anon.

An information number can be found online for each organization, with contact information and for the larger organizations, such as AA, NA, and Al-Anon, printed in a meeting directory. Volunteers with local Intergroups, the clearinghouses for meetings in a particular city or area, provide meeting times and locations, and "on-call" fellowship members respond to personal requests for help as part of their own Twelve Step commitment. Urban areas with numerous meetings publish a directory with meeting information classified by location, day of the week, time of day, and type of meeting. Directories, often called "Where and When" guides, are available at open meetings or by calling the information number listed online or local telephone directory where one is still available. Many addicted people and their family members find their way to Twelve Step meetings through referrals from community organizations, such as schools, hospitals, and churches.

As we saw in the previous chapter, formal inpatient or outpatient addiction treatment lasting four weeks or longer is commonly used as a bridge to lifelong recovery and Twelve Step programs for addicted people and their families. The criminal justice programs, such as DWI programs, parole, and probation, as well as state physician health programs and similar programs for attorneys, can all be lead-ins to Twelve Step fellowships. Urine testing for drugs of abuse and employee assistance programs at work play similar roles for many addicted people today—they provide the incentive and the road map to addicts to help them find recovery in Twelve Step fellowships.

There are a number of Twelve Step meetings online now, including some identifying as AA, NA, or another addiction-specific program and others that are non-affiliated and simply offer a forum for addicted people to interact. These meetings open up many new possibilities for homebound individuals. Similarly, people who live in rural areas can now participate in more meetings per week online than are available in the immediate vicinity. Some of these meetings are set up on an ad hoc basis among a small group of users. Others are scheduled meetings with a more traditional format where users log in at an appointed time. You can find these meetings through a search using the key words "12 Step meetings," AA or NA meetings online, and so on. It's good to try out a number of meetings to find the right match for you. Be cautious about sharing any personal information until you're certain that this is a safe and valid Twelve Step forum.

Even then it is unwise to share details about behaviors that could be dangerous or self-incriminating if revealed. You don't have the same protections at a Twelve Step meeting that you do with a priest, lawyer, or doctor. At an NA meeting several years ago, I heard a woman describe her job as a police dispatcher and how she sold information about police drug busts to her drug dealer for drugs. She said people died as a result of her information. She was immediately advised by members of the group that, for her own protection, details like this are not appropriate for the meeting but that these facts could be discussed with her sponsor.

How to Find and Use a Twelve Step Program

1. Identify your addiction problem (for example, addiction to alcohol or other drugs, or loss of control over food, debt, or gambling).

2. Find a friend in the fellowship that deals with your particular addiction who can get you started, or look online for the telephone number of your fellowship and call for information. Choose meetings at a convenient time and place for you.

3. Go to three or four different meetings to find your home meeting, the one in which you are most comfortable. At each meeting ask people like you to recommend good meetings for you to go to. After a few inquiries like this, it is usually easy to find appropriate meetings.

4. Find someone of your own gender (or the opposite if you're gay or lesbian) who has at least one year of successful time in that program. Choose someone you like and respect, and ask that person to be your temporary sponsor.

5. With the guidance of your sponsor, work the Twelve Steps, in order, going to ninety Twelve Step meetings in ninety days if you haven't been in treatment and are using a Twelve Step program as your only means of recovery. Read and discuss the written material provided by your fellowship. Speak up, or "share," at every meeting you attend.

6. If you fail to make further progress after an initial positive experience, consider changing sponsors and find other meeting because, as you grow in the program, your needs change and different sponsors and meetings can give you different sorts of help.

7. Help other people find and use your fellowship, sharing your own experience, strength, and hope with those you know who have similar problems.

8. If you've given several Twelve Step groups a fair chance and just don't find this program helpful, find other non-Twelve Step mutual aid groups or systems of support in your family, community, religious organization where you can practice the principles and practices behind the Steps on a daily basis.

The Role of Literature and Media in the Twelve Step Movement

Although the Twelve Step fellowships do not encourage publicity, an extensive variety of literature is available through AA's or NA's world service headquarters, AA Intergroups, and at local meetings. AA and NA offer an extensive array of books and pamphlets. Most of the pamphlets are distributed free of charge, and the books, including their textbooks, are inexpensive. Literature published by the Twelve Step national organizations is written primarily for the alcoholic or addict entering and continuing in recovery. Alcoholics Anonymous also distributes a monthly periodical, *Grapevine*, that contains articles of interest to the recovering community.

Major publishing houses are now printing books based on the Twelve Step themes of spirituality, meditation, and recovery. In larger urban areas, there are stores that devote their entire stock to books, tapes, and other inspirational materials related to Twelve Step recovery. Most libraries and bookstores now have major sections devoted to books dealing with addiction and recovery, and of course the Internet offers a wide array of information from reputable sources.

Integrating Twelve Step Fellowships with Therapy

Going to Twelve Step meetings is no guarantee of success in overcoming with addiction, although I have never known an addict who went to meetings consistently, had a sponsor, and worked the program who did not get well from their addiction. Going to meetings is not an alternative to mental health or other medical treatment. The Twelve Step programs of recovery are not addiction treatment or treatment for any other problem, illness, or disease. AA and NA are not treatment for any other personal or psychiatric problems. Many addicted people find their ways to Twelve Step programs through formal addiction treatment programs as well as through the recommendations of therapists and doctors. Once in Twelve Step fellowships, addicted people with co-occurring psychiatric disorders often are better able to make use of mental health care and other forms of treatment. It is common for recovering addicted people who are in active psychotherapy to also attend Twelve Step meetings. I find in my own practice that working with someone in a Twelve Step fellowship facilitates our mental health work because the same principles that support recovery from addiction commonly, but not always, support recovery from mental disorders.

No medical or psychiatric treatment has proven as successful as Twelve Step programs specifically in getting people well from addiction. All too often, not only is formal, professional treatment for addiction not successful, it actually proves to be a screen behind which addiction continues and worsens as addicts and their families believe that they are doing something useful to cure the addiction by participating in a publicly or privately funded health care program. However, a major goal of the medical and psychiatric treatment of addiction is to help the addict find and use lifelong help in the Twelve Step fellowships.

For example, methadone treatment and other medication-assisted treatment regimens can help desperately ill addicts stabilize their lives, stop nonmedical drug use, and prepare for living drug free. There is no medical need to ever stop methadone or other MAT, but most MAT patients stop using medications including methadone, buprenorphine, naltrexone, and other medicines like Antabuse, acamprosate, and naltrexone for alcoholism. Both while taking medicines for addiction and after stopping their use, the Twelve Steps facilitate and support recovery. The Twelve Step fellowships do not replace medicines and medicines do not replace the Twelve Steps. They both have useful roles for many addicted people.

Sometimes, once alcoholics and addicts are clean and sober in recovery, they and their families want to use formal health care treatments including psychotherapy, the "talking cure." Many times, I have seen addicted people who did not benefit from years of psychotherapy join and use a Twelve Step program, get clean and sober, and then benefit from psychotherapy for the first time in their lives. Many addicted people, once in stable recovery, also are able to make religion a positive part of their new lives.

When addicts are actively using alcohol and other drugs, they are in no position to benefit from counseling or therapy, to say nothing of religion or education. Their minds are so obsessed with and impaired by their use of alcohol and other drugs that they can think of nothing else, certainly nothing that might come between them and their chemical lovers. Once addicts are abstinent, they have a chance of benefiting from diverse forms of therapy. Sometimes, as part of their medical and psychiatric care, addicted people in recovery need and benefit from the use of non-addictive psychiatric medicines, such as antidepressants. This is widely accepted in Twelve Step fellowships and AA has supported this in recent publications. I recommend caution by people in recovery for prolonged use of any controlled substance—especially benzodiazepines like Xanax, Klonopin, and Valium and stimulants like methylphenidate and amphetamine, such as Ritalin and Adderall. It is important that the prescribing physicians know of your status as a recovering alcoholic or addict and that your family and sponsor know all of the facts about your use of these medicines. The same applies to the use of opioids for pain by people in recovery. The first choice is not to use these drugs unless they are absolutely necessary. These drugs are mostly used for symptom relief, meaning they do not cure the problems for which they are used. In all cases, there are alternative treatments for these conditions that should be tried and that often are very effective. I have seen people in recovery use controlled substances successfully. But I have also seen many spectacular failures, so I am very cautious about using any controlled substances, especially prolonged and/or high-dose use, by people in recovery.

Twelve Step Fellowships: The Heart of Stable Recovery

For most people, Twelve Step fellowships are central to the experience of recovery from addiction. Some people, however, are able to give up their use of addictive drugs without going to a Twelve Step meeting. They discover the impossibility of living their lives with the addictive substance, and they find ways to stop using it and to avoid using it again in the future. Most cigarette smokers who stop smoking do so without the benefit of any treatment or program, and many of them remain abstinent for years, and often for their lifetimes. Sometimes that same pattern occurs for people addicted to alcohol and other drugs. Those who are successful have usually found a way to replicate the recovery principles and practices found in Twelve Step programs, often in their place of worship and through a network of friends and family.

There are those alcoholics and addicts who try to go it on their own and attempt to stay sober by willpower alone. My experience leaves me troubled by such attempts, especially by people who had a prolonged period of addiction to these substances and especially when the person has had repeated failures to achieve or sustain abstinence. I have seen too many of these people who try to stay abstinent by self-will relapse to addiction. This fragile state is called "white-knuckle sobriety" by members of the Twelve Step fellowships. Similarly, I have seen many people who have entered recovery through regular membership in a Twelve Step fellowship and who then stop going to meetings, only to relapse. Without continuing attendance at Twelve Step meetings, denial is all too likely to creep—or spring—back into the abstinent person's life, setting the stage for a painful, dangerous, and often prolonged relapse.

When people first go to Twelve Step meetings, they are usually confused, upset, and demoralized. They do not think they can be helped by anyone, least of all a group of nonprofessionals such as those who attend Twelve Step meetings. They fear making changes in their lives and cling to their old ways of handling their problems, even though their old ways have worked so poorly for them.

Newcomers reluctant to commit themselves to a Twelve Step program may notice that others at the meeting seem different from them in ways that seem important. The problems of other members of the Twelve Step group can seem dissimilar and often much worse than newcomers perceive their own problems to be. The rituals they may encounter at the meetings can seem foreign and off-putting. These rituals can even appear to have religious overtones as well, confirming some people's fears that Twelve Step groups are just a disguised form of religion. Most addicted people and their families have not found help in religion, and many are profoundly anti-religious by the time they go to their first Twelve Step meetings. Newcomers may find the same failures at meetings and conclude that the fellowships do not really work. These perceptions and the tendency to "affiliate out" are often part of denial: The disease of addiction is whispering to the addict to flee from the Twelve Step program.

After a few meetings, many addicted people conclude that they have given the Twelve Step program a chance and "it didn't work for me." This unfortunate pattern is an expression of the denial that perpetuates the addictive disease in the addict and in the family. My suggestion for newcomers is to keep going to meetings, get a sponsor, and work the program. Find the successful people at the meeting and work with them. Give your fellowship a solid chance to work for you. What is a "solid chance"? In my experience, it is ninety meetings in ninety days. I have never seen anyone do that and not find value in the Twelve Step fellowships. What I have seen often are people who go to a few meetings for a while and then drop out—usually without benefit of a sponsor or any serious working of the Steps. That sort of toe-in-the-water approach is bound to fail and the failure is not of the Twelve Step programs but of the half-hearted exposure to the programs.

Early in recovery, the best course is daily meeting attendance, followed, after several years of abstinence from the use of alcohol and other drugs, by attendance at Twelve Step meetings at least once a week—and more often when temptations to use and life challenges warrant. Just showing up at meetings is better than not showing up, but full participation with a sponsor and serious Step work is the most reliable ticket to lasting recovery. When addicted people are in stable recoveries—meaning they are certain that they continue to be alcoholics and/or addicts and that this status includes the lifelong risk of relapse—and when they have been clean and sober for many years, the frequency of attending meetings can sometimes safely be reduced. Stopping meetings, and not having a sponsor, is risky for any addicted person in recovery. Most often in successful and stable recovery, reasonably frequent attendance at meetings continues, with the focus shifting over time from sobriety itself to the quality of life that underlies the Twelve Step fellowships. With more experience under their belts, these people can give back by sponsoring newcomers and taking on active leadership roles in meetings. After working the first eleven Steps, all members can work Step Twelve by being of service to other alcoholics and addicts and to their communities. Dedicated and successful Twelve Step fellowship members continue to have a clear picture that a relapse is always just "one drink or drug use away" and that continued attendance at meetings and working the Twelve Step programs are essential to maintaining a healthy and rewarding recovery.

Experienced members of the Twelve Step fellowships also find that more frequent participation in meetings, even years into sobriety, can be helpful in dealing with personal crises of all kinds. For example, a member whose spouse dies or who loses a job may find it helpful to attend meetings once a day for a period of weeks or months to help deal with the feelings unleashed by the crisis, feelings that, if not dealt with, might lead to a relapse to alcohol or other drug use.

When I see a pattern of regular use of Twelve Step meetings, I am much more secure about the stability of the recovery and the long-term welfare of that person. This pattern is most often associated not only with being free of alcohol and drug use over the long haul, but with a positive and satisfying lifestyle.

Typically, people addicted to alcohol and other drugs start going to meetings when their lives are in shambles and they are desperate to find a path out of their deepening misery, out of their self-imposed chemical slavery. When their lives are stabilized in recovery, they keep going to meetings for two reasons: to reduce the risk of relapse into addiction and to find support in building better lives. It starts with a search for freedom from suffering and it shifts over time to a program of living a better life, including finding ways to handle the multitude of other problems besides addiction that come with living. There is an additional bonus: the satisfaction of helping others find freedom from chemical slavery and better ways to live their own lives.

Risks at Twelve Step Meetings

Twelve Step meetings are filled with addicted people in various states and stages of their disease. Most of them are stable in their recoveries and doing well in their lives. They are honest and responsible people. However, there are some dishonest people who are in the same meetings and who are still active in their addictive disease. A few people attend Twelve Step meetings while they continue to use alcohol and other drugs. Others may believe they can stop using their primary "drug of choice," such as alcohol or cocaine, and safely use other drugs. Many of these people will get clean and sober if they continue to attend meetings, get sponsors, and work the program. Some of the successful members will relapse for longer and shorter periods of time as they struggle with this difficult disease over their lifetimes.

When newcomers go to their first Twelve Step meetings, it can be hard for them to sort out the people serious about their recovery from the people who aren't. This is especially true of adolescents attending general Twelve Step meetings with adults. They are likely to be uniquely vulnerable to some of the more colorful characters who aren't serious about working a responsible program; this is particularly true of girls who might encounter predatory adult males. In fact, female newcomers of any age need to be aware of one of the most notorious risks of the Twelve Step meetings, the "Thirteenth Step." This is the sexual exploitation of newcomer women by sophisticated-appearing, malicious men in the program, who take advantage of the atmosphere of intimacy and trust that develops in the program. This is not meant to scare you about Twelve Step meetings but to alert you to the realities of the serious and challenging process of recovery.

A treasured colleague with abundant policy and clinical experience in addiction late in mid-career confronted addiction in his teenage son. His education included a lot of humility and respect for families confronting addiction in a loved one. "With my son and his addicted friends I found that as they began the journey of recovery they found the Twelve-Step programs to be particularly helpful since they could not continue to associate with their former drug using 'friends' and did not feel comfortable with peers who had not used drugs and suffered painful consequences. The Twelve-Step fellowships offered them a place where people like them who were in recovery could understand what they were going through. They felt uniquely comfortable in these fellowships of recovery where they found lots of support and many good ways to navigate their new drug-free lives. My wife and I who were horrified by many of our son's drug using friends were delighted to open our home to his new friends in recovery."

The most risky Twelve Step meeting, however, is vastly safer than the everyday experiences of addicts of either sex or any age. When addicted people pursue their addictive careers, there are fewer controls over whom they meet and what is to become of them than there are at any Twelve Step meetings. At least at meetings there is a culture of recovery, and at most meetings the great majority of members are good people who can help the newcomer get and stay well. I have never felt physically endangered or observed any violence at a meeting of a Twelve Step fellowship. The tamest suburban bar is, in my experience, a riskier place than the scariest Twelve Step meeting.

To handle the small but real risks at Twelve Step meetings, it is best for adolescents and young women to go to meetings limited to other young people, or to go to regular Twelve Step meetings with a trusted and sober friend. If it is possible to find a trusted adult, usually of the same sex, in the program who can accompany the young person to meetings, so much the better. As mentioned earlier, in larger communities there are often women's groups available that focus on the special challenges of women in recovery. Once the newcomer starts going to meetings, it is important for him or her to find a sponsor of the same sex who can help sort out the important issues, including risks such as "Thirteenth Stepping."

Critics of the Twelve Step Fellowships

Not everyone agrees with my positive view of the Twelve Step programs for addicted people. There is a vociferous group of intelligent, well-motivated professionals, and others, who resist the long-standing public recognition of the value of the Twelve Step programs and the principal articles of faith of these groups, including the central role of admitting that you are powerless over your addiction, the disease concept of addiction, and the importance of the spiritual foundation of the program including the role of the Higher Power in recovery.

These alternative voices commonly urge addicts be more rational and to take personal responsibility for their behaviors. Some of the critics of the Twelve Step programs also argue that the medical treatment of addiction with or without the Twelve Step programs is less effective than forcing addicts to accept responsibility for their own behaviors. This criticism of the Twelve Step approach misunderstands the admission of powerlessness in Step 1 as an abdication of personal responsibility for the addiction and the behavior to which it led. Recall that the two central features of addiction are loss of control of one's use and life (or unmanageability) and dishonesty (often with denial). The admission of powerlessness in Step 1 is a direct confrontation of both of these problems and is the first, the most difficult, and the most important step on the road to recovery. This is not about rejecting personal responsibility. It is about admitting that all efforts to quit drinking and using under your own power have failed and becoming willing to get help from a "power greater than self," which includes this time-tested program of recovery.

Critics of the Twelve Step fellowships sometimes object to physicians referring patients to Twelve Step programs, the way I do in this book, because they think of these organizations as brainwashing cults or religions. Other people are offended by the requirement that members of Twelve Step fellowships admit openly at meetings that they are addicted to alcohol and other drugs, that they have lost control of their lives, and that they can never again drink alcohol or use other drugs socially and moderately. These requirements are all part of the disease concept of addiction held by Twelve Step groups.

When I meet actively addicted people who are skeptical of my advice to use the Twelve Step programs, I encourage them to look around for other models of getting well, to find people who have overcome addiction to alcohol and other drugs in other ways, and to learn how they did it. I suggest that they try alternative mutual aid groups, such as SMART recovery (Self-Management and Recovery Training), which differ from, and are even antagonistic to, AA and NA. SMART recovery is a cognitive behavioral self-help program that emphasizes self-reliance, rational thought, and altered behavior during events that trigger relapse.

In recovery, it is not one-size-fits-all. One of the glories of the recovery community is the diversity it contains. One thing my patients who are uncomfortable with the Twelve Step fellowships notice when they try alternatives is how many Twelve Step meetings there are and how relatively few alternative meetings there are. I ask them to reflect on the meaning of that disparity. It is not because the government or some rich philanthropist has poured money into AA and NA. I also remind them that when they have gone to one AA meeting or one NA meeting they have gone to one meeting. Every single Twelve Step meeting is different from every other Twelve Step meeting. That means that within the Twelve Step fellowships there is enormous variety. Furthermore the Twelve Step fellowships have proven to be highly adaptive over time. The meetings are always evolving with the elements that are most helpful preserved and new elements incorporated. This is how the meeting are culturally sensitive because their membership is so diverse on every dimension, age, ethnicity, gender you name it. There are Twelve Step meeting to fit just about every person.

I encourage you to "meeting shop," to go to many meetings and find the ones that best meet your particular needs. Helpful meetings for one person can be unhelpful meetings for someone else. Helpful meetings at one time in the lifelong process of recovery can be less helpful meetings at other times for the same person. All meetings of a Twelve Step fellowship have foundations that they share, so they are instantly familiar to anyone who is accustomed to the fellowship. On the other hand, each meeting is unique in relation to all others, and meetings change in subtle and important ways over time. The rich diversity of meetings within a single AA or NA fellowship is one of the many valuable features of these programs. In the end, meetings that meet the real needs of its members flourish, and those that do not, disappear.

A few years ago a longtime patient, herself a physician, returned to see me. She was about sixty years old and saw me for her problems with obsessive compulsive disorder. She was never addicted to alcohol or drugs and had in her life rarely used any alcohol. She had two grown children and was looking forward to living out her life with her husband after a sometimes troubled relationship. She told me that a year prior to her visit to me, he was diagnosed with cancer. He died within a few months of the diagnosis. She was bereft—alone and scared. She told me she turned for support to her friends, who were in recovery from alcohol and drug addiction and active members of the Twelve Step fellowship. I asked her why she had not returned to see me at that time. She said, "I turned to these friends because these people live life at a deeper spiritual level and that was what I needed then." Rather than feeling deflated by her choice, I told her that I understood exactly what she meant, and I felt the same way about people in recovery.

8. THE FAMILY'S ROLE

The family sees the addict's life unfold up close and personal. The family lives addiction with the addict. And, it is hoped, that the family is able to experience the joys of recovery alongside the addict as well.

While an individual's path to addiction is always unique, there is a clear pattern among individuals with substance use disorders: addiction begins with seemingly benign drug and alcohol use, often in adolescence. From this start, the substance use plays out over many years in ways that are inescapable for the addict's family. The addict's family did not cause the addict's disease and cannot control the addict's alcohol and drug use. The addict's family also cannot cure the addiction. Nevertheless, the addict's family is not only caught up in the addict's perilous journey but what the family does about the addict's alcohol and drug use and about the addiction itself can either worsen the consequences of addiction or contribute to the journey's ending in recovery. Recovery of the addict also has a huge positive impact on the addict's family. That said, the addict's family, while not helpless, can at best only facilitate the addict's sustained hard work that is ultimately required for the addict to achieve lasting recovery.

Addiction is a family disease. First, most addicts (and lots of non-addicts) have family members who have substance use disorders. Thus, families have their own stories of addiction—some successful, many not successful—sometimes over many generations. All of these family stories of addiction offer useful lessons. Second, the family participates in the life of the addict, typically showing evidence of both enabling and tough love at various times and with various frequencies over many years. As we'll see, many family members have their struggles with codependency to work through to realize their own recovery.

The family's role with the addict's recovery commonly begins after the treatment experience. Whether by attending family sessions with the addict or otherwise, it's essential for family members to understand the disease of addiction and their roles in promoting and sustaining recovery. The family needs to develop a plan to prevent, identify, and quickly intervene with their addicted loved one if relapse occurs. The family also needs help in dealing with the problems that exist within the family, including alcohol and other drug problems among other family members. Most of all, the family needs to learn why the addicted family members behave the way they do and to recognize just how difficult this disease is to overcome. In short, the family needs help accepting the disease and respecting the addict for the challenges that lie ahead. The family also needs to learn how to promote recovery and use an episode of addiction treatment to begin some maintenance on the family itself. The family problems that surface in addiction treatment commonly existed for many years and have often been ignored. It is important for the family to confront and resolve these ignored problems for the benefit of the addicted family member—and for the benefit of all other family members.

Codependency

The modern understanding of the disease of addiction to alcohol and other drugs includes the recognition that the addict's family members, which for our purposes includes partners and other loved ones, are often more than passive victims of the addict's harmful and sick behavior. This was recognized in 1951 with the founding of Al-Anon, a group whose members use the Twelve Steps of AA to acknowledge unmanageability of the alcoholic's relationship with alcohol and their inability to control the alcoholic's behavior. When Melody Beattie published her bestselling book *Codependent No More* in 1987, she expanded on these ideas by defining a set of behaviors that characterize codependency, which has been embraced by many addiction professionals and family members of addicts. They agree that some members of the addict's family show signs of codependency, which is broadly described as relying on other people's approval and well-being for one's sense of worth and identity.

Codependence often has its roots in childhood exposure to addiction, usually the addiction of a parent, but one can also develop these tendencies as an adult in a close relationship with a spouse or a child who is addicted to alcohol or other drugs. While not a diagnosable disorder, this problem is common enough that it has spawned its own treatment and recovery movement, including the Twelve Step–based organization Codependents Anonymous (CoDA). The following characteristics of codependency apply to many people who find it hard to detach from the harmful behaviors of the addicts in their families and lead separate, healthy lives.

- They typically try extremely hard to always do the right thing and to please others, even to their own detriment.
- Their self-esteem is to some degree tied to being able to manage or control others' behavior.

- They, usually unconsciously, continue to try to save the addicted family member through selfless, dedicated, and tireless efforts in the face of repeated failure to do so.
- They neglect their own inner, deeper needs as they try desperately but futilely to fix themselves by fixing the addicted person in their lives.
- Their lives and self-concepts, to a large extent, are defined by their relationships with their addicts.

Learning from Suffering

Addicts are often strong personalities. Their addictive behaviors outwardly dominate their families. Because such awful things happen to addicts over time, it is difficult for families not to center much of their lives around the addicts and the destructive dramas they create in family life. In some cases, it appears as if the codependent family member acts in ways that unwittingly enable their loved one's addiction by making excuses for early problems that arise from the excessive use of alcohol or other drugs. Another all-too-common pattern for the person who grew up in an alcoholic or drug-addicted family is to develop his or her own addiction to alcohol and other drugs, thus repeating the role of both parents simultaneously—the addicted spouse and the enabling spouse.

Codependent family members may even come to believe that almost all of their problems can be traced to the addicted person. They think that if the addict would only get well, would only stop drinking and using drugs, then the other members of the family would be well also. Salvation, it appears, is just around the next corner. All that is needed is for the alcoholic or drug addict to become alcohol or drug-free. To destroy this myth, families need to eventually learn that addiction is a far larger problem than the reward caused by the drug high. Addiction is a disease of the entire self and afflicts not only the addict but the addict's family, which is why family members need to find healing for themselves separate from the addict.

Many professionals working in the field of addiction have recognized this pattern in families and have developed techniques for helping families afflicted by alcohol and other drug addictions. The first step on the road to recovery is to recognize that addiction in the addict is not simply physical dependence or even merely a result of alcohol or drug use. The addict's disease is rooted in not just the brain's out-of-control quest for the pleasure of the high, but commonly also in the addict's self-centeredness and resentments which are sustained by deep-seated dishonesty. Alcoholics or other drug addicts get well by working a program of recovery where they can regain their ability to be honest with and genuinely care about others. The same healing process needs to take place for people struggling with codependency where they break through their denial of the addict's disease.

For family members dealing with codependency, recovery includes giving up on the dream of fixing the addict and, instead, going about their own lives, whether or not the addict gets well. It means "detaching with love" and setting clear boundaries while still supporting the addict's recovery in healthy ways, such as going to treatment family programs and joining them in their Twelve Step recovery path by attending Al-Anon or other family support groups. Though understandable and inescapable at some stages of the recovery process, anger and resentment are not helpful in the long run. The simple understanding that the codependent person cannot be responsible for the addict is the start to recovery. Family members caught up in a loved one's addiction can manage only their own lives with effort, but they cannot manage their addicts' lives, no matter how hard they try. In working with family members, I encourage them to find and develop their own identity and self-worth. They need to restructure their views of themselves and their whole lives in ways that do not reflect the behavior or character of their addicted family members. They need to figure out what to do to become themselves, and they need to give up on fixing the addict.

Characteristics of Codependency

The family member:

- Wants to please others and do the right thing to his or her own detriment
- Focuses on controlling the addict's drinking or other drug use, ties self-esteem to managing the addict's behavior
- May be shame-based with low self-worth
- Neglects own needs while trying to fix the addict
- Believes personal success and happiness lie in stopping the addict's alcohol and drug use

This discussion of codependence has largely referred to the family's relationship with adult addicts. When it comes to addicted youth, especially teenagers, "detaching with love" is a non-starter. The family cannot do that and fulfill its responsibility to the child. On the other hand, the family has much more leverage in dealing with a teenager than in dealing with a spouse or an adult child living independently. It is imperative that the family, mostly this means the parents, act "parental" in dealing with a drug-using, or addicted, child. The family must to do what is necessary to get the young person to stop using drugs and to enter and stick with treatment if that is needed. Further, it is critical that the family support the young person's long-term recovery. Strategies for the family's roles in doing this are detailed in chapters 5 and 6 on prevention and treatment.

One final point on codependence: The codependent spouse or parent did not cause the addiction and is not to blame for the addiction. The person responsible for the addictive behavior is the addict alone. On the other hand, the family is enmeshed in the family disease of addiction. Some behaviors of family members are helpful and other family behaviors are not helpful, or even enable the addictive behavior to continue. Understanding codependence can help family members find more healthy and effective ways to promote recovery to the benefit of both the addicted family member and all other family members.

Addiction is an old diagnostic label. Codependence is a relatively new idea. Addiction, following the lead of AA and consistent with a rapidly growing body of neurophysiological research, has been redefined in recent years. When addiction was thought to be a function of simple pharmacology, the family was irrelevant. Once addiction was understood to be an enduring way of living, rooted in biology and shaped by the characters of addicts interacting with their specific environments, it suddenly became clear that the family was the most important environment for the progression of addiction. The family was also the most important engine of change for recovery. Just as recovery was a great gift for the addict, so too was recovery a great gift for family members struggling with codependence.

Another Perspective

One of my professional colleagues has shared another perspective on codependency from her own experiences with addiction in her family. Her husband is in long-term recovery and two of their three children suffered from serious and prolonged addiction. One child made it to recovery in adulthood and the other died of an overdose at a young age despite repeated determined efforts at treatment. She feels that families need to know that they cannot cure their addicted family members no matter how hard they try—that the disease of addiction is often fatal, despite the best efforts of the addicted person and the family. She told me that she felt the most comfortable when her addicted children were in residential treatment because for a while, at least, she was confident that they were safe. She noted that many experts diagnose family members of addicts, especially those with addicted children, as codependent because of their persistent enabling behaviors and because they often give up their own interests to serve the interests of their addicted children. Rather than seeing this common parental behavior as a diagnosable disorder or a disease, my colleague has come to see codependence as an understandable and all-but-unavoidable behavior of loving parents scared to death for their sick and suffering addicted children. She noted she did not take credit for her child who is in recovery or blame for her child who died of addiction. She felt they both made major efforts to get well, efforts that she respected. She saw the devastating impact of addiction on her family over many generations. She was humbled by it and grateful for the two members of her immediate family who had found their ways into recovery. Her own professional life was devoted to passing on this respect for the disease of addiction and the hope for recovery to the suffering families of addicts with whom she works.

When I was a psychiatric resident, the principal mental illness we focused on was schizophrenia. One of the common views then was the disturbed thinking and behavior of the schizophrenic patient was caused by pathological communication patterns between these mentally ill patients and their mothers. This led to the concept of the schizophrenogenic mother, a theory perpetrated by many psychiatrists and professors of psychiatry that in essence blamed the schizophrenic's mother for that often tragic disease. This has long been disproven as brain research demonstrated the biological basis for schizophrenia. The schizophrenogenic mother theory of causation is an embarrassment today. Sensitized by this experience, I want to be sure that my readers know that I am not saying the addict's family, or any "codependent" member of that family, causes addiction. What I am saying is that addiction in the family has a dramatic effect on the family as a whole. One way that family members react to addiction is the syndrome or behavioral pattern I, and many others, have labeled codependence. This behavior pattern is a reaction to addiction—not the cause of it. Most of the characteristics of co-dependence are common, and understandable, behavior patterns that may be maladaptive. It may also be generational, so that the pattern adopted in childhood by children growing up in a family dominated by alcoholism or drug addiction sometimes carries this behavior pattern and the feelings and thoughts that characterize it into marriage and children. I focus on this character trait here to encourage its recognition and, when appropriate, to help break the cycle of repetition of codependence for the good of the addict—and for the good of the codependent family members.

Twelve Step Family Fellowships

As Twelve Step recovery organizations devoted to alcoholics and addicts flourished, it became clear that their families needed programs for their own recovery. Al-Anon was co-founded in 1951 by Anne B. and Lois Wilson, the wife of AA's co-founder Bill W., with Al-Ateen soon to follow. A similar group for families of NA members sprang up and eventually Nar-Anon was formed. Adult Children of Alcoholics (ACOA) and Codependents Anonymous came later as other more specific needs of family members were identified.

These recovery programs, based on the Twelve Steps of AA, have identified and developed time-tested approaches to dealing with the problems of the addict's family.

Al-Anon

In its literature, Al-Anon describes itself as a Twelve Step mutual aid fellowship offering a program of recovery for relatives and friends of alcoholics based on the Twelve Steps and the Twelve Traditions of Alcoholics Anonymous. Al-Ateen is a part of Al-Anon for younger family members who have been affected by someone else's drinking.

Al-Anon began as a natural outgrowth of Alcoholics Anonymous called the Family Group. Little is known about the first meeting of Al-Anon, but the founders realized that families of AA members needed the Twelve Steps as a means of restoring normalcy to their own and to their families' lives.

The alcoholics in AA, most of whom initially were men, went to meetings more or less every evening. They were working the new program and finding new ways to deal with their old problems. What were their spouses to do? They were not welcome at the AA meetings, and they were alone night after night. They did not have a way of understanding what was wrong with their families and with themselves. Family members of addicts needed their own program of recovery from the disease of addiction. Al-Anon met the important needs of the spouses of alcoholics.

Two common characteristics of mental health treatment for addiction were dramatically absent from Al-Anon. First, the Al-Anon groups did not combine the alcoholics and their spouses in the same groups, as traditional family therapy does. Throughout the history of AA, the meetings have been separate. Many addicts are themselves married to, or are the children of, people addicted to alcohol and other drugs, since addiction is both a family and a generational disease. Thus, many addicts also need help in dealing with addicted people in their families of origin and in their current families. When addressing these issues, addicts themselves may go to Al-Anon or ACOA meetings. But in keeping with the singleness-of-purpose concept, addicts are urged to give top priority to their own sobriety, which means their attendance at AA and NA meetings takes precedence.

Second, when family members of alcoholics get together, they often do so to complain about the addicts who run (and ruin) their lives. In contrast, Al-Anon's program, surprisingly to most newcomers, does not build on blaming addicts for the pain in their families. Instead, Al-Anon focuses on ways that family members contribute to the problems in the alcoholic's family. Al-Anon is not for complainers and blamers; it is a program that is tough and clear-eyed in its view of the family disease of alcoholism.

Al-Anon, like AA, focuses with singleness of purpose on alcoholism in the family, not on the broader definition of addiction to all nonmedical drug use. Nevertheless, family members of people addicted to drugs other than alcohol are usually welcome at Al-Anon meetings. Al-Anon defines recovery as including abstinence from use of all nonmedical drugs by addicts, not merely abstinence from alcohol use. Although many members of Al-Anon do not drink alcohol—some being themselves recovering alcoholics or addicts—Al-Anon does not require abstinence from alcohol use by its members who are not alcoholic.

The Al-Anon Family Group Headquarters publishes a number of books and pamphlets about recovering from the family disease of alcoholism.

Al-Ateen

Al-Ateen, a part of Al-Anon, was established specifically for adolescent Al-Anon members to share experiences, learn coping strategies, and offer encouragement to one another. Key issues are the shame of having an alcoholic parent or sibling and learning about their own predisposition to addiction to alcohol and other drugs. Al-Ateen is a fellowship of teenagers whose lives have been affected by the drinking of family members, not a teenage AA program.

Each Al-Ateen group has an adult sponsor who is a member of Al-Anon. The sponsor is an active participant in the Al-Ateen meeting who provides guidance and knowledge about the disease of alcoholism and about the Steps and Traditions of AA. These groups, like Al-Anon groups, usually meet at the same time and location as AA meetings to facilitate participation of family members not yet old enough to drive. Members are guided toward awareness that they are not the cause of a loved one's alcoholism or addictive behaviors and that they cannot change or control anyone but themselves. By developing their own spiritual and intellectual resources, based on Al-Anon principles, adolescent members of this fellowship can develop a satisfying personal life despite alcohol-related family problems.

Nar-Anon

Nar-Anon, known officially as Nar-Anon Family Groups, is to NA as Al-Anon is to AA. After efforts to launch the program originally failed, it was revived in 1968 by Robert Stewart and incorporated in 1971. As in NA, AA, and Al-Anon, members run the groups, which meet on a regular weekly or monthly schedule. Members focus on their own enabling and codependency issues, not their addicted family members, while following the same Twelve Step principles and practices in working their own program of recovery.

Adult Children of Alcoholics and CoDependents Anonymous

Around 1978, ACOA (or ACA) was founded by Tony A. and others to provide education and support to adult children of alcoholics. The name was said to have come from the seminal text on the topic, Adult Children of Alcoholics, by Janet Woititz. ACOA groups follow the same Twelve Steps and Twelve Traditions as Al-Anon and Nar-Anon; however, the focus is on recovery from painful childhood experiences related to parental alcoholism.

The first meeting of CoDependents Anonymous (CoDA), took place in 1986 and it grew to around 1,000 meetings with groups reported in 30 countries. While it's not affiliated with Al-Anon, it has a similar mission in that its members uses the Twelve Steps as their program of recovery and apply them to attaining freedom from dysfunctional codependent behaviors, usually in relation to an addicted family member. Many members deal with codependence that traces back to their early childhood and the influence of being raised by alcoholic, addicted, or otherwise dysfunctional parents. Codependence was defined at the First National Conference on Codependency in 1989 in Scottsdale, Arizona, as "a pattern of painful dependency upon compulsive behaviors and on approval from others in a search for safety, self-worth, and identity. Recovery is possible."

The Family's Role When Intervention or Treatment Fails

When the addicted family member refuses treatment or, even more commonly, fails to complete treatment or returns to alcohol and drug use after treatment, the family is tested. This is the most common pattern for families facing addiction in a family member, whether in the first effort at treatment or the tenth. When relapse occurs, the family will benefit from working with a specialist in dealing with addiction.

The family typically, with painful ambivalence, initially starts by accepting this disappointing failure to achieve lasting recovery. In this situation, the family often limps along not wanting to set off an explosive crisis in the addict. I understand this decision to avoid the pain that comes with tough love. I understand the common family concern that if they directly and forcefully confronted the addict, they would be drawing a hard line that could lead their loved one to a depression, life on the street, or even a suicide. In this tough love scenario, the family gives the addict a choice—continued participation in the family life or continued use of alcohol and drugs—a choice without compromise.

There are endless variations in this picture, but sooner or later most families face it in dealing with the disease of addiction. No one can tell the family what to do or take responsibility for the family's actions, because no one can know what the outcome will be of their decision. Either choice—enabling or taking a stance of tough love—can produce severe negative and even fatal consequences. The family can insist on no use of alcohol and other drugs as verified by frequent random drug tests, or the family can verbally insist on recovery but accept continued alcohol and drug use. Both are uncertain and dangerous. Clearly, I favor the choice of tough love when there is abundant evidence that the addicted family member has had repeated serious negative consequences of alcohol and drug use and still continues to use. I also favor drug testing after treatment to verify the drug- and alcohol-free status. But I do so with humble uncertainty because there is no guarantee that this hard line will succeed and, if it fails, the consequences can be catastrophic. In my experience, the outcome from this approach is more likely to be successful than not. It is certainly more likely to be successful than the harm reduction–tolerant approach to continuing addictive drug use. Unfortunately, I have seen that tough love only comes after trying everything else, usually repeatedly, and seeing the failures of the more patient and more tolerant approach to addiction.

Families confronting rebellion in the addicted family member and failure of treatment, either by early termination or relapse, sometimes adopt an ambivalent enabling strategy. This road, usually, leads to more suffering for the addict and for the family; however, this path also presents endless opportunities to reassess the family's strategy for dealing with the addicted family member. Remember, however, that down this tolerant path death is also a very real possibility, most often from overdose but also from infections, accidents, and violence.

Families facing the difficult choices when recovery is not achieved should seek assistance from a trained professional with experience treating addiction. The family decisions—either tough or tolerant—need to be talked about with everyone in the family. When possible, a coherent, consistent, and explicit family strategy should be adopted.

It is important for the family confronting an addicted family member to do an inventory of how other family members and they themselves use alcohol and other drugs. This family crisis is an opportunity to confront substance use problems in other family members. It is also important for the family in crisis and conflict to open themselves up to receiving help from addiction professionals as they s confront the contradictions and complications that inevitably erupt.

Strategies for Parenting:
Addressing the Effects of Addiction in the Family on Youth

Learning effective parenting practices and building trust is vital in establishing a safe family structure for young people who are abusing alcohol or other drugs, who are in recovery, or who have an addicted or recovering family member.

Parents who are themselves impoverished and troubled by drugs and alcohol or other problems are often so preoccupied with their own painful lives that they are unable to give much love or attention to their children. Some of these parents are harsh with their children; many others are neglectful. Children do best with parents who encourage them to solve their own problems, parents who are involved with them on a daily basis but who do not soften the often painful blows of reality for them. Parents help their children when they celebrate their children's successes, but also when they allow them to learn—to grow—from their failures. This is not easy, but it is the most rewarding way to be a parent. It is also the most likely to lead to a happy outcome of family life for both parents and children regardless of the level of the parents' or child's success.

Families with addiction or mental health disorders in the parents and families with high-risk adolescents will have the most difficulty with parental authority and family goals. Nevertheless, such families have, paradoxically, a great opportunity for raising healthy and strong children by helping them to see how the family team copes with adversity, including being able to ask for help, both from professionals and from family members and friends. Children in families that have few problems do not necessarily have an easier time than those in families with more problems, because the children are likely, sooner or later, to confront many serious problems in their own lives. The sooner young people learn that the measure of their characters is their ability to deal with adversity and failure, the better off they will be. On the contrary, families that are closed (humiliated, frightened, or in denial), families that pull apart rather than together when they encounter adversity, and families that lie to and deceive each other are unlikely to thrive. They are especially susceptible to substance abuse and addiction, which is a disease of spiritual impoverishment as much as a disease of disordered brain chemistry.

Families need to help their children face the fact that having great abilities is of little value unless those abilities are harnessed in productive ways. Children with high IQs and exceptional talents who are performing poorly in school and elsewhere need to learn that unless they make the necessary effort, these abilities won't lead to success. Life is scored on performance, not on ability. The biggest determinant of success in life is the ability to do hard and goal-oriented work over long periods of time. This is lesson that we can all learn from alcoholics and addicts who have committed to recovery. If people, including youth, are not able to work hard and to maintain their efforts, they are unlikely to prosper no matter how great their talents. Many people with modest talents do extremely well in life because of their good work habits. Adults need to explain these facts to youth and to help them develop sound work habits. There is plenty of room in life for a highly diverse range of interests and talents, but success in any area of activity—from music to mathematics, from creative writing to athletics—is impossible without steady, hard, and productive work. And so it is in dealing with addiction in the family.

Strength in Weakness

It's helpful for parents to talk about both their successes and their failures with their children. Doing so helps children accept their own flaws and move beyond them if they hear about their parents' own failures, mistakes, and deficiencies, and the ways that they worked to cope with their difficulties, including addiction. For many parents, such discussions are disturbing because they seem to undermine the children's view of the parents as having all the answers and of being strong. The opposite is more often the case. Although it is not desirable for parents to harp on their heroic exploits in overcoming problems, it is nonetheless generally useful to children to know of the more serious problems their parents have confronted and what the results of those confrontations have been. Besides addiction issues, failures in school or at work, health problems, divorce, financial failure, and personal rejection are the typical problems that most families confront at one time or another. These problems are growth opportunities for all family members.

Preventing substance abuse by adolescents is a shared family project that fits well in the overall family goal of raising children who pursue their own destinies, independent of their parents. Families that have a history of addiction and families with high-risk children are those most likely to be put to the test in preventing their children from having substance abuse problems, especially during their teens and early to mid-twenties. Confronting these problems can be a source of strength. Parents who have overcome addiction themselves can bring their personal experience with the devastation of substance abuse to bear on establishing a no-use policy. Similarly, parents who have overcome codependency issues with an addicted family member can help children learn to set healthy boundaries in their relationships.

Parents, working together if there is more than one parent caring for children, need to define clearly what the family's expectations are with respect to certain vital behaviors in adolescence. First and foremost, the parents need to deal with the issues of alcohol and other drug use by their children. A clear message setting the family rules for no alcohol or drug use needs to be consistently given, and the consequences for violating those rules need to be clearly communicated. Likewise, the reasons for the rules need to be clearly spelled out so the child knows, from an early age, that the rules are not arbitrary or mean-spirited.

How much of a hard line parents should take cannot be scripted; it has to be worked out in the family over time. But as we said in chapter 5 about the family's role in preventing substance abuse, the more clarity and determination there is in the family's message of "no use of alcohol, nicotine, marijuana, and other drugs for health," the better. The more this message is couched in concern for the young person's long-term success, health, and welfare, the better. Most of all, the earlier it is delivered the better. There will be abundant opportunity to return to this discussion given the high rate of drug use and drug-caused problems in the youth culture. While examples of drug-caused problems for youth are abundant, they are unavoidable.

When youth use any drug and have serious consequences from doing so, like problems at school, motor vehicle crashes, or illnesses, then it is time to shift from a more tolerant stance to a more directive and strict insistence on the no-use standard, including considering substance abuse treatment. In these situations, it is often useful for the family to get the help of a counselor experienced with youth drug problems to guide the family.

Substance abuse and other health-related behaviors also should be discussed openly in the family with the clear understanding that, ultimately, the maturing child will be responsible for his or her behavior and decisions. The family rules should be designed not only to make the family function better, but to help the child grow up to be a healthy, productive, reasonably happy, and independent adult living outside the parents' home. This is the best insurance that new generations will develop the healthy attitudes and behaviors around alcohol and drug use that will help prevent future drug epidemics and ensure that those who do develop addiction can get the best help possible to put them on the road to long-term recovery.

***

Together we have explored what the modern drug epidemic is and why it is happening now. At root the shared human problem is that drugs of abuse super-stimulate brain reward more than any natural reward. This chemical brain stimulation hijacks the drug user's motivation and thinking prioritizing repeating the drug using experience even in the face of multiple negative consequences of the drug use. We have seen that addiction usually starts in adolescence because of the unique vulnerability of the adolescent brain. We have seen how the negative consequences of drug use commonly play out over the entire life cycle. We have focused on the importance of family and others in prevention, intervention and treatment. We have seen that the modern global illegal drug distribution system is rapidly increasing its ability to deliver a wider variety of addicting drugs at lower prices and more conveniently than ever before. The drug problem is an American problem but it is increasingly adversely affecting people all over the world. We have seen that attitudes that accept or even encourage drug use, especially by youth, and the normalization of drug use have facilitated this epidemic.

There is a misguided choice often presented about the roles of the criminal justice system and the health care system as if the country needs to choose one and reject the other. This is usually presented today as favoring the health approach and rejecting the role of criminal justice in addiction policy. I began my five decades in wrestling with addiction by helping to shift the country from a nearly exclusive focus on law enforcement to a new balanced approach to the rising drug epidemic. Beginning in the early 1970s the long-standing law enforcement efforts were linked to prevention, treatment and research. It is essential today that the linkage to law enforcement be strengthened and not abandoned. That can be done while reducing incarceration by using a range of new programs like drug courts to link community corrections to treatment. It is essential that law enforcement reduce the supply of illegal drugs and that it function as an engine of recovery. Many addicts confront their addiction and decide to enter recovery as a direct result of their involvement in the criminal justice system.

Most significantly the book has presented action steps to turn back the drug epidemic not only at the individual and family level but also at the national and international levels. Addiction is a cruel and powerful teacher of individuals, families and communities. It is vital to learn lessons from the confrontation with addiction at all these levels. We have seen the remarkable growth of the recovery movement as millions of the people and families that have overcome the deadly threat of addiction have emerged as a powerful antidote to the drug epidemic. Their journeys to recovery provide a roadmap for others to follow, for our nation to follow.

In this book, I have focused on the human brain. The most basic feature of the brain, unlike the lungs, kidneys, and heart, is its plasticity. Life changes the brain. Neurons are continually making new connections, or synapses, in response to experiences. Although it is true that once it is addicted to alcohol and other drugs the brain has changed forever, it is also true that all human experience permanently changes the brain. Not only is the vulnerability to addiction hardwired into the brain, but the human brain has the capacity to acquire new operating instructions from experience and from the environment in which the brain exists. Recovery changes the brain. The brain-changing environment includes, first and foremost, the family but also the community where the addict learns how to live a good, drug-free life. The emergence of the recovery movement is changing American culture. Human cultures are shared, but ever-changing responses to human experiences over long periods of time.

Not just addicted people and their families learn from addiction but so do communities, nations and even the global community. Policies and programs matter. Drugs are more than personal challenges. Prevention and recovery must be achieved one person and one family at a time. But social attitudes and the institutions of society must also facilitate both prevention and recovery.

At a deeper level, learning from addiction means learning what makes a good life, for individuals, families, and communities. Real recovery from addiction, and real prevention of addiction, can only come one person at a time, from the inside out. Recovery and prevention are as much about the heart as the head, which is why addiction is a spiritual disease and not just a problem of chemicals acting in the synapses of the brain. This is the secret to the success of Twelve Step recovery.

Most impressively the driving force for all of the Twelve Step fellowships and other recovery communities, for addicts and for families, is that helping others find and sustain recovery is essential to the recovery of everyone touched by addiction. Addiction is isolating. Addiction shrinks the soul. Recovery, in clear contrast, requires being with and caring about other people. Recovery does not just restore addicted people and their families to their pre-addicted selves. Recovery enhances and expands the soul—the souls of the addicts, of the addicts' families, and of all people who are touched by them.

EPILOGUE: WHERE DO WE GO FROM HERE?

What's in the future for our relationship with drugs of abuse? When I look into the crystal ball to divine the future of drug use, I first look at the recent past and the current state of drug abuse and mostly predict a continuation of current trends, including a focus on those trends that I find hopeful. Before taking some guesses, I confess that over the past fifty years of working on drug prevention and drug treatment, I have had many surprises. It bears repeating Bill W.'s description of the disease of addiction as "cunning, baffling, and powerful," a disease that often evolves quite rapidly in dramatic and unexpected ways.

With that disclaimer, I'll start with my threat assessment of potential bad news ahead about the drug epidemic. First, in the public and among leaders a view is growing that the future of drug policy hangs on the choice between law enforcement and treatment, with the obvious answer being more treatment and less law enforcement. At the extreme extension of this line of thought there will be little or no law enforcement dealing with either drug sale or drug use. Instead drug policy will become a "tax and regulate" scheme of legalization for drug sale and use, more or less modeled on the current way the country handles alcohol and tobacco.

Marijuana is leading this charge today as legalization of medical and recreational use spreads to more states, but many additional illegal drugs are in line for this policy trend, beginning as did marijuana, with the perception that these addictive drugs have some legitimate use that justifies taking them outside of medical controls for "self-medication." The response to the negative health consequences of the abuse of these drugs is to recommend voluntary treatment for those who want it, along with obligatory admonitions about the risks of using them. I believe that down this road is more drug use, and more drug-caused problems, with the most vulnerable populations. However, our long experience with alcohol and tobacco tells us that not everyone will use "legal" drugs and there are many useful strategies to discourage use despite a drug's legality. Nevertheless, legalization significantly increases drug use and problems, especially for the young, the disadvantaged, and the seriously mentally ill.

A second current negative trend is the rapid expansion of the global drug supply system with more effective distribution, including the sale of drugs in neighborhood stores and delivered to homes like pizza, as package delivery and routine mail. Not only is drug distribution expanding, the prices of abused drugs are steadily decreasing, the potency of drugs is steadily increasing, and the number and variety of drugs being sold are dramatically increasing. There is now a widening range of abused drugs that includes agriculturally grown drug crops increasingly supplemented by untold numbers of purely synthetic drugs produced in mobile clandestine laboratories in all parts of the world. These agriculturally and laboratory produced drugs and their hybrids are increasingly seen as attractive income generators for a wide variety of people who don't fit the drug dealer stereotype. They make up a multi-tiered sophisticated global network that efficiently feeds these drugs into communities across this country and around the world. Global illegal drug supply is increasingly lucrative and increasingly sophisticated. It is delivering more different, usually synthetic and not agriculturally-produced, drugs, at higher potencies, at lower prices, to more people more conveniently than ever before. That is a business model likely to grow, probably dramatically.

A third negative trend is the rise in harm reduction policies that accept continued drug use while trying to reduce some of its negative consequences, such as giving clean needles to intravenous drug users to reduce their risk of contracting HIV and hepatitis C and providing addicts "safe and clean" places with medical supervision to use drugs until they are ready to go to treatment and perhaps even choose to give up using drugs. I believe that this retreat from a drug-free goal, while clearly a humanitarian effort that may be helpful in some cases, also reduces the motivations for many people to stop drug use.

These increases in the acceptance of recreational drug use and increases in drug supply with falling prices need to be considered in the context of the growing science that shows the vulnerability of the brains of all mammals, including all humans, to the powerful super stimulation of brain reward that defines what a drug of abuse does. This same science is showing ever more clearly the negative effects of drug use on health, safety, education, productivity, and family life. The new brain science also shows ever more clearly the unique vulnerability of the adolescent brain to addiction and the fact 90 percent of alcohol and drug addiction begins in adolescence.

Fortunately, not all drug-related news is menacing. There are many changes occurring today that hold the promise of lowered drug use going forward. The most recent major milestone is the US Surgeon General's report *Facing Addiction in America* on alcohol, drugs and health in in 2016. This report calls for the integration of addiction into the fabric of all health care from disease prevention to identification, intervention, and treatment all the way to lifetime monitoring in healthcare for any relapse to drug use with swift and effective intervention when relapse occurs.

The positive trends, while widespread, are much less dramatic and therefore less visible than the negative trends. First, there is a steady growth of the percentage of youth who have decided not to use any alcohol, cigarettes, marijuana, or other drugs. In 2014, one quarter of American twelfth-graders had never used any alcohol, cigarettes, marijuana, or other drugs, up from about 3 percent in 1982. Equally important, half of high school seniors had not used any alcohol, cigarettes, marijuana, or other drugs in the prior thirty days, up from about 16 percent.[1] This widely overlooked strong and consistent trend toward ever higher percentages of youth who do not use any addictive drug—youth that I label "abstainers"—has been going on for more than three decades. The identification of this trend has encouraged the simple, straightforward—but brand-new—drug prevention message for youth that has been one of the key recommendations of this book: "One Choice: no use of alcohol, tobacco (nicotine), marijuana, or other drugs by youth under age twenty-one for health." This message needs to be widely embraced and promoted. It holds great promise in replacing earlier highly ambiguous drug prevention messages.

A second positive change is the definition of the goal of treatment as sustained recovery—the five-year recovery standard. This standard for evaluating drug treatment holds the promise of dramatically improving treatment outcomes and at last making recovery the expected outcome of substance abuse treatment rather than relapse, as is it is today. The state physician health programs not only show that this transformation is possible; they also show the way that is done—by combining excellent but brief substance abuse treatment with long-term monitoring to discourage and to identify relapses to any alcohol or other drug use. The great hope for the future of effective recovery-oriented addiction treatment is to integrate this distinctive model into all health care as is increasingly now being done with other serious chronic illnesses.

Third, the overprescription of opioid pain medicine has begun to drop thanks to the leadership of the US Centers for Disease Control and Prevention (CDC), which has declared this, and the related explosive growth in drug overdose deaths, an epidemic. It is important to recognize that many of the people who became addicted to opioids, including

---

[1] Levy, S., Campbell, M., Shea, C. L., & DuPont, R. L. (2018). Trends in abstaining from substance use in adolescents: 1975-2014. *Pediatrics*. doi: 10.1542/peds.2017-3498

prescription opioids, had long and continuing histories of alcohol and drug abuse. This makes the point that opioid addiction and overdose deaths are a part of the larger problem of the use of addictive drugs for pleasure.

Fourth, and most important, the emergence into the public eye and of the recovery movement changes how the country thinks about addicts and addiction. Today there are more people in recovery than there are people with addiction. The recovery movement not only shows the path out of addiction to recovery in life stories but it is also visible and active in the shaping of national drug policy. It also offers lessons in how millions of real people get and stay clean and sober and how their work of recovery transforms them from dishonest addicts into exemplary citizens through their lifetimes of hard work in recovery communities. This newly visible, global miracle, begun in Akron, Ohio, in 1935, is the heart of this book.

Taking a global look at drug policy, I believe that the US and the entire global community will develop new ways to respond to the menacing and still growing drug epidemic. I predict that sooner or later, after the policy equivalents of family "enabling" have produced relentless negative results, there will be a powerful global rejection of increasing drug use. This will lead to a new widely-shared restrictive drug policy that discourages the sale and use of all addictive drugs with limited use of the criminal justice system. This policy will no longer condone what I have called recreational pharmacology—the personally controlled use of drugs that super-stimulate brain reward for fun. How this new drug policy direction will deal with continued illegal drug use and sales remains to be seen, but one thing appears certain: As the problems caused by drug abuse—including crime, family dysfunction, rising health care and legal costs, and overdose deaths—increase, the public tolerance of drug use and policies that accept or even promote drug use are sure to decrease.

This is the global equivalent of what happens within families facing drug use problems, especially addiction. At first the family ignores the problem. Then the family tries modest measures to get the addicted family member to stop using drugs. As the drug use escalates into devastating drug abuse, the family shifts from tolerance of the drug use to intolerance. More aggressive interventions then replace the earlier, gentler efforts: enabling leads to tough love because it fails. So it will be with national and global drug policies. Only when the softer approaches fail do tougher approaches gain wide acceptance. This is what happened in 1978, when the explosive growth of drug use and drug-caused problems in the prior decade finally led to a strong bipartisan shift of national sentiment about drug use away from tolerance—especially drug use by youth. We are now, likewise, seeing this shift in dealing with the excessive prescribing of opioid medicines.

It should be clear by now that I strongly support the view widely shared among addiction professionals that the right drug policy promotes the message that the use of chemical stimulants of brain reward—recreational pharmacology—is unhealthy and unwise for individuals and for society as a whole. In recent decades, we have witnessed this shift from acceptance or even encouragement of nicotine use to a widely shared social disapproval of sales and use of this drug. I expect a similar shift to take place with respect to all drugs of abuse in the coming decades.

In summary, the better drug policy of the future rejects any youth drug use and protects vulnerable adolescent brains from the chemical slavery of addiction. The better drug policy promotes recovery from addiction, including not only abstaining from alcohol or other drugs of abuse but prioritizing the development of healthy character. The better drug policy is not a choice of law enforcement or treatment: It uses both the criminal justice system and health care to prevent and treat drug use disorders. Working together, with limited use of incarceration, they can produce positive results that neither the criminal justice system nor health care can achieve alone.

We can all make this policy shift happen. We learned in chapter 5 about the role of families, schools, and health care in preventing substance abuse. Communities also have a role in not only improving prevention education, but also changing policies and practices regarding addictive drug use. As responsible members of our communities, we can support:

- More support of the One Choice goal of no-use drug by youth by families, health care, schools, and other institutions;
- More stringent and effective government interdiction to prevent drug trafficking and track down and punish drug dealers, both within the US and internationally including supply reduction of illegal drug growth in source countries;
- Continued health care reform to effectively manage substance use disorders just like other serious chronic diseases, from prevention to identification, treatment, and long-term monitoring to detect and immediately intervene with any relapse;
- Funding for brain research and the development of more effective addiction intervention and treatment strategies, including medically assisted treatments, that are evaluated based on their ability to produce sustained recovery;
- Broader understanding and acceptance of the disease model of addiction and the success of Twelve Step fellowships and other mutual support groups in promoting abstinence for lifelong recovery;
- More research and public education on the harms of addictive drugs, especially drugs like marijuana that are perceived to be safe to use recreationally and medicinally. Research should focus not on smoking marijuana as a medicine but on the use of pure individual

chemicals in marijuana and other drugs, and their synthetic analogues, to treat specific diseases;
- Strategic, judicious use of drug testing for substance abuse prevention, intervention, and relapse prevention; and
- Strong legal interventions that discourage drug use while limiting incarceration for the use of drugs. At the same time holding alcoholics and addicts responsible for crimes and other harms they have caused. Addiction is not a "get out of jail free" card. It is a serious chronic disease that requires specific and effective treatment.

Unfortunately, this shift to a better drug policy will come only after the deaths and ruined lives mount beyond the nation's ability to tolerate them. From pain, loss, and catastrophe comes determination and commitment. It is tragic that the cost must be so high to trigger more responsible and effective efforts to deal with addictive drug use. This is a pattern common to families, communities, and even nations. I have shown how valuable lessons about addiction can be learned that can be labeled "recovery": The inspiring, hopeful, and positive reality of recovery for addicts also has great relevance to those who spend their time around or live with addicts. Sharply reducing recreational pharmacology has benefits not only for individuals and families but also for communities, for nations, and for the entire world. The addict's journey from addiction to recovery is mirrored by the global community's journey confronting addiction, a journey that has a very long way yet to go.

APPENDIX A: PREVENTION, TREATMENT AND RECOVERY RESOURCES

The following resources are broken out into three sections: organizations that provide general information, recovery support groups, and recommended reading.

General Information

Addiction Policy Forum
718 7th Street, NW, 2nd Floor
Washington, DC 20001
http://addictionpolicy.org

American Society of Addiction
Medicine (ASAM)
5515 Security Lane, Suite 700
North Bethesda, MD 20852
(301) 656-3920
www.asam.org

Center for Alcohol and Addiction
Studies
Box G-S121-5, Brown University
Providence, RI 02912
(401) 863-6600
www.caas.brown.edu

Center for Substance Abuse
Prevention (CSAP)
Substance Abuse and Mental Health
Services Administration
5600 Fishers Lane, Rockwall II
Rockville, MD 20857
(301) 443-0373
www.samhsa.gov

Center on Young Adult Health and
Development (CYAHD)
University of Maryland School of
Public Health
4200 Valley Drive, Suite 2242
College Park, MD 20742

College Life Study
1234 School of Public Health
Building, College Park, MD 20742
www.cls.umd.edu

Community Anti-Drug Coalitions
of America (CADCA)
625 Slaters Lane, Suite 300
Alexandria, VA 22314
800-54-CADCA
www.cadca.org

Community of Concern
c/o Georgetown Preparatory
School
10900 Rockville Pike
North Bethesda, MD 20852
(301) 656-2481
https://thecommunityofconcern.org

DEA's Get Smart About Drugs
DEA Headquarters
Community Outreach Support and
Prevention Section
8701 Morrisette Drive
Springfield, VA 22152
(202) 307-7936
www.getsmartaboutdrugs.gov

Drug Free America Foundation
5999 Central Avenue, Suite 301
Saint Petersburg, FL 33710
(727) 828-0211
www.dfaf.org

Drug Watch International
P.O. Box 45218
Omaha, NE 68144
(402) 384-9212
www.drugwatch.org

DUID Victim Voices
www.duidvictimvoices.org

Facing Addiction with the National
Council on Alcoholism and Drug
Dependence (NCADD)
100 Mill Plain Road, Third Floor
Danbury, CT 06811
www.facingaddiction.org

Family Resource Center (from the
Treatment Research Institute)
600 Public Ledger Building
Philadelphia, PA 19106
(215) 399-0980
www.familyresourcectr.org

Institute for Behavior and Health
6191 Executive Boulevard
Rockville, MD 20852
www.IBHinc.org
www.PreventTeenDrugUse.org
www.StopDruggedDriving.org

Mentor Foundation USA
1775 Tysons Blvd, 5th Floor
Tysons, VA 22102
(571) 458-7050
http://mentorfoundationusa.org

Mothers Against Drunk Driving
(MADD)
511 East John Carpenter
Freeway, Suite 700
Irving, TX 75062-8187
(877) 275-6233
www.madd.org

National Association of Alcoholism
and Drug Abuse Counselors
(NAADAC)
44 Canal Center Plaza, Suite 301
Alexandria, VA 22314
(800) 548-0497
www.naadac.org

National Association of Drug Court Professionals (NADCP)
625 N. Washington, Ste. 212
Alexandria, VA 22314
(703) 575-9400
www.allrise.org

National Center on Addiction and Substance Abuse
633 Third Avenue, 19th Floor
New York, NY 10017-6706
www.centeronaddiction.org

National Clearinghouse for Alcohol and Other Drug Information (NCADI)
http://store.samhsa.gov

National Institute on Alcohol Abuse and Alcoholism (NIAAA)
(301) 443-3860
www.niaaa.nih.gov

National Institute on Drug Abuse (NIDA)
6001 Executive Blvd
Rockville, MD 20852
(301) 443-1124
www.nida.nih.gov

National Organization on Fetal Alcohol Syndrome
200 Eton Court, NW, 3rd Floor
Washington, DC 20007
(202) 785-4585
www.nofas.org

National Safety Council
1122 Spring Lake
Itasca, IL 60143-3201
(800) 621-7615
www.nsc.org

Partnership for Drug-Free Kids
352 Park Avenue South, 9th Floor
New York, NY 10010
www.drugfree.org

Rutgers University Center of Alcohol Studies
Smithers Hall
607 Allison Road
Piscataway, NJ 08855-0969
(848) 445-2190

Shatterproof
135 West 41st Street, 6th Floor
New York, NY 10036
1-800-597-2557
www.shatterproof.org

Smart Approaches to Marijuana (SAM)
400 N. Columbus Street
Alexandria, VA 22314
www.learnaboutsam.org

Teen-Safe (from the Center for Adolescent Substance Abuse Research at Children's Hospital Boston)
www.teen-safe.org

We Save Lives
2850 S Quincy Street #6943
Arlington VA 22206
(571) 970-1989
http://wesavelives.org

World Federation Against Drugs
Box 10136, 100 55 Stockholm
Sweden
www.wfad.se

Recovery Support and Recovery Advocacy Organizations

Adult Children of Alcoholics
World Service Organization
P.O. Box 3216
Torrance, CA 90510
(310) 534-1815
www.adultchildren.org

Al-Anon Family Group
Headquarters
1600 Corporate Landing Parkway
Virginia Beach, VA 23454
(757) 563-1600
www.al-anon.alateen.org

Alcoholics Anonymous World
Services, Inc.
P.O. Box 459
Grand Central Station
New York, NY 10163
(212) 870-3400
www.aa.org

Association of Recovery Schools
6221 Main Street
Houston, TX 77030
https://recoveryschools.org

Cocaine Anonymous World
Services, Inc.
21720 S. Wilmington Ave. #304
Long Beach, CA 90810
(310) 559-5833 (office)
(800) 347-8998 (meeting info)
www.ca.org

Co-Dependents Anonymous
Fellowship Services Office
P.O. Box 33577
Phoenix, AZ 85067-3577
(602) 277-7991
www.coda.org

Dual Disorders Anonymous
World Network Central Office
P.O. Box 8107
Prairie Village, KS 66208
www.draonline.org

Emotions Anonymous
International
P.O. Box 4245
St. Paul, MN 55104-0245
(651) 647-9712
www.emotionsanonymous.org

Faces and Voices in Recovery
840 1st Street NE, 3rd Floor
Washington, DC 20002
www.facesandvoicesofrecovery.org

Gam-Anon Family Groups
P.O. Box 157
Whitestone, NY 11357
(718) 352-1671

Gamblers Anonymous
P.O. Box 307
Massapequa Park, NY 11762
(718) 352-1671
www.gam-anon.org

International Doctors in
Alcoholics Anonymous
8514 E. Maringo Drive
Spokane, WA 99212
(509) 928-4102
www.idaa.org

Marijuana Anonymous World
Services
340 S Lemon Ave # 9420
Walnut, CA 91789-2706
(800) 766-6779
www.marijuana-anonymous.org

Nar-Anon Family Group
Headquarters
23110 Crenshaw Blvd, Suite A
Torrance, CA 90505
(800) 477-6291
www.nar-anon.org

Narcotics Anonymous World
Services, Inc.
P.O. Box 9999
Van Nuys, CA 91409
(818) 773-9999
www.na.org

National Association for
Children of Alcoholics
(NACOA)
10920 Connecticut Avenue,
Suite 100
Kensington, MD 20895
(301) 468-0985
www.nacoa.org

Overeaters Anonymous
PO Box 44020
Rio Rancho, NM 87174
(505) 891-2664
www.oa.org

Oxford House International
1010 Wayne Avenue, Suite 300
Silver Spring, MD 20910
(301) 587-2916; (800) 689-6411
www.oxfordhouse.org

QUITPLAN (for smokers)
(888) 354-7526
www.quitplan.com

Self-Management and Recovery
Training (SMART Recovery)
7304 Mentor Avenue, Suite F
Mentor, OH 44060
(866) 951-5357
www.smartrecovery.org

Women for Sobriety
Box 618
Quakertown, PA 18951-0618
(215) 536-8026
http://womenforsobriety.org

Young People in Recovery
150 Oneida Street
Denver, CO 80220
http://youngpeopleinrecovery.org

Recommended Reading

- Adams A. J. Undrunk: A Skeptic's Guide to AA. Center City, MN: Hazelden, 2009, 216 pp.
- Anonymous. A Program for You: A Guide to the Big Book's Design for Living. Center City, MN: Hazelden, 1991, 192 pp.
- Anonymous. Help for Helpers: Daily Meditations for Counselors. Center City, MN: Hazelden, 1994, 384 pp.
- Beattie M. Codependent No More: How to Stop Controlling Others and Start Caring for Yourself. Center City, MN: Hazelden, 1986, 229 pp.
- Black C. Straight Talk from Claudia Black: What Recovering Parents Should Tell Their Kids about Drugs and Alcohol. Center City, MN: Hazelden, 2003, 144 pp.
- Bradshaw J. Bradshaw On: The Family: A Revolutionary Way of Self-Discovery. Deerfield Beach, FL: Health Communications, 1988, 242 pp.
- Carnes P. A. Gentle Path through the Twelve Steps: The Classic Guide for All People in the Process of Recovery, revised edition. Center City, MN: Hazelden, 2012, 340 pp.
- Cermak T. L. A Primer on Adult Children of Alcoholics, 2nd edition. Deerfield Beach, FL: Health Communications, 1989, 87 pp.
- Conyers B. Everything Changes: Help for Families of Newly Recovering Addicts. Center City, MN: Hazelden, 2009, 168 pp.
- Covington S. S. A Woman's Way through the Twelve Steps. Center City, MN: Hazelden, 1994, 264 pp.
- Dufton E. Grass Roots: The Rise and Fall and Rise of Marijuana in America. New York, NY: Basic Books, 2017, 320 pp.
- DuPont R. L. and McGovern, J. P. A Bridge to Recovery: An Introduction to 12-Step Programs. Washington, DC: American Psychiatric Press, 1994, 184 pp.
- DuPont R. L. Getting Tough on Gateway Drugs: A Guide for the Family. Washington, DC: American Psychiatric Press, 1984, 352.
- Fox C. L. and Forbing, S. E. Creating Drug-Free Schools and Communities: A Comprehensive Approach. New York, NY: HarperCollins, 1992, 344 pp.
- Gamill J. Painkillers, Heroin, and the Road to Sanity Real Solutions for Long-Term Recovery from Opiate Addiction. Center City, MN: Hazelden, 2014, 208 pp.
- Gold M. S. The Good News About Drugs and Alcohol: Curing, Treating and Preventing Substance Abuse in the New Age of

Biopsychiatry. New York: Villard Books, 1991, 348 pp.

- Goldstein A. Addiction: From Biology to Drug Policy, 2nd edition. New York, NY: Oxford University Press, 2001, 368 pp.
- Gorski T. T. Passages through Recovery: An Action Plan for Preventing Relapse. Center City, MN: Hazelden, 1997, 176 pp.
- Gould M. Staying Sober: Tips for Working a Twelve Step Program of Recovery. Center City, MN: Hazelden, 1999, 200 pp.
- Hamilton B. Getting Started in AA. Center City, MN: Hazelden, 1995, 228 pp.
- Hamilton T. and Samples P. The Twelve Steps and Dual Disorders: A Framework of Recovery for Those of Us with Addiction and an Emotional or Psychiatric Illness. Center City, MN: Hazelden, 1994, 48 pp.
- Hill, K. Marijuana: The Unbiased Truth about the World's Most Popular Weed, Center City, MN: Hazelden, 2015, 240 pp.
- Jay J. and Jay D. Love First: A Family's Guide to Intervention, 2nd edition. Center City, MN: Hazelden, 2008, 360 pp.
- Johnson V. E. Everything You Need to Know about Chemical Dependence: Vernon Johnson's Complete Guide for Families. Center City, MN: Hazelden, 1998, 528 pp.
- Johnson V. E. I'll Quit Tomorrow: A Practical Guide to Alcoholism Treatment, revised edition. San Francisco, CA: Harper San Francisco, 1990, 192 pp.
- Johnson V. E. Intervention: How to Help Someone Who Doesn't Want Help. Center City, MN: Hazelden, 1998, 116 pp.
- Ketcham K. and Pace N. Teens Under the Influence: The Truth About Kids, Alcohol, and Other Drugs: How to Recognize the Problem and What to Do About It. New York, NY: Ballantine Books, 2003, 414 pp.
- Kurtz E. Not God: A History of Alcoholics Anonymous. Center City, MN: Hazelden, 1991, 456 pp.
- Kurtz E. and Ketcham K. The Spirituality of Imperfection: Storytelling and the Search for Meaning. New York, NY: Bantam, 1993, 304 pp.
- May G. G. Addiction and Grace: Love and Spirituality in the Healing of Addictions, reissue edition. New York, NY: HarperOne, 2007, 240 pp.
- McGovern G. Terry: My Daughter's Life-and-Death Struggle with Alcoholism, reprint edition. New York, NY: Plume, 1997, 224 pp.
- Milam J. R. and Ketcham K. Under the Influence: A Guide to the Myths and Realities of Alcoholism. New York, NY: Bantam, 1981, 256 pp.
- Mooney A. J., Eisenberg A. and Eisenberg H. The Recovery Book. New York, NY: Workman Publishing, 1992, 624 pp.

- Musto D. F. One Hundred Years of Heroin. New Haven, CT: Yale University, 2002, 250 pp.
- Nakken C. The Addictive Personality: Understanding the Addictive Process and Compulsive Behavior, 2nd edition. Center City, MN: Hazelden, 1996, 144 pp.
- Nowinski I. and Baker S. The Twelve-Step Facilitation Handbook. Center City, MN: Hazelden, 2017, 224 pp.
- Quinones S. Dreamland: The True Tale of America's Opiate Epidemic. New York, NY: Bloomsbury Press, 2015, 284 pp.
- Robertson N. Getting Better: Inside Alcoholics Anonymous. New York, NY: William Morrow, 1988, 298 pp.
- Sabet K. A. Reefer Sanity: Seven Great Myths About Marijuana, 2nd edition. New York, NY: Beaufort Books, 2018, 210 pp.
- Schaefer D. Choices and Consequences: What to Do When a Teenager Uses Alcohol/Drugs. Center City, MN: Hazelden, 1998, 168 pp.
- Slater D. Wolf Boys: Two American Teenagers and Mexico's Most Dangerous Drug Cartel. New York, NY: Simon & Schuster Paperbacks, 2017, 368 pp.
- Tighe A. A. Stop the Chaos: How to Get Control of Your Life by Beating Alcohol and Drugs. Center City, MN: Hazelden, 1998, 200 pp.
- Twerski A. J. Addictive Thinking: Understanding Self-Deception, 2nd edition. Center City, MN: Hazelden, 1997, 152 pp.
- Washton A. and Boundy D. Willpower's Not Enough: Recovering from Addictions of Every Kind, reprint edition. New York, NY: HarperPerennial, 1990, 288 pp.
- Wegscheider-Cruse S. and Cruse J. R. Understanding Co-Dependency: The Science Behind It and How to Break the Cycle, updated and expanded edition. Deerfield Beach, FL: Health Communications, 2012, 192 pp.
- White W. L. Slaying the Dragon: The History of Addiction Treatment and Recovery in America, 2nd edition. Bloomington, IL: Chestnut Health Systems, 2014, 558 pp.
- Whitfield C. L. Healing the Child Within: Discovery and Recovery for Adult Children of Dysfunctional Families, updated and expanded edition. Deerfield Beach, FL: Health Communications, 2006, 151 pp.
- Wing N. Grateful to Have Been There: My 42 Years with Bill and Lois and the Evolution of Alcoholics Anonymous, revised and expanded edition. Center City, MN: Hazelden, 1998, 208 pp.
- Winters K. C. and Sabet K. A. (Eds.). Contemporary Health Issues on Marijuana. New York, NY: Oxford University Press, 2018, 336 pp.
- Woititz J. G. Adult Children of Alcoholics, 2nd edition. Deerfield

Beach, FL: Health Communications, 1990, 135 pp.
- Wolin S. J. and Wolin S. The Resilient Self: How Survivors of Troubled Families Rise Above Adversity. New York, NY: Villard Books, 1993, 256 pp.

APPENDIX B: THE TWELVE STEPS AND TWELVE TRADITIONS OF ALCOHOLICS ANONYMOUS*

The Twelve Steps

1. We admitted we were powerless over alcohol—that our lives had become unmanageable.
2. Came to believe that a Power greater than ourselves could restore us to sanity.
3. Made a decision to turn our will and our lives over to the care of God as we understood Him.
4. Made a searching and fearless moral inventory of ourselves.
5. Admitted to God, to ourselves, and to another human being the exact nature of our wrongs.
6. Were entirely ready to have God remove all these defects of character.
7. Humbly asked Him to remove our shortcomings.
8. Made a list of all persons we had harmed, and became willing to make amends to them all.
9. Made direct amends to such people wherever possible, except when to do so would injure them or others.
10. Continued to take personal inventory and when we were wrong promptly admitted it.
11. Sought through prayer and meditation to improve our conscious contact with God, as we understood Him, praying only for

*Note: The Twelve Steps and the Twelve Traditions are reprinted with permission of Alcoholics Anonymous World Services, Inc. ("AAWS"). Permission to reprint the Twelve Steps and the Twelve Traditions does not mean that AAWS has reviewed or approved the contents of this publication, or that AA necessarily agrees with the views expressed herein. AA is a program of recovery from alcoholism only - use of the Twelve Steps and Twelve Traditions in connection with programs and activities which are patterned after AA, but which address other problems, or in any other non-AA, does not imply otherwise.

knowledge of His will for us and the power to carry that out.

12. Having had a spiritual awakening as the result of these Steps, we tried to carry this message to alcoholics, and to practice these principles in all our affairs.

The Twelve Traditions

1. Our common welfare should come first; personal recovery depends upon AA unity.
2. For our group purpose there is but one ultimate authority—a loving God as He may express Himself in our group conscience. Our leaders are but trusted servants; they do not govern.
3. The only requirement for AA membership is a desire to stop drinking.
4. Each group should be autonomous except in matters affecting other groups or AA as a whole.
5. Each group has but one primary purpose—to carry its message to the alcoholic who still suffers.
6. An AA group ought never endorse, finance, or lend the AA name to any related facility or outside enterprise, lest problems of money, property, and prestige divert us from our primary purpose.
7. Every AA group ought to be fully self-supporting, declining outside contributions.
8. Alcoholics Anonymous should remain forever nonprofessional, but our service centers may employ special workers.
9. AA, as such, ought never be organized; but we may create service boards or committees directly responsible to those they serve.
10. Alcoholics Anonymous has no opinion on outside issues; hence the AA name ought never be drawn into public controversy.
11. Our public relations policy is based on attraction rather than promotion; we need always maintain personal anonymity at the level of press, radio, and films.
12. Anonymity is the spiritual foundation of all our Traditions, ever reminding us to place principles before personalities.

APPENDIX C: REDUCING FUTURE RATES OF ADULT ADDICTION MUST BEGIN WITH YOUTH PREVENTION[*]

The United States is confronting a public health crisis of rising adult drug addiction, most visibly documented by an unprecedented number of opioid overdose deaths.[1] Most of these overdose deaths are not from the use of a single substance – opioids – but rather are underreported polysubstance deaths.[2] This is happening in the context of a swelling national interest in legalizing marijuana use for recreational and/or medical use. As these two epic drug policy developments roil the nation, there is an opportunity to embrace a powerful initiative. Ninety percent of all adult substance use disorders trace back to origins in adolescence.[3][44] New prevention efforts are needed that inform young people, the age group most at-risk for the onset of substance use problems, of the dangerous minefield of substance use that could have a profound negative impact on their future plans and dreams.

---

[*] Note: This is a commentary authored by Robert L. DuPont, MD dated February 16, 2018. Additional commentaries and publications from the Institute for Behavior and Health, Inc. are available at www.IBHinc.org.

[1] Hedegaard, M., Warner, M., & Minino, A. M. (2017, December). Overdose deaths in the United States, 1999-2016. NCHS Data Brief, 294. US Department of Health and Human Services, Centers for Disease Control and Prevention, National Center for Health Statistics. Available: https://www.cdc.gov/nchs/data/databriefs/db294.pdf

[2] Florida Drug-Related Outcomes Surveillance and Tracking System (FROST), University of Florida College of Medicine. http://frost.med.ufl.edu/frost/

[3] The National Center on Addiction and Substance Abuse at Columbia University. (2011). Adolescent Substance Use: America's #1 Public Health Problem. New York, NY: Author. Available: https://www.centeronaddiction.org/addiction-research/reports/adolescent-substance-use-america%E2%80%99s-1-public-health-problem

[4] Among Americans age 12 and older who meet criteria for substance use disorders specified in the Diagnostic and Statistical Manual of Mental Disorders, 4th edition (DSM-IV).

Moving Beyond a Substance-Specific Approach to Youth Prevention

The adolescent brain is uniquely vulnerable to developing substance use disorders because it is actively and rapidly developing until about age 25. This biological fact means that the earlier substance use is initiated the more likely an individual is to develop addiction. Preventing or delaying all adolescent substance use reduces the risk of developing later addiction.

Nationally representative data from the National Survey on Drug Use and Health shows that alcohol, tobacco and marijuana are by far the most widely used drugs among teens. This is no surprise because of the legal status of these entry level, or gateway, drugs for adults[5] and because of their wide availability. Importantly, among American teens age 12 to 17, the use of any one of these three substances is highly correlated with the use of the other two and with the use of other illegal drugs.[6] Similarly for youth, not using any one substance is highly correlated with not using the other two or other illegal drugs.

For example, as shown in Figure 1, teen marijuana users compared to their non-marijuana using peers, are approximately 8 times more likely to use alcohol, 12 times more likely to binge drink or drink heavily, 13 times more likely to smoke cigarettes and 9 times more likely to use other illicit drugs, including opioids. There are similar data for youth who use any alcohol or any cigarettes showing that youth who do not use those drugs are unlikely to use the other two drugs. Together, these data show how closely linked is the use by youth of all three of these commonly used drugs.

---

[5] Marijuana remains illegal under federal law but is legal in some states for recreational use the legal age is 21, and in some states for medical use, the legal age is 18. Nationally the legal age for tobacco products is 18 and for alcohol it is 21.
[6] DuPont, R. L. (2017, October 23). For a healthy brain teens make "One Choice". Rockville, MD: Institute for Behavior and Health, Inc. Available: www.PreventTeenDrugUse.org

Figure 1. Past Month Prevalence of Alcohol, Cigarette and Other Illicit Drug Use among Youth Aged 12-17 by Past Month Marijuana Use

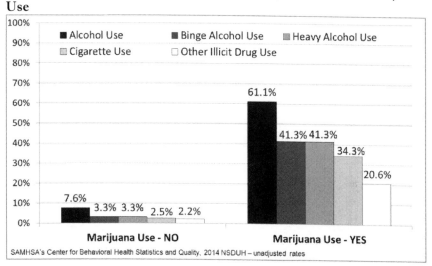

SAMHSA's Center for Behavioral Health Statistics and Quality, 2014 NSDUH – unadjusted rates

These findings show that prevention messaging targeting youth must address all of these three substances specifically. Most current prevention efforts are specific to individual substances or kinds and amounts of use of individual drugs (e.g., cigarette smoking, binge drinking, drunk driving, etc.), all of which have value, but miss a vital broader prevention message. What is needed, based on these new data showing the linkage of all drug use by youth, is a comprehensive drug prevention message: *One Choice: no use of any alcohol, tobacco, marijuana or other drugs for youth under age 21 for reasons of health.*[7] [8] This no use prevention message provides clarity for young people, parents, physicians, educators, communities and for policymakers. It is not intended to replace public health prevention messages on specific substances, but enhances them with a clear focus on youth.

Some claim adolescent use of alcohol, cigarettes and marijuana is inevitable, a goal of no use of any drug as unrealistic and that the appropriate goal of youth prevention is to prevent the progression of experimentation to later

[7] DuPont, R. L. (2015). It's time to re-think prevention: increasing percentages of adolescents understand they should not use any addicting substances. Rockville, MD: Institute for Behavior and Health, Inc.

[8] Chadi, N., & Levy, S. (2017). Understanding the highs and lows of adolescent marijuana use. *Pediatrics, 140*(6). Available:
http://pediatrics.aappublications.org/content/pediatrics/early/2017/11/02/peds.2017-3164.full.pdf

heavy use or problem-generating use. These opinions are misleading and reflect a poor understanding of neurodevelopment that underpins drug use. Teens are driven to seek new and exciting behaviors which can include substance use if the culture makes them available and promotes them. This need not be the case. New data in Figure 2 show over the last four decades, the percentage of American high school seniors who do not use any alcohol, cigarettes, marijuana or other drugs has increased steadily. Fifty-one percent of high school seniors have not used any alcohol, cigarettes, marijuana or other drugs in the past month and 26% have not used any alcohol, cigarettes, marijuana or other drugs in their lifetimes. Clearly making the choice of no use of any substances is indeed possible – and growing.

Figure 2. Past Month Trends among High School Seniors in Abstaining from Alcohol, Cigarettes, Marijuana and Other Illicit Drugs

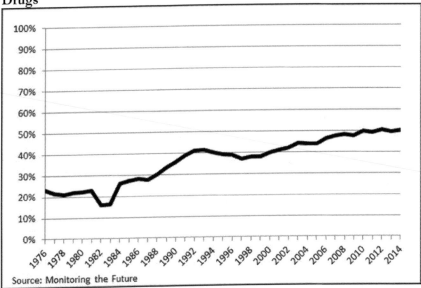

Source: Monitoring the Future

Sowing the Seeds for a New and Enduring Parents' Movement

Key lessons for the future of youth prevention can be learned from the past. Substance use peaked among high school seniors in 1978 when 72% used alcohol, 37% used cigarettes, and 37% used marijuana in the past month.[9] These figures have since dropped significantly (see Figure 3). In

---

[9] Miech, R. A., Johnston, L. D., O'Malley, P. M., Bachman, J. G., Schulenberg, J. E., & Patrick, M. E. (2017). Monitoring the Future national survey results on drug use, 1975–2016: Volume I, Secondary school students. Ann Arbor: Institute for Social Research, The

2016, 33% of high school seniors used alcohol, 10% used cigarettes and 22% used marijuana in the past month. This impressive public health achievement is largely unrecognized.

Figure 3. Percentage of US High School Seniors Reporting Past Month Substance Use, 1975-2016

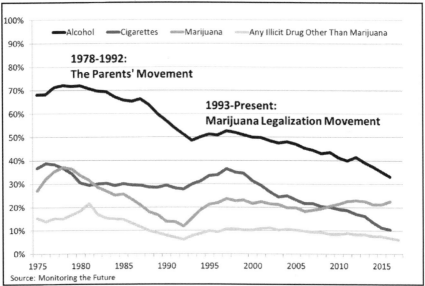

Although the use of all substances has declined over the last four decades, their use has not fallen uniformly. The prevalence of alcohol use, illicit drug use and marijuana use took similar trajectories, declining from 1978 to 1992. During this time a grassroots effort known as the Parents' Movement changed the nation's thinking about youth marijuana use[10] with the result that youth drug use declined a remarkable 63%. Rates of adolescent alcohol use have continued to decline dramatically as have rates of adolescent cigarette use. Campaigns and corresponding policies focused on reducing alcohol use by teens seem to have made an impact on adolescent drinking behavior. The impressive decline in youth tobacco use has largely been influenced by the Tobacco Master Settlement Agreement which provided funding to anti-smoking advocacy groups and the highly-respected *Truth* media campaign. The good news from these long-term trends is that alcohol and tobacco use by adolescents now are at historic lows.

University of Michigan. Available at:
http://monitoringthefuture.org/pubs.html#monographs
[10] Dufton, E. (2017). *Grass Roots: The Rise and Fall of Marijuana.* New York, NY: Basic Books.

It is regrettable but understandable that youth marijuana use, as well as use of the other drugs, has risen since 1991 and now has plateaued. The divergence of marijuana trends from those for alcohol and cigarettes began around the time of the collapse of the Parents' Movement and the birth of a massive, increasingly well-funded marijuana industry promoting marijuana use. Shifting national attitudes to favor legalizing marijuana sale and use for adults both for medical and for recreational use now are at their highest level[11] and contribute to the use by adolescents. Although overall the national rate of marijuana use for Americans age 12 and older has declined since the late seventies, a greater segment of marijuana users are heavy users (see Figure 4).

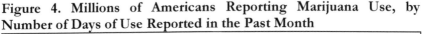

Figure 4. Millions of Americans Reporting Marijuana Use, by Number of Days of Use Reported in the Past Month

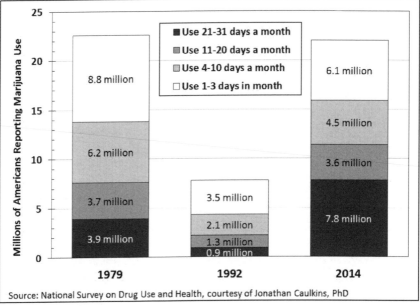

Source: National Survey on Drug Use and Health, courtesy of Jonathan Caulkins, PhD

Notably, from 1992 to 2014, the number of daily or near-daily marijuana uses increased 772%.[12] This trend is particularly ominous considering the breathtaking increase in the potency of today's marijuana compared to the product consumed in earlier decades.[13] [14] [15] These two factors – higher

---

[11] Geiger, A. (2018, January 5). About six-in-ten Americans support marijuana legalization. Washington, DC: Pew Research Center. Available: http://www.pewresearch.org/fact-tank/2018/01/05/americans-support-marijuana-legalization/

[12] Caulkins, J. (2017, November 7). Psychoactive drugs in light of libertarian principles. *Law and Liberty*. Available: http://www.libertylawsite.org/liberty-forum/psychoactive-drugs-in-light-of-libertarian-principles/

potency products and more daily use – plus the greater social tolerance of marijuana use make the current marijuana scene far more threatening than was the case four decades ago.

Through the Parents' Movement, the nation united in its opposition to adolescent marijuana use, driving down the use of all youth drug use. Now is the time for a new movement backed by all concerned citizens to call for *One Choice: no use of any alcohol, tobacco, marijuana or other drugs for youth under age 21 for reasons of health*. This campaign would not be a second iteration of the earlier "Just Say No" campaign. This new no-use message focuses on all of the big three drugs together, not singly and only in certain circumstances such as driving.

We are at a bitterly contentious time in US drug policy, with front page headlines and back page articles about the impact of the rising death rate from opioids, the human impact of these deaths and the addiction itself.[16] At the same time there are frequent heated debates about legalizing adult marijuana and other drug use. Opposing youth substance use as a separate issue is supported by new scientific evidence about the vulnerability of the adolescent brain and is noncontroversial. Even the Drug Policy Alliance, a leading pro-marijuana legalization organization, states "the safest path for teens is to avoid drugs, including alcohol, cigarettes, and prescription drugs outside of a doctor's recommendations."[17]

This rare commonality of opinion in an otherwise perfect storm of disagreement provides an opportunity to protect adolescent health and thereby reduce future adult addiction. Young people who do not use substances in their teens are much less likely to use them or other drugs in later decades. The nation is searching for policies to reduce the burden of addiction on our nation's families, communities and health systems, as well

---

[13] ElSohly, M. A., Mehmedic, Z., Foster, S., Gon, C., Chandra, S., & Church, J. C. (2016). Changes in cannabis potency over the last 2 decades (1995-2014): Analysis of current data in the United States. *Biological Psychiatry, 79*(7), 613-619.

[14] World Health Organization. (2016). *The Health and Social Effects of Nonmedical Cannabis Use.* Geneva, Switzerland: Author. Available:
http://www.who.int/substance_abuse/publications/cannabis/en/

[15] Rocky Mountain High Intensity Drug Trafficking Area. (2017, October). *The Legalization of Marijuana in Colorado: The Impact, Volume 5.* Denver, CO: Author. Available:
https://rmhidta.org/

[16] E.g., Seelve, K. Q. (2018, January 21). One son. Four overdoses. Six hours. A family's anguish. *New York Times*, p.A1. Available:
https://www.nytimes.com/2018/01/21/us/opioid-addiction-treatment-families.html

[17] Drug Policy Alliance. (2018). Real drug education. New York, NY: Author. Available:
http://www.drugpolicy.org/issues/real-drug-education

as how to save lives from opioid and other drug overdoses.[18] Now is precisely the time to unite in developing strong, clear public health prevention efforts based on the steady, sound message of *no use of any alcohol, tobacco, marijuana or other drugs for youth under age 21 for reasons of health.*

Robert L. DuPont, MD
President, Institute for Behavior and Health, Inc.
Former Director, National Institute on Drug Abuse (1973-1978)
Former White House Drug Chief (1973-1977)

www.PreventTeenDrugUse.org
www.OneChoicePrevention.org

---

[18] The President's Commission on Combatting Drug Addiction and the Opioid Crisis. (2017). Final Draft Report. Available:
https://www.whitehouse.gov/sites/whitehouse.gov/files/images/Final_Report_Draft_11-15-2017.pdf

INSTITUTE FOR BEHAVIOR AND HEALTH, INC.

Founded in 1978, the Institute for Behavior and Health, Inc. is a 501(c)3 non-profit organization that develops new ideas to reduce the chemical slavery of addiction. Non-partisan and non-political, IBH facilitates creative public and private sector collaboration to achieve this important public health goal.

IBH relies on funding from individuals and organizations. We need your help to continue our work. Tax-deductible contributions can be made directly to the organization at the following address:

Institute for Behavior and Health, Inc.
6191 Executive Blvd
Rockville, Maryland 20852
Tax ID: 52-1138173

For more information, visit the IBH websites:
- www.IBHinc.org
- www.PreventTeenDrugUse.org / www.OneChoicePrevention.org
- www.StopDruggedDriving.org
- www.PreventionNotPunishment.org

ACKNOWLEDGEMENTS

Without my first editor, Sid Farrar, this book would not exist, let alone be half as good as it is. He twisted my arm to start this project and held my hand throughout the writing process. He had a clear vision for the new book and he had the determination to see it through to a successful conclusion. Sid also has a unique understanding of the wide-ranging literature and the hard-earned reality of recovery. He shares my awe of and pride in the uniquely American, world-changing institution of Alcoholics Anonymous and the other Twelve Step fellowships.

My second editor, Cathy Broberg, worked magic to get the book ready for publication. She too shares the book's commitment to the miracle, the emancipation and the joy of recovery from addiction.

I also thank General Barry R. McCaffrey (Ret.), President Clinton's second White House Drug Czar. I worked closely with him in that job. He invited me to his office to autograph five copies of the first edition of my book, *The Selfish Brain: Learning from Addiction.* I asked General McCaffrey to whom I should address them. He said he wanted inscriptions for his three grown children and for the President and the Vice President. General McCaffrey is the dean of the 17 White House Drug Czars. I treasure him as a colleague and friend. He remains uniquely devoted to drug prevention and treatment. I thank him especially for his generous Foreword to this new book.

Thanks to Corinne Shea, my alter ego, my tireless assistant and my brilliant collaborator for ten years at the Institute for Behavior and Health, Inc. Words of thanks are not enough to express my gratitude to Corinne for her support of the work of IBH.

Finally, and most importantly, thanks to my wife, Helen, my partner in life for 56 years, and the co-founder and Executive Director of the Institute for Behavior and Health, Inc. Helen not only cheerfully put up with the disruptive demands of this book project but she also has contributed directly to the writing. It was Helen who insisted on IBH's commitment to prevention. She was the source this book's new vision of youth prevention, the goal of "no use of alcohol, nicotine, marijuana and other drugs by youth under twenty-one for reasons of health." Helen is the originator of IBH's innovative One Choice prevention vision.

ABOUT THE AUTHOR

Robert L. DuPont, MD, is a practicing psychiatrist who has specialized in the prevention and treatment of addiction to alcohol and other drugs for five decades. He was the first director of the National Institute on Drug Abuse (NIDA) (1973 to 1978), serving under Presidents Nixon, Ford, and Carter. Dr. DuPont was the second director of the White House drug abuse prevention office (1973 to 1977), a position known as the drug czar. He is president of a nonprofit research organization, the Institute for Behavior and Health, Inc. (1978 to the present). A second major area of professional interest is anxiety disorders such as agoraphobia, panic disorder, and obsessive-compulsive disorder. He was the founding president of the Anxiety Disorders Association of America in 1980.

Dr. DuPont is clinical professor of psychiatry at Georgetown University School of Medicine in Washington, DC. He received a bachelor's degree from Emory University in 1958 and an MD degree from the Harvard Medical School in 1963. He received residency training in psychiatry from the Harvard Medical School and the National Institutes of Health from 1964 to 1968.

Dr. DuPont was born in Toledo, Ohio, and now lives with his wife, Helen, in Chevy Chase, Maryland. He is a life fellow of the American Psychiatric Association (APA) and distinguished fellow of the American Society of Addiction Medicine (ASAM).

That is the short official version of his biography.

**

Many readers want to know nothing more about me, preferring to let the book speak for itself. Other readers may want to know the author more personally. For you I offer the following information about me and how I came to write this book. More personal information is important to many readers because some of this book can be misinterpreted as political or as reflecting odd personal proclivities. This additional biographical material is offered to answer some of the questions that may crop up as you read the book.

First, to answer the most obvious question, I am not related to the du Pont family that started the vast chemical company in Wilmington, Delaware. They spell their family name with a small d and write it as two words, whereas my family, from Toledo, Ohio, uses a capital D as one word. My mother taught seventh grade, and my father was a salesman. My father was Robert L. DuPont, so I grew up as "Bob Jr." Since his death in 1986, I usually do not use "Jr." because with "MD" tacked on, my name got lost in terminal abbreviations.

My extended family has had its full share of problems with drug abuse and alcoholism. Especially hard hit have been family members born after 1950. A few years ago, a much-loved cousin died as a result of his cocaine and alcohol use despite substantial family efforts to help him. One of my uncles was an early member of Alcoholics Anonymous, which was founded in nearby Akron, Ohio, less than one year before my birth.

I am a psychiatrist, having graduated from the Harvard Medical School. I took a full year off from medical school to travel 25,000 miles in a Land Rover through twenty countries in Africa on a personal adventure. My choice of Africa reflected both my growing up in the South during the breakup of legal segregation after 1954 and my enthusiasm about the emergence of many independent African nations after a century of colonial rule. I went to Africa with a letter of introduction from Martin Luther King, Jr. whom I met in Atlanta. That letter, a lifetime treasure, is included here. In that year I fell in love with Africa and Africans.

When I finished my postgraduate medical training and military service at Harvard and the National Institutes of Health, I went to work in 1968 for the District of Columbia government as a full-time psychiatrist in the Department of Corrections. Inspired by my two heroes, President John F. Kennedy and Dr. Martin Luther King Jr., I chose public service for my life's work, hoping to use my medical knowledge to help solve the two serious problems that most attracted me: crime and drug abuse.

Martin Luther King, Jr.
Ebenezer Baptist Church
407 Auburn Avenue, N. E.
Atlanta, Georgia

Jackson 2-4395

March 6, 1961

TO WHOM IT MAY CONCERN:

Dear Sir:

This is to introduce Mr. Robert DuPont, Jr., a medical student at Harvard Medical School, who is now on leave spending a year in Africa. He is intensely interested in Africa and its problems. He is desirous of knowing the people of Africa and extending the frontiers of understanding. Any cooperation that you can give him during his travels will be highly appreciated and very helpful.

Mr. DuPont plans to write about his experiences and observations when he returns to the United States, and I am sure that he will do this in a most objective, creative, and understanding manner. I hereby introduce him to you as a person of genuine good will and humanitarian concern.

Yours truly,

Martin Luther King, Jr.

Km

Work in the Nation's Capital

When I went to work for the city government, Washington, DC, had recently been declared the "crime capital of the nation," leading to an intense bipartisan concern about sharply rising crime. With a handful of unemployed college students, we tested the urine of all the men admitted to the District of Columbia Jail in August 1969, finding that 45 percent were positive for recent heroin use. The epidemic of heroin addiction that we identified was a major cause of the city's crime wave. The first mayor of the

243

nation's capital, Walter E. Washington, asked me to develop a plan to respond to the problems of heroin and crime in Washington.

With a group of dedicated colleagues, on February 18, 1970, I started the Narcotics Treatment Administration (NTA) as part of the District of Columbia government's Department of Human Resources. That was my introduction to high-profile public service, with frequent testimony before congressional committees and active involvement with the mayor's office and the White House, as well as with the electronic and print media. Using the treatment approach to heroin addiction known as methadone maintenance NTA treated 15,000 heroin addicts at 20 sites in the city between 1970 and 1973. We helped to cut heroin overdose deaths in Washington, DC from sixty-five in 1971to five in 1973. The monthly rate of serious crime was cut approximately in half between late 1969 and mid-1973. My interest in reducing crime was not in punishing criminals but in helping people arrested to live better, happier, crime-free lives with the use of addiction treatment. I cared about the health and welfare of arrested offenders.

The Federal Phase

In June 1973, I moved from the city government to the federal government to head the White House Special Action Office for Drug Abuse Prevention as the nation's second drug czar. In September of 1973, I became simultaneously the first director of the National Institute on Drug Abuse (NIDA). Most people considered these jobs a promotion, but I regretted the loss of direct involvement with drug abuse treatment and the addict patients I was working to help. For me, there were as many losses as there were gains in this move up the ladder.

My Professional Life after Government Service

My government career came to an abrupt end in July of 1978 when the new Secretary of Health, Education, and Welfare decided that he wanted his own new directors in the three institutes dealing with mental health, alcohol abuse, and drug abuse. Since leaving the government, I have remained continuously active in the drug abuse field in a variety of private roles, including founding in 1978, with my wife, Helen, the Institute for Behavior and Health, Inc., a nonprofit organization located just outside Washington, DC. The mission of IBH is to find, promote, and evaluate big new ideas to improve drug abuse prevention and treatment. In recent years my daughter, Caroline M. DuPont, MD has become the Vice President of IBH. She is a psychiatrist who is board certified in both psychiatry and in addiction medicine.

In 1978, I also became fascinated by the suffering of a patient of mine with agoraphobia who was unable drive to and from her job as a teacher.

This led to my involvement in new ways to treat the anxiety disorders and to my founding the Phobia Society of America in 1980. This still vigorous national nonprofit organization later changed its name to the Anxiety and Depression Association of America (ADAA).

Since 1969 I have had my own practice of general psychiatry, the core of my professional identity. I have a deep respect for my patients. I am grateful to them for permitting me to enter into their lives, in some cases briefly and in other cases for decades, as I have attempted to help them and their families. My patients have taught me far more about suffering from addiction and about recovery than any research studies, books, or lectures.

In 1970, I was certified in psychiatry by the American Board of Psychiatry and Neurology, and in 1989 I was certified in addiction medicine by the American Society of Addiction Medicine (ASAM). I value my ASAM membership especially highly because the organization is composed not only of psychiatrists, but of physicians from all specialties who share a professional and often a deep personal commitment to the hard-won miracle of recovery from addiction. In 1994, I was certified in Addiction Psychiatry.

Family and Political Life

On the personal side, my wife and I have been married for fifty-six years. We have lived in the same home near NIH for more than nearly fifty years. In many ways, we have been raised by two wonderful daughters, who are now grown, married, each with two children and living independent lives. Elizabeth is a social worker; Caroline is a physician specializing in psychiatry. Their husbands are my sons.

With respect to my politics, I am a lifelong Democrat who has proudly served as White House drug czar under two Republican presidents, Richard Nixon and Gerald Ford. I was director of the National Institute on Drug Abuse under these presidents and under the Democratic president Jimmy Carter. I have worked with the White House Drug office, which has had many names since it began in 1971, proudly helping every president and every White House Drug Czar since. I believe that I am the only person who has known all 15 White House Drug Czars, all 13 Administrators of the Drug Enforcement Administration (DEA) and all 5 Directors of the National Institute on Drug Abuse (NIDA). I have liked and respected all of them as they in turn led the federal government's efforts to confront the evolving modern drug epidemic.

My Personal Exposure to Alcohol and Other Drugs

To round out this biographical section, I stopped drinking alcohol on August 15, 1978, because of my work with so many people who had alcohol and drug problems. Also, I wanted to raise our daughters—then eight and ten—to know me as a nondrinker. I am not an alcoholic, although I did drink what I now consider to be too much in my late teens and early twenties. I have never been a member of a Twelve Step fellowship, such as Alcoholics Anonymous. However, based on my attendance at open meetings and on my work with hundreds if not thousands of addicted patients, I consider myself to be a respectful and devoted friend of these remarkable programs. I am proud to be an American for many reasons but high on that list of reasons for national pride is the creation of Alcoholics Anonymous in Akron Ohio nine months before my birth down the road a few miles in Toledo, Ohio. AA is free to anyone who wants to stop drinking. No licenses to lead, no buildings no certifications, just people who as part of their programs of recovery devote their time to helping others with the same problem. Nothing could be more American. I encourage readers of this book who are not personally familiar with the Twelve Step fellowships to go to three or four open meetings to see the miracle of recovery.

With respect to my personal drug use, I tried marijuana once at a social occasion while I was a medical student. This became an issue in 1974 when, as director of NIDA, I was asked about my marijuana use in a national press conference releasing an annual report on the health effects of marijuana. My admission of youthful pot use prompted a brief period of celebrity as talk shows across the country made much of this revelation about a "high official in Washington."

Many years ago, a patient told me that while she was cooking dinner for her family, she heard my voice coming from her living room. She poked her head into the room and saw me on the network evening news show, saying one sentence. Here it is as reported by this patient: "The secret weapon in the war on drugs is the Twelve Step programs." I thought a lot about that. The modern media knit us together in a remarkably intimate and personal community, a new electronic global village. That TV show was my fifteen seconds of fame. I would have missed it if my patient had not brought it to my attention because I never saw the program. The more I thought about it, the better I felt about that experience. If I were going to pick a single sentence to summarize my fifty years of work with the problem of addiction, I would not have changed even one word. Here, if nowhere else, television news did a great job of condensing and communicating a lifetime of work.

Today the news is full of stories about two drug-related subjects—the legalization of marijuana and the epidemic of opioid overdose deaths there is a historic focus on drugs. This intense attention gives people all over the world an opportunity to learn from the tragedy of addiction. One of the most important projects in my life today is my work with His Holiness Pope Francis and Her Majesty Queen Silvia of Sweden, who have teamed

to promote a better global drug policy. It is my privilege to work with them and others on this project. They are my heroes. This book is inspired by and dedicated to them. I spoke at the workshop "Narcotics: Problems and Solutions of This Global Issue" led at the Vatican on November 23-24, 2016. My presentation and prepared remarks are available at the website of the Pontifical Academy of Sciences:
http://www.pas.va/content/accademia/en/publications/scriptavaria/narc otics/dupont.html

There you have it, a short summary of my life in the world of alcohol and other drugs and a review of a few of the events that shaped the perspective expressed in this book.

Made in the USA
Columbia, SC
26 October 2018